# EASIER SAID THAN DONE

## A Life in Sport

'Alan's been an integral part of many great sporting events and sports lovers from around the world will enjoy his story. He is the consummate professional and, having witnessed at first-hand the silky skills he possesses, the "silver fox" from Wales justifies his tag as one of the "best in the business".'

**Stephen Fleming**


'Working with Alan Wilkins has been great fun. When we're broadcasting he's articulate and knowledgeable but he's also excellent company socially with his endless supply of hilarious stories, all told with his amazing ability to perfectly mimic accents. Alan has certainly led an interesting life and his book makes enjoyable reading.'

**Ian Chappell**

# EASIER SAID
# THAN DONE

## A Life in Sport

## Alan Wilkins

ST DAVID'S PRESS

Cardiff

Published in Wales by St. David's Press, an imprint of

Ashley Drake Publishing Ltd
PO Box 733
Cardiff
CF14 7ZY

www.st-davids-press.wales

First Impression – 2018

ISBN
Hardback: 978-1-902719-61-0
eBook: 978-1-902719-62-7

British Library Cataloguing-in-Publication Data.
A CIP catalogue for this book is available from the British Library.

Typeset by Replika Press Pvt Ltd, India
Printed by Akcent Press, Czech Republic

# Contents

*'To my parents, Anne and Haydn, who gave me everything in life I could have wished for, and ensured that whatever sport I played, at least I looked the part. I couldn't have asked for more.'*

# Acknowledgements

This has been a long-term project and goodness knows how many years I have said that I would write a book. I am sure that many of my close friends have grown tired of my saying "It's in the book" for so many years but, after living in Singapore for a decade or more, I began to put my thoughts down on paper and, slowly but surely, the manuscript started coming together. There are so many people to thank, and please forgive me if I leave anyone out, because this has been a long journey and my cricket career happened a hell of a long time ago.

Early encouragement to write a book came from Scyld Berry, cricket correspondent for *The Telegraph*, who kept telling me that I had a story to tell and that he, for one, would like to read it, which surprised me initially because Scyld's focus would generally be on international cricket, and I of course did not play international cricket. I would ask him: "Who on earth would be interested in my story?" To which Scyld would reaffirm: "There are many people who haven't played the cricket you have, or played with and against the cricketers you have, or led the life of a broadcaster that you have, so in my view, you have a story to relate."

Getting facts and figures accurate is crucial in writing an autobiography and for all that he has done, not just for me but for television cricket commentators all over the world, Mohandas Menon from Mumbai, is peerless. Time after time I have asked Mohan for some information on someone, or for reminding me what I might have done in places as far removed as Canterbury and Calcutta (now Kolkata, of course) and each time I have asked, the answer has come through without fuss. Mohandas Menon is the extra commentator in the commentary box, a human encyclopaedia of cricket. Thank you, Mohan, and to all the cricket statisticians around the world whose endeavours are so appreciated by the broadcasters and our audiences alike.

I didn't ever imagine that I would require physiotherapy to carry out my duties as a cricket commentator, but I have been kept in one piece for years by the unstinting efforts and genuine care of John Gloster, a physiotherapist-cum-psychologist who I first met in Dhaka when he was looking after the Bangladesh cricket team. When illness engulfed me on my first tour to Bangladesh, John gave me a dose of pills. I have never asked what exactly they were, but they got me back on to my feet, and we have been close friends ever since. In more recent years, he has looked after the Indian cricket team, Surrey County Cricket Club and the Rajasthan Royals in the IPL. Before that, in my playing days and even when the shoulder problem and the neck joints were still not fully recovered, I must thank Dean Conway, physiotherapist to Glamorgan CCC (and one time with the England cricket team) for keeping me in decent shape for my new role in broadcasting. Across the water in Bristol, Gloucestershire's Les Bardsley had the task of working with my dysfunctional shoulder that ultimately brought an end to my playing days. The medical people and physiotherapists who worked on me were unsung heroes who always gave me belief that it wasn't the end of the world, even if it felt like it at the time. How right they were.

Away from the studios and commentary boxes, golf is a passion and a means of relaxing. Although my game would be described as 'an honest endeavour' at best, I must thank one of my great friends in Singapore, Rick Brown, for making me look like a Titleist staff ambassador whenever I ventured out onto the golf course. As with my cricket, at least I looked the part, even if my performance didn't.

Embellishing the manuscript with photographs has been a lengthy procedure, going back into family photo albums and into scrapbooks for newspaper articles and preparing them for publication, so thanks go to Charlie Johnson and David Thomas of Davies Colour in Cardiff for working wonders with old black-and-white photographs. My thanks also to Siân Trenberth, for her patience in photographing the subject matter for the cover shot. It can't have been easy.

It was my four years at Loughborough University which made me think differently about so many aspects of life and where ambition was driven by the pursuit of excellence. For that I especially thank Rod Thorpe and Rex Hazeldene, two of Loughborough's foremost lecturers of physical education, who had a profound influence on my sporting career. They, with my dear friend and psychology lecturer, the late Duncan Case, made me feel like a Titan who could face any challenge in life.

I must thank my colleagues (who are now more like friends) who have contributed personal endorsements for the book. Every one of you has been a part of my life from my early playing days to more recent times in broadcasting. I can't thank you enough for the truly humbling words you have written. Responding to my late call for help in launching this book, I am so grateful to my friend of getting on for 20 years, the inimitable Gautam Bhimani, a true champion in broadcasting from our early days with ESPN Star Sports and more latterly with Star Sports India. When Gautam asked if he could help with emcee duties I couldn't have asked for a more capable man to do the job.

To my teammates at both Glamorgan County Cricket Club and Gloucestershire County Cricket Club for the wonderful years we shared in county cricket in England and Wales, for the laughs and the camaraderie, for taking the catches when I needed wickets and for putting up with the wayward bowling on many a long day in the field.

To the families and friends in South Africa who welcomed me into your lives from my first visit to the country in September 1978 until I left in August 1987. The love and friendship that shaped my life in those emotional, informative years in your beautiful country helped me start a new life away from the land of my birth and it was with a heavy heart when I left.

Playing cricket and working as a broadcaster in South Africa during the height of the *apartheid* regime was clearly a controversial decision and perhaps, in hindsight, far more controversial than I realised at the time. The *apartheid* laws were inhuman, cruel and wrong, and I was delighted to see them end in 1991 as the 'Rainbow Nation' was born. Back then I didn't consider my visits to, and subsequent employment in, South Africa as an endorsement of *apartheid*, although I do understand why others did, but I certainly disliked the hypocrisy which targeted sporting but not business links. My yearning to travel to the country can be traced back to my father's rugby tour with

Cardiff RFC in 1967. Hadyn was an inspirational man and a big influence on my life, so when he encouraged me to one day go and see the country for myself, it was something I just had to do. South Africa became the place I dreamed of and I felt a strong sentimental pull to follow in my father's footsteps. I saw a lot there that I felt very uncomfortable about, but I also made many good friends – across the racial divide – and began my broadcasting career in South Africa, for which I remain extremely thankful. I don't regret going, but I do understand and sympathise with the motives of those who criticised me for doing so. While recalling and describing my experiences in South Africa for *Easier Said Than Done*, I sincerely appreciated the input and support of two extremely good friends, who made similar journeys and willingly shared their thoughts and emotions with me. Firstly, Roger Jones who, like myself, wanted to make his own judgement on the country through the auspices of sport – in his case it was rugby. Also Edward Griffiths, a Zimbabwean-born writer, former editor of Johannesburg's *Sunday Times*, general manager of SABC TopSport, and former chief executive of Saracens Rugby in England, who has been an invaluable confidant over the years, particularly when our careers ran parallel during those early days in South Africa. Roger's and Edward's honesty and constructive advice is much appreciated.

Almost 16 years were spent in Singapore where I was fortunate to forge new friendships, many for life, not just in south-east Asia but across the Indian Ocean to the Indian subcontinent where Bangladesh, India, Pakistan and Sri Lanka have become integral parts of my life. Also, of course, to all our friends here in Britain, all of whom must be wondering if the story would ever end!

The summer of 2017, whilst completing the book, was an emotional time with, on June 1st, the sudden passing of my sister, Marian. A complete and utter shock to our family and friends. Something as devastating as this makes you appreciate even more the people who are close to you and in this regard my deepest thanks go to my brother-in-law, Andrew, my brother Howard and his family, and also to Susie's family.

My thanks to Ashley Drake and his company, St. David's Press, for having faith and confidence in me and for believing in my story, thus enabling this book to be published. In our very first meeting

# ACKNOWLEDGEMENTS

Ashley said to me: "I want you to have a book that you, your family and your friends will be proud of." I sincerely hope you will be.

The task of editing my initial manuscript was undertaken by Huw Richards, whose writing – in many globally respected newspapers and several excellent books – I have long admired. From Huw's editorial perfection to the stamp of approval from Dr. Andrew Hignell, Glamorgan CCC's official historian, who cast his expert eye over the proofs, I am indebted to their excellence.

My thanks are also extended to Ayaz Memon, whose introduction to Pramod Kapoor – the founder and publisher of Roli Books – has resulted in *Easier Said Than Done* also being published across the subcontinent. The enthusiastic and professional support of Pramod's son, Kapil, and daughter, Priya, has been invaluable and has given me the opportunity tell my story and to express my gratitude to so many wonderful people in a special part of the world that has made my life in sport a journey I thought I could only dream of.

Which brings me to the person who has shared this journey for the past 19 years, my wife, Susie, who has shown a level of patience throughout the entire project beyond the call of duty; everything in this book has been run past her for her thoughts because her sense of fairness and qualities of judgement are exceptional. Susie's support and understanding has never wavered. I couldn't have done it without her.

My final word of thanks goes to my mother and father, Anne and Haydn, who have always been my guiding lights and the inspiration that enabled me to enjoy *A Life in Sport*. My mother, now into her nineties, is an amazing person whom I cherish dearly. 'Haydo' sadly passed away on May 16th, 2003, but there's not a day that goes past when I don't think of him and what he did for me and my career. God knows how good a cricketer he might have been had he been fortunate enough to have my opportunities, but he was happy that I took up the game and followed his path. I couldn't have had a better mentor and was honoured to call him my father. He made me believe it was all possible.

**Alan Wilkins**
**May 2018**

# Preface

It's not often you come across people at work, and informally, who you can completely jell with and also call a dear friend. To me, that's Alan. Over the 20 years that I have known and worked with Alan he hasn't changed much, except grow older, and our chemistry continued to entertain audiences, live 'on air' and at the many events we've done together. Everyone knows how good he is at doing what he does on television, but his off-camera demeanour has endeared him to everyone he's met, especially me, and this is reflected by the humour and trust in each other that we share whenever we work together.

I first met Alan in 1999 when he joined me to anchor Wimbledon for ESPN Star Sports, as it was called then, and I thought, 'OK, here is this former cricketer' – to be honest I didn't even know that either – 'joining me to cover the world's number one tennis event from London. What does he know?' He walked in very fast – a bit of a funny walk I thought – and after a few minutes chatting, he opened the show, 'live'. I had already worked for the network for a good five years and I wasn't ready to partner someone who wasn't experienced but, immediately, I knew that he was excellent as a host, but just as quickly realised that he knew very little about my sport.

A quick learner with a magical memory for names and pronunciations, he can make the tough job of presenting look easy. He is always better when he works off the cuff and not from a script. From that Wimbledon fortnight we were inseparable, as we traveled the Grand Slam circuit, and the viewers' positive feedback energised us even more.

Over the years we've become very good friends and shared a lot of fun times but there are two very special things that Alan's done for me that I will always remember. The first was when I asked if he would travel from Singapore to MC my foundation's inaugural charity evening in Los Angeles. Alan said "Yes" immediately, without hesitation, and many years later he would do it again as we celebrated the first decade of the foundation's operations in India.

The second, which was even more meaningful, was when he asked if he could come and visit my parents in Chennai. I was truly touched and wondered whether he would actually come to visit. He did, and my parents were absolutely delighted to see him and spend time with him.

I was delighted when he married Susie and the two of them seem so made for each other. Sometimes it takes a lifetime to find your lifetime partner.

There is nothing we can't discuss when we sit down together over a glass of wine, wherever we are in the world. Our conversations are always serious, yet entertaining and relaxed, and there never seems to be enough time. That's Alan Wilkins. Easier Said Than Done reads the same way as our chats, so enjoy the book in the same way as I am fortunate to enjoy his friendship – with a warm smile!

Alan, good luck and God bless you and Susie.

**Vijay Amritraj**
**March 2018**

# Foreword

Whenever sports people write their autobiographies they invariably have the introduction or the foreword written by their idol, role model or a person who has inspired them or helped them in the early years. Some ask their contemporaries whom they admired as opposition players, but this must be the first time that a 'bunny' has been asked to write the foreword to an autobiography.

Derek Underwood, the left-arm England spinner dismissed me the most times in Test matches – 12 – followed closely by Michael Holding and Imran Khan with 11 dismissals each, though we played against each other in a fair few Test matches. Alan Wilkins, however, dismissed me in both of the matches when we faced each other, and Wilko is only the second bowler to have bowled me around my legs. Michael Holding was the other, but while his ball deflected off my leg-guards and went on to hit the stumps, with Wilko there was no contact with bat or pads as the leg-stump went flying.

With Holding, it was trying to get in line early that got me, but in Wilko's case I was doing the unconventional thing and running towards gully rather than towards square-leg, as batsmen are wont to do against fearsome quick bowling. So, clearly, I am his 'bunny' for being dismissed by him every time we played against each other. Something Wilko has never let me forget.

Alan Wilkins has to be the nicest man in broadcasting. There is nobody who is so gentle, so kind, so generous with his time and someone who laughs at himself as much as Wilko does. He also has a great sense of mimicry and his impersonations of the South Africans are hilarious, but nothing beats his impressions of his former Gloucestershire teammate, Sadiq Mohammad's way of speaking. That will have you rolling on the floor, holding your sides.

Always aiming to please, Wilko is hugely popular in the subcontinent where, for some strange reason, people call him

Wilkinson, whilst across the Indian border to the east he is known as the Banglawaleshi for his affinity towards Bangladesh cricket.

Wilko has decided to pen his memoirs and I know they are going to be widely read all over the world as, after his playing career, he has put down his tent in many other cricketing countries. The subcontinent, though, is where there will be a great reception for his book for we all know Wilkinsonsaheb will not let us down.

**Sunil Gavaskar**
**March 2018**

# Introduction

I first met Alan when I joined the sports department at BBC Wales in 1990 where he was already a well-established voice and face of Welsh sport. Over the coming years we became good friends as well as colleagues and I soon came to see why he had made the challenging transition from talented cricket and rugby player to accomplished and respected broadcaster.

The camera does not lie and he did look the part, right voice, engaging personality, great sense of humour, a natural communicator – just like his father, Haydn, who I always enjoyed chatting to – a great guy.

He rarely talked about his own playing career, preferring to ask others about their experiences. It was only when I researched his days with Glamorgan and Gloucestershire that I saw what a talented sportsman he had been – his career sadly and prematurely ending due to a severe shoulder injury.

Throughout the 1990s we remained good friends, enjoying a few pints after a round of golf, working together on a few charities and taking the occasional 'spin' in his Porsche 944. Ask him about it if you get the chance!

During this time at BBC Wales other opportunities knocked and it was no surprise to me that his reputation and talent was being recognised more and more on the international stage, and his move to Singapore to join ESPN Star Sports in February 2000 provided that stage for the next 15 years.

Now, before mine and all the other glowing tributes go to his head, let me tell you that he is not always the sharp, alert personality that we see on our screens. He and his lovely wife, Susie, used to visit us at Christmas and after a few glasses of wine, maybe more, he would soon nod off to sleep on Susie's shoulder for an hour or so. My wife, Meriel, saw this as a great compliment of making him feel at home, but it annoyed me greatly as it was always halfway through one of my very interesting stories!

Despite this, I've been looking forward to reading his book as Alan has many tales to tell. *Easier Said Than Done* educates, informs and entertains us, as so many of his commentaries have.

Meriel and I always look forward to welcoming Alan and Susie to our house, with their dog Leo, to drink some of my best white wine and to watch him drifting off, dreaming of scoring a century at Lord's to win the final Test against Australia.

**Lynn Davies CBE**
**March 2018**

# 1

# Early Days

*'Alan Wilkins played for Glamorgan with great enthusiasm before an injury to his bowling shoulder cut short the career he loved. He then became an outstanding television sports broadcaster, utilising that very same personal attribute in the commentary box.'*

**Majid Khan**

In my sporting life I didn't really make it onto the big stage, but I had a pretty good time trying. This is a two-fold story. The first part is about a schoolboy ambition to play sport at the highest level. Every Welsh boy wants to wear the red rugby shirt of Wales, and I also desperately wanted to wear the three lions of the England cricket sweater. That neither happened is, looking back, of no surprise. I'm not sure I was ever quite good enough, and I'll never know, but a shoulder injury at an inopportune time put paid to any ambitions I might have had.

When is an injury ever opportune? Some might say that the injury that ended my sporting career *was* opportune, as it ignited a passion for a new career.

This is the second part of the story: my decision to stop playing professional cricket and seek a career in sports broadcasting, a transition from playing to talking that was far from straightforward. I didn't play international rugby, neither did I play Test cricket, but in both sports I enjoyed a first-class career that gave me a taste of what it was all about.

That taste for sport made me want to play for a living, although there was not much of a living to be made from county cricket since the financial rewards were negligible, unless you played long enough for a club to earn a 'Benefit Season'. I jeopardised any chance of that by leaving one county, Glamorgan, to play for another, Gloucestershire, and I didn't stay long enough at either club to warrant recognition.

The first part of my story is about my life in cricket and the people I met while playing. It took me to parts of the world I could never have dreamt of seeing had I taken up teaching, for which I qualified, or computer science, in which I failed miserably with a token attempt at getting to grips with the real world after leaving school.

English county cricket was a bizarre way of making a living. It was hardly a livelihood. For one thing, the season lasts barely six months, so you had to find a 'real' job for the other six. But it was a captivating way of life once you managed to get into it.

It was captivating for me because I was fortunate enough to play in an era that some folk might regard as cricket's halcyon times, playing with and against some of the greatest players to have graced the game. It was the era of the four talismanic all-rounders: Ian Botham, Kapil Dev, Imran Khan and Richard Hadlee. A perennial debate was which would be the first pick in your World XI. In my honest opinion, the name of Mike Procter should always be in that list. Mike Procter, a little older but still a force at Gloucestershire, was in my view the equal of any of them.

It was a time of great batsmen: Viv Richards, Sunny Gavaskar, Barry Richards, Gordon Greenidge, Desmond Haynes, Clive Lloyd, Collis King, Alvin Kallicharran, Zaheer Abbas, Majid Khan, Javed Miandad, Asif Iqbal, Graham Gooch, Geoff Boycott, Allan Lamb, David Gower, Peter Kirsten and Glenn Turner.

It was the era of ferocious West Indies firepower: Michael Holding, Andy Roberts, Joel Garner, Colin Croft, Malcolm Marshall, Wayne Daniel, Sylvester Clarke, Winston Davis and Ezra Moseley.

There were others who were no slouches, including the intensely-driven, supremely talented South African all-rounder, Clive Rice. His countrymen Garth le Roux and Vincent van der Bijl were magnificent fast bowlers.

2

My university years coincided with the visit of Clive Lloyd's wonderful West Indian team of 1976, when Viv Richards and his colleagues made England's South African-born captain, Tony Greig, pay for his ill-advised and insensitive promise – made during the era of *apartheid* – to make the West Indians 'grovel'. A year on and Tony Greig was again making headlines with his part in Kerry Packer's World Series Cricket, the biggest schism in the game's history.

Every county player had a front-row view of these changes. We were on the ground as Tony Greig was booed off the field by his home supporters in Sussex; an England captain becoming a pariah in English cricket.

In recounting my years as a professional cricketer, I have tried to recall how things seemed to me at the time. What was it like to bowl to Viv Richards? Or to Gordon Greenidge. What was it like facing Michael Holding? Or Joel Garner, when you knew that the target was either your throat or your toes? How could you one day feel so good about your game, and the very next day so bad?

Was it *that* professional? Or was it just a summer pastime for those of us with the ability to play in those cherished months from April to September? Unless you were selected for an England tour you had to find work in the winter months, so what was the motivation for playing day in, day out county cricket if we were not destined for an England place?

My first county, Glamorgan, used two main cricket grounds and neither of them had proper practice nets. St. Helen's in Swansea, where the cricket ground shared half of its playing area with the rugby pitch, had no practice nets at all! At Glamorgan's base in Cardiff, the practice nets shared the end of the rugby pitch that belonged to Cardiff RFC. The last thing you wanted to do was go into the nets to face anyone of any pace, because the surfaces were not good enough. So how did a club like Glamorgan compete with the likes of Middlesex, whose headquarters were at Lord's Cricket Ground? Or with Surrey at The Oval, or with Warwickshire at Edgbaston? The clubs were a dispiriting distance apart in so many areas, yet we competed in the same tournaments for the same trophies.

The fact is that there was something utterly compelling about playing County Championship cricket. After all, we were getting paid to play cricket and that was better than doing a 'proper' job, even if the salary was never going to help you retire with plenty of money in the bank. You didn't really think about the long-term. No, once you got into a county club, you just played cricket, and you would think about the winter later in the season.

There were 17 county clubs, each with their full-time staff players, so I played with and against a battalion of around 300 men who called themselves professional cricketers.

Alongside the best home-grown players, each county had its star overseas players, and that is what made the years I played so utterly memorable. Somerset, for instance, had Vivian Richards and Joel Garner. Nottinghamshire had Richard Hadlee and Clive Rice. Hampshire had West Indians Gordon Greenidge, Andy Roberts and then Malcolm Marshall. Gloucestershire had Mike Procter, Zaheer Abbas and Sadiq Mohammad. Sussex had Imran Khan and Garth Le Roux. Lancashire were skippered by Clive Lloyd. They also had Michael Holding, who later moved to Derbyshire, and then Colin Croft. Northamptonshire had Kapil Dev and Bishan Singh Bedi.

The biggest England star was Ian Botham at Somerset, and you also had players like Allan Lamb at Northants and Graham Gooch and John Lever at Essex. Middlesex was virtually a full international team led by Mike Brearley with Wayne Daniel, Vince van der Bijl, Phil Edmonds, John Emburey and Mike Gatting in their line-up. Glamorgan had at different times Majid Khan, Javed Miandad, Ezra Moseley and Winston Davis.

Amongst the array of international stars were the journeymen of English county cricket, plying our trade as professional cricketers. Nobody yet thought of cricketers as athletes. Some were decent athletes but it was a disparate mix of men who played day in, day out, for six months of the year. One might sell you a second-hand car, many would give you tips for a horse to win you a small fortune, but it never did; you might get invited to someone's pub which he part-owned with a local businessman, or might end up in a glitzy nightclub in London if you knew the right people. Imran knew a few. You might have to share your car journeys with a heavy smoker,

4

because smoking in cars and in changing rooms was still acceptable, or with a large family going from one end of Britain to the other. Sadiq Mohammad had a large family, and I met them all on a few occasions and always in the same full car.

But in a strange way, we were all one big family. All shapes and sizes, bright boys from Cambridge and Oxford Universities, not-so-bright boys straight from school, former insurance salesmen, former teachers, a few athletes, many non-athletes, smokers, drinkers, dreamers and nutters, English county cricket had them all. But it was fun to be amongst them, and it was a wonderful way to spend six months of the year.

Then, when injury strikes, it is suddenly taken away from you. You are not a part of it anymore; you are on the sidelines. A darkness envelopes your world, the escapist world that you once cherished so much, the world of being a professional cricketer. Some players found it too much like drudgery and chose to get out, but most of the journeymen would stay on in the game for as long as they possibly could. A 20-year career was not uncommon. After finishing they might retain their connection to the game by going into a coaching capacity with the club, while others became umpires. After completing the necessary courses, they would start in the first-class game with ambitions to become an international umpire.

Financial rewards have escalated so markedly in the last 20 years that the game is virtually unrecognisable, and not just for players. Now, umpires on the ICC's Elite Panel command good salaries, and there are, I am told, very decent rewards for those who go on to become ICC match referees.

The new member of cricket's family – Twenty20 cricket – is awash with money and players and umpires have jumped on to the speeding wagon, afraid they'll miss the spoils if they don't. The Twenty20 leagues around the world have changed the very base of the game, and it is almost like a different sport. Players can make serious money by plying their trade all over the globe, and there is a new breed of specialist who plays Twenty20 and nothing else. You can't blame any player for choosing to showcase his skills purely in Twenty20, where there is a handsome living to be made. Umpires are also in the mix. If you're one of the umpires standing in the Indian Premier

League, then you're on a better day rate than if you're standing in Cardiff or Canterbury.

Those options did not exist when injury struck me down. I missed an entire first-class season at a time when I felt I was at my peak and could go on to better things. It all came crashing down around me. While I recovered from my injury, I wasn't the same bowler afterwards, either in my own mind or, probably, in that of others. I knew that. I also knew that I could have carried on as a journeyman on the county cricket treadmill, but it just wasn't for me. Although my motor skills were still at a reasonable level, my brain and my heart were both telling me that my best cricketing days were behind me. I needed a new challenge. I didn't want to coach. I saw a new horizon in sports broadcasting.

And that brings me to the second part of the story: the desire to find a position in sports broadcasting. As with cricket, it has not been a straightforward path, but a journey of peaks and troughs, triumphs and adversity, emotion and drama, fun and tears. It's a journey I am still on and, after 30 years, I felt that now was the time to share some of the journey with you. In *Easier Said Than Done* I hope to convey to you some of the challenges which have come my way in the world of sports broadcasting. Who was it who said: 'It's a funny old game'?

Of course, I would rather have fulfilled my boyhood ambitions to have played rugby for Wales or cricket for England, but the journey of trying to make both a reality hasn't been the worst. As one of my school reports once remarked: 'Not a bad effort, but could have achieved more.' I guess I knew that; I couldn't really disagree with them.

My early years at school were memorable. I was fortunate to attend the wonderful Rhiwbina Junior School, on the outskirts of Cardiff, and then Whitchurch Grammar School [now Whitchurch High School], more recently attended by both the world's most expensive footballer, Gareth Bale, the Wales and British and Irish Lions rugby captain Sam Warburton, and the gold medal winning cyclist Geraint Thomas.

Cricket, rugby and football were played at all levels in both schools, but it was cricket and rugby that grabbed my attention. This was mostly because I played them reasonably well, but it also helped that my father had excelled in both.

My parents were the main influence on my academic and sporting aspirations – not necessarily in that order of priority, as I constantly jostled school examinations with sporting ambitions.

My mother had one big influence in sporting terms; even if I couldn't cut it as a cricketer all the time, at least I would look like one! Every game I played, my white flannels were freshly washed and ironed and, because my idol – the great West Indian Garry Sobers – wore his shirt collar up, I was prepared to take the ribbing from my school mates for wearing my collar the same way.

I managed to play cricket at every age level at school, and felt as proud as hell when I wore my first Wales Schools Under-15 sweater. Rugby at Whitchurch Grammar School was a challenge. The school had one of the toughest fixture lists of all, with matches against the top grammar school teams in south Wales such as Neath, Llanelli, Bridgend, Bassaleg, Cardiff High, Porth, Lewis (Pengam) and Caerphilly. There weren't many easy games. I loved rugby but, as an outside half who wanted to play like Barry John, I don't think I ever got over a raucous shout from the touchline in one of our school matches. I wasn't having the best of games wearing the number 10 jersey, when, bellowed across the field, came the words: "Alan ... go to the wing, Boy!" The barking order came from our rugby master, Tim Harris, a legend at Whitchurch Grammar School but, on that particular day, not my biggest fan!

Although I would continue to play rugby, cricket held my interest. I loved the sport! As a young schoolboy, I used to sit in front of our black and white television at home wearing my father's pads and holding his Gunn & Moore Autograph bat. Both were miles too big for me, but I guess it made my parents chuckle! I devoured the sport at every opportunity, and watching at home on a small television set seemed perfectly normal.

One day in my school life stands out more than most. It came during the summer holidays of 1971. As a 17-year-old, I caught the bus early morning from Radyr, a suburb on the outskirts of Cardiff, to watch the visiting Indian team play Glamorgan at Sophia Gardens, little knowing what that hot summer's day had in store for me.

Led by Ajit Wadekar, a formidable Indian line-up included a young Sunil Gavaskar, who opened the batting with Abbas Ali Baig; then there was Wadekar, Gundappa Vishwanath, Syed Abid Ali, Farokh Engineer – who was playing for Lancashire CCC that season but was released to play for the touring Indians – Srinivas Venkataraghavan, Syed Kirmani (wicket-keeper), Devraj Govindraj, Bishan Bedi and Bhagwat Chandrasekhar.

I sat in the small enclosure in front of the pavilion, enjoying both the beautiful batting of an array of stylish stroke makers warming up for the following week's first Test against England, and the atmosphere of a large holiday crowd. The pleasant, relaxed atmosphere suddenly changed when a huge man stood in front of me, completely blocking out the late morning sunshine.

"Young Wilkins, do you have any cricket kit with you?" was the question he directed at me, overheard by half the enclosure. It was the unmistakable shape and sound of the Glamorgan secretary, Wilfred Wooller, a terrifying proposition at the best of times, leaving this 17-year-old schoolboy feeling like the subject of an inquisition.

"No, sorry Mr. Wooller," I replied, completely in the dark – literally and metaphorically – as to why he was asking.
"Then follow me upstairs right now!" came the swift reply. I knew that this meant the players' dressing rooms since Sophia Gardens was also the home ground of Cardiff Cricket Club, my team at weekends. But today I was being led into the Glamorgan players' inner sanctum.

Wilf Wooller, one of the greatest all-round sportsmen that Wales had ever produced, was a huge man with a booming voice to match. He was a formidable personality, indestructible in spirit and all-powerful in deed.

A renowned all-rounder, he had captained Glamorgan for 14 years, leading them to their first County Championship title in 1948. He was also club secretary for 30 years and president for six. His rugby union career was perhaps even more impressive: first picked as a schoolboy in 1933, he won 18 caps as a giant-striding centre for Wales, including the famous victory over the New Zealand All Blacks in 1935, won Blues at Cambridge University and played for Cardiff Rugby Club, which had some claim to its boast of being 'the greatest rugby club in the world'. He had also survived wartime

8

incarceration by the Japanese in the notorious Changi prisoner-of-war camps in Singapore.

Everyone in the sporting world knew him. He had become a familiar face and voice on BBC radio and television, especially in Wales, and he was a leading sports journalist for the *Sunday Telegraph*. He even played football for Cardiff City and squash for Wales! He was an imposing personality in every sense, so when he barked an order there was no alternative but to listen.

I followed Mr. Wooller into the Glamorgan dressing room. Since I stood behind him in the doorway it is doubtful anyone in the room could see me. I could hardly see them, but could hear the banter amongst the players and smell the cricket paraphernalia peculiar to changing rooms – leather pads, linseed-oiled bats, sweat-stained flannels – and the horrible clouds of cigarette smoke that filled the room, which had a view across the players' balcony onto the playing area below.

"Right, quiet!" came the instruction from Wilf, moving me, with one sweep of his arm so that I stood alongside him. "This is young Alan Wilkins – some of you will know his father, Haydn, who played for Glamorgan – and young Wilkins plays his cricket here for Cardiff Cricket Club. He is going to be fielding for you this afternoon, but he hasn't got any kit with him, so I want to see him properly dressed to go out there in 20 minutes' time. Is that clear?"

He turned to me as I gazed up with my mouth open. "Young Wilkins," came the booming voice, "we have a few sick players and we are short of a 12th man, so you are going to play for us today. Get out there and enjoy yourself. I'll see you at tea."

Wooller then strode out of the changing room and left me standing there in front of the entire Glamorgan team, who had had a tough time containing the Indian batsmen in the morning session. Sunil Gavaskar had stroked an attractive 39, Abbas Ali Baig had fallen three short of a 50. Ajit Wadekar had fallen cheaply for just 1, but Gundappa Vishwanath and Abid Ali were well set.

I have no idea quite what the Glamorgan players thought but the captain, Tony Lewis, beckoned me as he handed me a pair of his cricket shoes. "Here you are, young Wilkins, try these on for size."

They fitted like a glove, but even if they hadn't, I wasn't going to turn them down. I was wearing the Glamorgan captain's cricket shoes!

I have to admit to being star-struck. They were the team I hoped one day to play for, but at that moment I was in awe of the collection of cricketers sitting around that changing room. Captain Tony Lewis, who would go on to captain England in India in 1972-73; Alan Jones, Glamorgan's most prolific opening batsman; Majid Khan, the great Pakistani top order batsman who had joined Glamorgan from Cambridge University; Roy Fredericks, the Guyanese left-hand opening batsman who was the epitome of calypso Caribbean batting; Peter Walker, all-rounder and one of the greatest close catchers of all time; Eifion Jones, wicket-keeper and brother of Alan; Tony Cordle, the Barbados-born quickie, but a home player based in Cardiff; Malcolm Nash, the left-arm swing bowler famed as the victim of Garry Sobers' six sixes from an over of ill-fated spin at St. Helen's, Swansea, three years earlier; Lawrence Williams, right-arm medium fast from west Wales; Mike Llewellyn, hard-hitting top order batsman from Swansea; and Kevin Lyons, a Cardiff top-order batsman who had been coaching me for a couple of years in the Wales schools coaching set-up. They were all household names in Welsh sport.

I think I wore one of the captain's shirts but I cannot remember if I wore his or Majid Khan's trousers. What I do know is that I was ready and willing to go out and give my all for Glamorgan on that swelteringly hot afternoon in Cardiff against the Indian tourists. Kevin Lyons and Peter Walker were especially helpful, since I was understandably nervous fielding in front of a good holiday crowd at Sophia Gardens. The ball was being hit to all parts of the ground and I seemed to be chasing it everywhere, but I enjoyed fielding and had a decent throw in my armoury. My Cardiff Cricket Club teammate, Reggie Shah, who also happened to be in the crowd and was also asked to put on the whites and field for Glamorgan when another player fell ill was less fortunate. Poor Reggie had a shocker! He let the first ball that came to him pass clean through his legs for four, kicked the next one over the boundary rope for another four and gave the next an escort to the boundary for four more! At that point Kevin Lyons shouted: "Hey Reggie, are you fielding for them or us?" It got a few laughs around the fielding side.

The afternoon was a blur of fabulous batting by Gundappa Viswanath, Syed Abid Ali and especially Farokh Engineer, who smashed an unbeaten 62. I ran my legs off, all over Sophia Gardens, and felt I had done a fairly decent job. As I was handing my borrowed Glamorgan cricket clothes and shoes back to their owners Wilf Wooller marched into the dressing room and gave me a glowing verbal report, followed by a full-on rant at the seasoned professionals sitting around the dressing room. Welcome as the praise was, hearing my efforts trumpeted while he bollocked these accomplished professionals for what he saw as a poor day in the field made me a little uncomfortable. If they were below standard, one reason was the sickness going round the dressing room which had led to me and Reggie getting our call-ups as emergency fielders.

I left Sophia Gardens with a huge grin after my unexpected dream day. I got home to my parents and began to relay the events of this remarkable day, but all of a sudden I felt quite nauseous. My temperature was high, I was sweating profusely and I was as pink as a new strawberry. I began to topple as I stood up from the dining table, took a turn for the worse and started talking absolute gibberish. The doctor was called and found me down with a nasty bout of sunstroke, lying feverishly in bed and unable to distinguish between dreams and reality. Had all this been a dream? Had I imagined all those wonderful moments in the field for Glamorgan? I didn't really care; even if they were just dreams I knew that one day I wanted to be a professional cricketer, and I wanted to play for Glamorgan.

India won the match by 102 runs, with Bedi and Venkataraghavan each picking up nine wickets and, a month later, made their mark on history. Victory in the third Test at The Oval – where England were undone by the bewitching spin of Chandrasekhar, Bedi and Venkataraghavan – made Ajit Wadekar's team the first of seven Indian touring squads since 1932 to win a series on English soil.

That first, unexpected contact with Indian cricket – precursor to many more – took place in the summer holidays before my final year at Whitchurch Grammar School. My school life was always a balancing act between achieving the academic grades needed to get me to move onto higher education and the demands of sport. In Wales it seemed that being recognised as a decent cricketer and rugby player was just as important. My sporting aspirations often came at the price of stern appraisals from teachers who were trying their level best to get me through my chosen A Level subjects: history, geography and economics. Looking back, I think they had it tougher than I did.

My final year at school was a self-inflicted botch of achievements, ideas, dreams and thought processes. I believed I was doing reasonably well in my three chosen subjects, but my idea of progress clearly differed from that of the headmaster and my teachers. I was ordered to give my sporting endeavours a rest and get down to some serious academic work, or face the consequences in years to come. It was a stern warning with the A Level examinations looming.

Then there was the utterly confusing proposition of choosing which university you wished to attend, assuming that you would achieve the required A Level grades. My dream was to head to Cambridge, play cricket and rugby, get a degree – see my order of priorities? – then take on the world!

Our family had a Cambridge University connection; my second cousin, R.B. Collier, was an outstanding rugby player, a blindside flanker who won a Cambridge Blue in 1966, played for London Wasps, but then suffered the devastating blow of breaking his leg in a final England trial. Bob had attended St Catharine's College, Cambridge, and suggested that I might like to do the same. It meant that I had to take the Cambridge University Entrance Scholarship examinations and, to put it mildly, they did not go well.

The Dean of St Catharine's College Cambridge at that time was Dr. A.L. Caesar, who must have sensed that I was trying to swim in deep waters at that time in my life. It was his advice, following my failure to make Cambridge through the entrance exams, that I should apply for a place at Loughborough College of Education. He gave me the example of T.G.R. (Gerald) Davies, one of the greatest Welsh wing or centre three-quarters of all time, who had taken the Loughborough path and qualified as a teacher before going on to Cambridge University where he won three Blues. It sounded very attractive to me and my heart was set: Loughborough, then Cambridge, cricket and rugby, and some academic work in between!

The trouble with all of this was that I had failed to submit my application form to UCCA, the admissions system for British universities, so that it didn't matter what my A Level grades were – I hadn't submitted the application form early enough to be considered by *any* university. To this day I am not altogether sure where I applied – Liverpool? Manchester? Birmingham? Maybe even Cardiff was on the list – but wherever it was, it wasn't of any use now because when the results came out – I passed all three subjects with decent grades – I would be going nowhere because I had failed to comply with the system.

How did I manage to make such a mess of applying to attend university? How did I manage to keep my failure to submit the forms from my parents? Dr. Caesar's words of advice were ringing loud and clear inside my head every day – "go to Loughborough and then come to Cambridge for a year" – but first, I had to apply for a place at Loughborough.

In the meantime a career counselling meeting, with someone whose name I still don't remember, pushed me in the direction of a computer sciences degree at the Polytechnic of Wales in Trefforest, near Pontypridd, about 12 miles north of Cardiff. It was always a long shot, since my aptitude for mathematics was at best satisfactory. Had anyone actually *seen* a computer in 1972? I don't think I had, but here I was learning about Fortran, Cobal and Prolog, the earliest computer languages. Within a week, I'd had enough. It could have been Greek hieroglyphics for all it meant to me, and I was determined to go no further.

Trefforest, which runs along the west bank of the River Taff – hence why Welshmen are sometimes referred to as 'Taffies' – is famous for being the birthplace of one of the world's great singers, Sir Tom Jones. Pontypridd was also home to the eccentric Dr. William Price (1800-1893) who was one of the first advocates of cremation and who actually performed the first modern cremation – in 1884 – on his deceased young son.

One more landmark was about to be made in the September of 1972: my computer sciences course was about to be cremated and there was nothing I was going to take with me from Trefforest except a file bursting with notes on a subject that I thought one day might catch on but, for now, was not my scene.

I had been an aspiring computer scientist for barely ten days, but I was happy to call it a day at Trefforest. My mind was set – I wanted to go to Loughborough College of Education at Loughborough University – the problem was that I had missed the boat for my year. What would I do for the next 12 months?

Travelling to Loughborough with my parents, by car, was easy enough which eased any worries about me being too far away from Cardiff, and as we walked around the beautiful campus I decided that this was the place to launch a thousand dreams. There was no doubt in my mind that this was where I wanted to spend the next chapter of my life, but gaining admission to England's premier academy for sporting excellence was anything but easy.

The physical examination was nothing short of brutal. Very few of us were prepared for the punishment of the day and it broke a few of the lads. At the end of the umpteenth bleep test, where you had to sprint flat out between certain distances – competing against everyone to be first – and where you wanted to be noticed for being fit, for being good enough for Loughborough; it was sheer, unadulterated relief to hear the words, "OK fellas, that's it. Out you go, get showered, get changed quickly and we'll see you back in the gym for a chat."

I was grateful that rugby training plus a few competitive games had kept me in reasonable condition and was quietly confident of getting in, if only because I had survived that tortuous time in the gym, when others had either physically or mentally broken down or just given up. But we all had to wait to see if we had passed the test.

The news eventually came that I had passed, and was offered a place to study physical education (sports science) and my secondary chosen subject, either history or geography; it would be history. The news was welcome but the matter remained of filling in the year before I could start there.

I had to do something to occupy my time, while also earning some money in readiness for life at university. In short, I had to find work. I had given up any faint ambition of becoming a computer scientist, but a new opportunity came about as a result of the generosity of a wonderful man, Bill Hardiman, the head groundsman at Cardiff Rugby Football Club. Bill, who never had an enemy in his life, was the man responsible for producing the renowned rugby pitches at the National Stadium and at Cardiff Arms Park, home to the Wales national team and Cardiff RFC respectively. The offer to be an assistant groundsman at Cardiff Arms Park undoubtedly came about because Bill had answered the call from my father, Haydn, then President of Cardiff RFC. After all, I was only an out-of-work student-to-be.

In September 1972 the Cardiff Athletic Club staff had sole responsibility for producing rugby pitches for both Cardiff RFC and the Welsh national team. The Welsh Rugby Union, in effect, leased their international match pitches from Cardiff Athletic Club. Glamorgan County Cricket Club had a similar sharing agreement with the Athletic Club for the use of Sophia Gardens a short distance away.

Cardiff Athletic Club also had the most beautiful tennis courts and bowling greens on the banks of the River Taff in the centre of Cardiff. Sophia Gardens, now a full Test Match cricket ground, is located a bit further up river but was then very much a property of Cardiff Athletic Club. Their hardworking groundstaff were about to be tested not only by the worsening weather of the approaching winter of 1972-73, but by the tangible ineptitude of their newest recruit, whose knowledge of groundsmanship was scant at best and, with the wrong implement in hand, positively dangerous. This would be another test, not so much for myself, but for the poor souls who had to work with me, often in horrible weather conditions. I said then, and still say, that the groundsmen's lot is probably the toughest of all in sport; they are a hardy bunch who often work in the foulest winter weather to ensure that pitches are playable.

Yet these were happy times. As well as working, I joined Cardiff RFC as a player, although I knew that there would be raised eyebrows in some quarters since my father, Haydn, was then secretary of the club. It was a challenge in many ways but I was made to feel welcome by the players at Cardiff RFC and it was a lot of fun.

I remember that 1972-73 rugby season for the cold, but also for the privilege of pulling on the famous Blue-and-Black jersey. In those days you learnt of selection for either the 1st XV, or the 2nd XV – known as the Cardiff Athletic XV, or more colloquially, as 'the Rags' – through the post. I will never forget that first postcard arriving through the letterbox at home: just a few typed lines but magical words to read:

*Dear Alan,*
*You have been selected to play for the Cardiff Athletic XV against Ebbw Vale Athletic at Cardiff RFC on Saturday 15th October 1972. Please confirm your availability to the Club Secretary by Wednesday latest. Please note that meeting time is 1.30pm. Kick-off 3pm.*

1972-73 was a record points-scoring season for the Rags. The side was ably led by the late A D 'Tony' Williams, who had played more than 300 games for the club. Throughout that season we played the most thrilling rugby, scoring over 1,100 points and conceding only 400. I was a novice outside-half in a side bristling with talent, and it was a joy to play for the Blue and Blacks. It was also the season after the great Barry John had announced his retirement following the successful British and Irish Lions tour to New Zealand in 1971. The club's chairman, Peter Nyhan, wrote at the time that 'the King is dead. Long live Barry John'.

It was the season when the mighty New Zealand All Blacks were touring the British Isles. There was no Barry John in the Cardiff team anymore but there were the great Gareth Edwards, Gerald Davies and John Bevan, all part of the victorious Lions team in New Zealand just a year earlier. The All Blacks came to Wales and were beaten by Llanelli RFC on October 31st, 1972. That famous win, with Llanelli triumphing 9-3, helped launch the career of one of the greatest Welsh entertainers of our time, Max Boyce. Even now the hair stands up on the back of my neck when I think of that day at Stradey Park, because ... I was there! My father had ensured that my brother, Howard, and I would always remember that indelible piece of Welsh rugby's folklore when he managed to get tickets for the match.

We stood for the entire 80 minutes on breeze blocks, jammed up against people we'd never met – but who became instant friends the moment the great Phil Bennett made his first sidestep – craning our necks to see that while Llanelli were getting physically mauled by the men in black, their scarlet hearts were bigger and pounded to a more powerful beat on that cold, grey October day.

Four days later, the All Blacks played Cardiff at the National Stadium. The club had been preparing for the New Zealand match for weeks with some high intensity training sessions but it hadn't bargained for Llanelli's magnificent win, which was the surest way to fire up the All Blacks.

Bad news came when Cardiff's mercurial outside-half, Keith James, reported to training with an injury three days before the match. Still worse news was that the incumbent outside-half in the Athletic XV was me, but there was never any likelihood of my playing. I had more chance of going to the moon. I will never forget the club's coach, Roy Bish, taking me aside in training on the Wednesday evening, just 24 hours after Llanelli's win. With Keith James merely a spectator at training, Roy confided that although I was next in line, in reality it just wasn't going to happen. I was shaking. I was white with anxiety. I knew in my heart that I was never up to a match of that standard, but now I wanted to be a doctor, because I saw it as my responsibility to get Keith James fit and ready to play against the All Blacks. The club even invited the former Wales scrum-half, Clive Rowlands, then the Wales coach, to give the squad a pep talk on how to beat New Zealand. How to beat the All Blacks! I just stared at Keith, and wished he would suddenly announce that he wasn't injured. Fortunately for me and for Cardiff RFC, Keith James announced on the Friday that he would be fit to play. The New Zealand All Blacks made amends for their defeat against Llanelli, beating Cardiff by 20–4 in what was a bad-tempered game. I was just happy to watch from the stands, and no doubt the selection committee was as well.

Rugby was very much my sport that winter. My last game of cricket for the Welsh Secondary Schools team had been a few months earlier, in July 1972, when we trounced the Irish Schools side at the Mardyke in Cork. I managed to make the ball do things I hadn't achieved previously for Wales, and ended up with first innings figures of 22 overs, 12 maidens, 8 wickets for 35 runs. I couldn't manage the two second innings wickets I needed for ten in the match, but I settled for nine, a win by an innings and an introduction to Guinness, for which I will always be in Ireland's debt.

As the cold winter months of 1973 gave way to a mild spring, sporting priorities changed from rugby to cricket. I was still working for Cardiff Athletic Club, but instead of tending to the rugby pitches I was now on the lawnmowers at Sophia Gardens preparing for cricket matches, a new cricket season, and with Loughborough on my mind.

# 2

# Loughborough, Eventually

*'When I first went to Cardiff Rugby Football Club I met Haydn Wilkins,
who was then president of the club, and no-one made me more
welcome at Cardiff than Haydo. Years later, his son Alan joined us for a
season, playing for the Rags, before he went up to Loughborough. I know
just how much Alan enjoyed his rugby at Cardiff that season, if the fun
at training was anything to go by!*

*Alan could do no worse than being a chip off the old block because
his father was a kind and giving person. Good Luck Alan. Haydo
would be proud.'*

**Sir Gareth Edwards**

September 1973, and the day arrived to head to Loughborough.
Accompanied by my parents, I arrived at my address for the
next year or so – 141 Ashby Road, the Storer Hall Annex. The first
person I met was to become not just my room-mate but my great
friend throughout the next four years, and to this day. Baron Bedford
was a very decent rugby player and a sprinter on the athletics track,
but he was also incredibly neat and tidy in the room, and he always
got his work assignments done on time. He was a model physical
education student, and was needed to balance up the rest of us in
the group.

The next four years would be taken up with learning all about
physical education and history for a Bachelor of Education degree.

This could lead to a job as a teacher, but I was already fairly certain that teaching would not really be my profession. I wanted to play sport at the highest level I could, and knew that I was in the right place to achieve that goal.

Loughborough was everything I had hoped it would be. We were all extremely fit, played exhilarating rugby and could cope with the alcohol intake – not that it was ever that great, but beer after rugby was part of college life. It also instilled a highly competitive instinct because the physical education course was based on the Standard Deviation Assessment. This meant that you were always competing against your friends in every subject, physical and academic, every day, because attaining high marks were needed to stay on the course. I saw friends crying with disappointment at the end of three years because their marks were not high enough to qualify for a fourth year and the B.Ed degree. It was a tough school, but that's what Loughborough was all about – the pursuit of excellence.

My first year of rugby at Loughborough was played the way I would always like it to be played. We were the Freshers XV, young guys from all over the British Isles who had come to Loughborough to experience the same thing – sporting excellence. We played fast, open rugby, generally against club sides who were physically bigger than us, but who couldn't match us for pace around the field. At the end of the season I was thrilled to be selected for the Loughborough Colleges Sevens squad to tour the Scottish Borders, going to the beautiful towns of Galashiels, Melrose, Hawick (home of the great BBC rugby commentator, Bill McLaren) and onto Edinburgh for the Edinburgh Academicals Sevens. Loughborough were known as one of the best sevens teams in Britain, and the Borders received us with a mixture of warm Celtic appreciation and the Scottish determination to bring us down. We didn't win either of the tournaments but we won friends, and appeared on the BBC's *Rugby Special* programme. That was something to boast about, although it would have helped if we had won more than we lost.

The rugby season finished in early May with the Middlesex Sevens, one of the world's outstanding tournaments. Four times winners previously, Loughborough made it to Twickenham by winning the qualifying tournament at the London Wasps ground at Sudbury. The

Middlesex Sevens finals day was an unforgettable experience. The sun shone on our backs and, in front of a full house of 55,000, we made the semi-final. With a couple of minutes to go we were pressing London Scottish, looking for the try that would take us into the final against Richmond.

Then, in a flash, it happened. An interception inside their 22, and in that split second we all looked at each other. Who was going to turn around and catch the galloping London Scottish player before he scored under our posts 75 yards behind us? There was no time to think. I got there first, jumped on this rampaging, bearded, Scottish flanker, and brought him down inside our 22; he didn't score, but his teammate did, and we lost the semi-final in those dying seconds.

I also lost my ability to stand up after making the tackle; sprinting at full tilt all I could do was grab him from behind and turn him. In doing so, he landed straight on top of me with such force that I gasped for breath as I felt a sudden, stabbing pain. I was struggling to take any kind of breath, and the medics informed me that I had torn my rhomboid muscles between my shoulder blades. The pain was excruciating; I was strapped up like an Egyptian mummy and that was the end of my rugby season.

Nor did it do much for the start of my new cricket season. It was my first real injury in a long time and, after months of highs at Loughborough, I came down to earth – literally and metaphorically – with a bump. I learned right then that in sport the high points and low points are no more than seconds apart. It was easy to cope with all the highs, scoring tries for the Freshers XV, and going on tour with Loughborough, but now how do you deal with a severe injury? Alas, I was to discover the hard way. As the two main sports in my life, rugby and cricket, got more intensive, so the injuries would take their toll. Physically and mentally, the next few years would be a huge test of character. An emotional roller-coaster period was ahead of me.

It was a painful spring and summer, but I knew I had to get fit again for cricket. As well as a full list of matches against universities, Loughborough played Leicestershire and Nottinghamshire, both first-class counties. After six weeks of physiotherapy I was fit for cricket, but ring-rusty after not bowling for months. We played Notts on a glorious day at Trent Bridge, then and now one of my favourite cricket grounds anywhere in the world. We had a decent team including players with first-class experience and enjoyed a good day against a full Notts team including the future England batsman, Derek Randall, who I managed to trap LBW during a lengthy spell from the pavilion end. In the evening, over drinks and food in the Trent Bridge pavilion, I was approached by the Nottinghamshire captain, Mike Smedley. He asked if I was contracted to any county. Naively I said no, leading to discussions of a possible professional contract with them.

News of this reached the *Western Mail*, the daily paper in Cardiff. I thought this looked rather good, but did not consider what my home county, Glamorgan, would say about it. I soon knew. Wilf Wooller, Glamorgan's secretary/president, contacted me on my return to Cardiff for the summer vacation, and let me know in no uncertain terms – with vocabulary much more colourful than he had used when I fielded for Glamorgan against India as a schoolboy – that I would not be playing my cricket for Nottinghamshire. The message was clear: don't mess with Wilf Wooller.

I heard from Wilf again in August 1975, only this time his tone on the telephone was different. I was due to go back to Loughborough for a summer training camp before my third year there, but the call from Mr. Wooller was the sort that every young sportsman wants to receive. "We need you at Taunton on Sunday to play for the 1st XI against Somerset in the Sunday League. Do you want us to arrange a lift for you?" There was no question of whether I was available or not, just the matter of how to get to Taunton for my Glamorgan debut. While the other players went in a convoy of cars, I travelled to this momentous occasion in my sporting career with my parents.

August 24th, 1975 was a blazing hot day and I was welcomed into the dressing room by Glamorgan's captain, the elegant Pakistan batsman Majid Khan. Majid had studied at Cambridge in the footsteps of his father, Dr. Mohammad Jahangir Khan, who had played four Test matches for India and was a college contemporary of Wilfred Wooller. He was also the cousin of Imran Khan and Javed Burki. He also did not say very much, just a polite handshake and then it was left to the other Glamorgan players to welcome the newcomer to their midst in the very cramped dressing room in the old stand at Taunton. It was a disparate group of cricketers: you couldn't have had two more different personalities than Glamorgan's two opening batsmen that day. Majid – princely, slightly aloof, quiet and unassuming – was paired with Geoff Ellis, a north Walian who was never short of a chippy comment, a mickey-taker and a decent batsman who hated fielding. There was the obvious east-west Wales differentiation and, in the middle of this group, was the talented East African, John Solanky, a very decent all-rounder who hailed from Dar es Salaam, Tanzania.

Everyone seemed to be talking about Viv Richards. Where would we bowl to him? 'Don't bowl short. Don't bowl full. Don't bowl on his legs. Don't bowl too wide. How many was Viv going to get?' Not quite the conversations to create a positive frame of mind for a debutant in professional cricket! 'Good Luck, Wilks!' was the general comment as I was preparing mentally for my first ever outing for Glamorgan County Cricket Club, and for a bowl against one of the greatest players of all time.

But this was not the first time I had seen Viv Richards, or bowled to him. That happened the previous year when Viv was playing for Lansdown, a historic club in Bath which had once fielded a 12-year old WG Grace. Viv had been spotted, and his fares paid, by a wealthy Lansdown member who was on holiday in Antigua.

I had played for Cardiff against Lansdown in the Western League in 1974. If my memory serves me correctly Viv, who already looked a fabulous player, smashed a whirlwind 99 against us, and holed out at long-off trying to hoist our leg-spinner into the grounds of the Royal United Hospital adjacent to Lansdown Cricket Club.

A year later, the County Ground at Taunton was absolutely packed, which was no surprise considering they had Viv Richards and the up-and-coming Ian Botham in their side.

Glamorgan made 188-8 in 40 overs and (unsurprisingly) I didn't bat but was given the new ball by Majid to bowl the first ball of the Somerset innings. I was suitably nervous, or rather, psyched up for the contest, but the ball left my hand pretty much as I wanted it to and I was relieved to get through my spell. In a dramatic finish Somerset also scored 188-8 and the match ended tied, my figures of 7-1-26-2 being respectable enough after an immensely enjoyable experience in front of a packed audience. I loved the thrill of being out there, on stage if you like, lapping up the attention and just enjoying playing cricket. Part of it, I felt, came naturally, but there was always the feeling of nerves throughout the contest. Was I the only one feeling nervous? Was it nerves or just adrenalin as the occasion demanded it? Whatever it was, I took it all in and wanted to experience the adrenalin flow again.

My wish was granted a fortnight later when I was selected in the team to play against Worcestershire, who were bidding for the Sunday League title. It was another full house at the beautiful New Road Cricket Ground, and Worcestershire, with the likes of Glenn Turner, Basil D'Oliveira, Imran Khan and Norman Gifford in their side, beat Glamorgan easily. Four overs from me cost 19 runs, and I was bowled by England's left-arm spinner, the wily Norman Gifford, for a duck, so my contribution was not exactly headline news.

Worcestershire, however, were pipped for the Sunday League title by Hampshire, who had the great South African, Barry Richards, in their side. Glamorgan finished rock bottom last, with just four wins in 16 matches. It could only get better couldn't it, for Glamorgan and for me? Twelve months' hence, I would be playing against Somerset again but the stakes, and the outcome, would be vastly different.

It always rains in the cricket season, but in 1976 it didn't. It was the hottest and driest summer in the United Kingdom since records began. Record temperatures of 35 degrees Celsius and the lack of rain meant that the green fields of England and Wales were scorched. Playing cricket that summer was an unprecedented experience.

The conditions that summer suited Clive Lloyd's touring West Indies, a magnificent side which entertained crowds all over the country. They played all 17 county clubs (Durham was still a minor county) and other teams as well including the MCC, Minor Counties and Combined Universities, before losing to TN Pearce's XI at Scarborough at the very end of the tour.

As a group of Loughborough students, we first got to see the West Indies at close quarters in early June at Trent Bridge, in the first Test of the five-match series. In those days, spectators were permitted to watch the Test on the grass outfield outside the ropes, and that's what we did, a bunch of Loughborough lads on a day out at Trent Bridge watching the extraordinary batting of the great Viv Richards who hit a majestic 232. Viv imperiously smashing the likes of England's John Snow back over his head was the most amazing sight.

It was the summer where England's captain, Tony Greig, made his infamous and somewhat ill-advised comment that England would make the West Indies "grovel" in the Test series. Clive Lloyd's team needed no further motivation to beat England. The first two Tests at Trent Bridge and Lord's were drawn, but the West Indies won the last three, at Old Trafford, Headingley and The Oval, where Viv scored a towering 291 and where Michael Holding bowled terrifyingly fast. Throughout the series, Holding, Andy Roberts, Wayne Daniel and Vanburn Holder bowled with a brutal, physical hostility. England recalled Brian Close, at the age of 45, to open the innings at Old Trafford, and the subsequent battering he received from Holding, Roberts and Daniel was one of Test cricket's most excruciating moments. Little did I know then, watching that ferocious pounding of England's batsmen, that I would be playing against the West Indies in a matter of weeks. Before then, we had university cricket to attend to.

We were in the semi-final of the British Universities Cup against Liverpool University at one of Oxford University's beautiful grounds, located alongside the River Isis. Our team was full of players with first-class experience, but we weren't at our best on that exceedingly hot summer's day. It came down to the last over of the game with Loughborough needing ten runs to win, and I was facing their key fast bowler. I am not sure if I had my eyes shut or maybe swung my trusty Gunn & Moore bat like a golf club, but the first ball he delivered was short and I just swung at it. The ball went flying over backward square leg for six! Two balls to go and four needed. This time he pitched it up and I took another swing. Four! Straight past the bowler, who stood there in the middle of the pitch as bemused as I was at what had just happened and that Loughborough had beaten Liverpool by the most unlikely manner; me scoring the runs to get us over the line. It should have been the best celebration of our summer, but in our haste to get crates of cold beers for the mini-bus to take us back to Loughborough, we stopped to fill up with petrol. Two minutes later, we came to a grinding halt on the M1 motorway, one of the busiest traffic arteries in Britain. The mini-bus was a diesel engine and we had just pumped 20 gallons of petrol into it. The long journey home, and our celebrations, quickly ran out of gas.

The Parks at Oxford University was the venue for my inaugural first-class match for Glamorgan, captained by Majid Khan. After three days of cricket against Oxford University, I realised that I knew little about the great Majid Khan, his personality or his thoughts on life, although he did invite me for a walk around the boundary during the match. The request took me by surprise, but it was a pleasant walk during which Majid asked a stack of questions. Majid had an aura about him: princely, regal, upstanding. I took it as a compliment that he invited me to walk with him around this most beautiful of cricket grounds.

Glamorgan won the rain-affected three-day match against Oxford University by 77 runs and I had to wait until the second innings to bag my first first-class wicket. The unfortunate fellow was John Claughton, LBW for 6. I then had Oxford's captain, Vic Marks, who would go on to play for Somerset and England, caught by Majid at first slip for nought. Nothing remarkable about my performance at all, but my first-class career was underway.

The West Indies had already won the Test series by the time they came to Swansea for two matches against Glamorgan. I wasn't selected for the three-day match, but was I happy about that! West Indies rattled up a total of 554-4 declared in just 83 overs, as the ball kept flying out of the St. Helen's ground. Gordon Greenidge and Viv Richards both hit typical centuries before Clive Lloyd annihilated the Glamorgan attack with an unbeaten 201 in two hours, equaling the fastest first-class double century ever. If it had been a boxing match, the fight would have been stopped by the referee. When Glamorgan batted I got onto the field as twelfth man for the tourists. On this occasion, it suited me just fine. I did, however, play in the Sunday 40-over match in front of a full house on the Bank Holiday weekend. We lost by 106 runs. Viv went for two runs, but Roy Fredericks hit 54 against his old club and Bernard Julien took great delight in trying to hit the cricket ball into the sea over the wall at the Mumbles End. He achieved it more than once, and we all gave him the opportunity to do it. My figures were 0-40 from my eight overs.

My County Championship debut followed a few days later against Middlesex – a powerhouse side chasing the title – at Swansea. As it happened, my first Championship wicket was their captain Mike Brearley, caught behind by Eifion Jones, and my second was Clive Radley, but not before he had scored a century and taken the game away from us. The St. Helen's pitch is a spinner's delight, and Mike Brearley had pulled off a masterstroke by calling up the long-retired England off-spinner, Fred Titmus, into the Middlesex side for this match. Brearley's genius and planning was rewarded, as Titmus took 7-34 in just seven overs in Glamorgan's second innings, bowling us out for a paltry 85. Middlesex won by 186 runs and were well on track for their first outright title since 1947.

What was most striking was the way in which Middlesex played the game. They were a supremely confident group. They strutted their stuff and made the occasional comment amongst themselves, loud enough to be heard by Glamorgan batsmen in the middle, but not remotely offensive enough to be called sledging. They didn't need to use offensive verbal methods, because they were ruthless enough with the bat and the ball and in the manner with which they fielded. This was only my first game of County Championship cricket, but I could already discern the gulf between a top side like Middlesex, and perennial strugglers like Glamorgan. We'd won the County Championship in 1948 and 1969, but the 1976 vintage was not going to make the BBC Sports Personality Team of the Year Award.

The fabulous 'West Indies' summer of 1976 gave way to winter at Loughborough. It was my last at University, and time for some proper work with final degree examinations due in the early summer of 1977. After that, I hadn't really made up my mind, apart from knowing I didn't want to teach. Professional cricket was probably top of my list, and I wanted to continue playing rugby, but the wonderful personality of my psychology lecturer, Duncan Case, had enthused me about continuing my academic career with sports psychology, a favourite subject. I was inquisitive by nature and I wanted to know more about so many things. I was naïve about a lot of things in life, but sport – and what made sportsmen and women perform or not perform – was something I thought a lot about.

That last year was a brute for the sheer volume of work. But having coasted for the three years to get my Certificate of Education – which qualified me as a teacher – I got my act together in the final 12 months and put in the hard 'yakka' for the Bachelor of Education degree I wanted more than anything else.

We all celebrated by heading to one of Loughborough's pubs on a warm, sunny day and did what students do when you think you are the most important people on earth – we drank too much and got drunk in the sun – but it was harmless stuff for those who managed to keep standing by the evening.

The morning hangover was reality sinking in that four years at Loughborough had come and gone. Now we all had to think about growing up, and start looking for a job. Many had long lined up full-time employment but I had no desire to go into teaching, and no teaching position lined up. Essentially, I was thinking of a summer of cricket, the summer of 1977. The final day at Loughborough, with a wonderful group of people from all parts of the UK, was an emotional assault on the senses. After four years of bonding through our triumphs and tortures, our highs and lows, our wins and losses, our results and our failures, it was now all over.

I was given a lift to Loughborough railway station, with my bags and all my paraphernalia collected over four years as a student. God knows how many of my close pals were in that car, but they managed to get me on the train to Cardiff on May 30th, 1977. Tears of joy and happiness engulfed us. Loughborough was over. I still didn't know my degree result, but top of my thoughts was the 1977 cricket season and my desire to play for Glamorgan.

# 3

## Glamorgan New Boy

*'Wilko and I were competitors on the cricket fields of England and now co-workers in commentary boxes around the world, and I can safely say he has been as genuine behind the microphone as he was when he trundled away at his medium-paced stuff for Glamorgan and Gloucestershire. Always caring about his fellow workers and especially willing to have a chat after working hours if a glass or two of wine was involved.'*

**Michael Holding**

The papers were full of Kerry Packer's plans for his rebel World Series Cricket competition in Australia, with 13 of the 17 Australian players currently on tour in England reported to have signed up and England captain Tony Greig having being sacked for his involvement, but my thoughts were much closer to home. Two weeks after arriving back in Cardiff, I was selected to play for Glamorgan against Somerset at Sophia Gardens. While Somerset still fielded Viv Richards, Ian Botham and Joel Garner, our overseas player that season was the West Indian all-rounder Collis King – 'Kingdom' to all in the dressing room. He endeared himself to the Welsh players and fans not just because of his infectious personality and his beaming smile, but because he had a middle name straight out of Wales – Llewellyn!

The welcome I received from Alan Jones, Glamorgan's captain, and the rest of the team was warm and generous. Six years after that day as a schoolboy fielder against the touring Indians, and two weeks out of university, I was back as a Glamorgan professional and about to be tested by one of the strongest county sides in England.

Heavy rain delayed the start of play but gloomy skies made way for bright sunshine late on the first day. However, there were no bright faces in the Glamorgan dressing room. We lost the toss and were put into bat on a damp, fast pitch where we were soon in trouble. The giant West Indian Joel Garner, known as Big Bird, was virtually unplayable on that pitch. With Ian Botham – looking to impress the England selectors – doing his best to bag wickets at the other end, it was no surprise that we went down like a row of dominoes. Big Bird went through us like a giant visitor from another planet, cutting us down with 15 overs of sustained pace, bounce and menace, taking 8-31 in the process. Kingdom strode out to bat without a helmet which, to us in the dressing room was a sign of madness, but to Big Bird it was playtime as a huge smile appeared upon his face. Together, those two Barbadian cricketers entertained us players as much as spectators; Joel bounced Collis and Collis swatted him away for four. Then came the yorker, which usually broke a batsman's toes, but with a Caribbean flick, that too travelled fast for four. Alas, the entertainment didn't last long; Kingdom was out for 22. My contribution, batting at 11, was a rather tentative five runs, with a marvellous edge through slips for four. The next ball from Joel smashed into my off stump as my bat was coming down as an afterthought to meet the oncoming ball. I was Big Bird's eighth wicket as Glamorgan were bowled out for a paltry 113. Joel and I were destined to have a few more duels out in the middle, but I can also assure you that it was not of my volition. I wasn't looking for a fight with Big Bird. No-one in their right mind would.

The light deteriorated (which was my excuse for missing the ball that demolished my stumps) sufficiently for the umpires to call play off for the day. Both sides adjourned to the bar which, in the original pavilion at Sophia Gardens, was no more than a small lounge in the middle of the two dressing rooms. But with Richards, Garner and Botham in town it was transformed into a Tardis, with seemingly hundreds there for a drink and a gawk at the cricketers on show. Joel Garner was a giant – the biggest cricketer I had ever seen, but he had the broadest grin and the deepest voice, which marvelously complemented his enormous skeletal frame. An hour earlier he had terrorised us; now here he was, with Collis and Viv, laughing raucously and having a great time together.

The following morning it was our turn to bowl. A much bigger crowd had turned up to see Viv, the biggest box office draw in the game. Malcolm Nash and Collis King opened the bowling and Collis removed the Somerset openers, Brian Rose and Peter 'Dasher' Denning, which meant that when I was given the ball as first-change bowler in the Glamorgan attack, I was going to bowl my first ball at Viv Richards.

With skipper Alan Jones, we set the field for Viv (did it really matter?) with a couple of slips, a gully and the rest in orthodox fashion. You had to appreciate what a magnificent physical specimen Viv was. It was not just when he stood at the crease leaning on his bat, even when he walked out to bat, there was a swagger to his stride that no-one else had. Garry Sobers had 'the walk', as did Michael Holding, but Viv's was different. If ever a cricketer exuded menace simply by walking, then Vivian Richards did just that. It was terrifying and beautiful at the same time.

The former Somerset and England off-spinner, Vic Marks, writing in the *Guardian* in 2009, summed up the menace of Viv Richards perfectly:

*These were the eyes that subjugated every bowler in the 1970s and 80s. One moment they allowed him to see the ball that millisecond faster than anyone else, the next they could stare down the pitch with such intensity that bowlers shrivelled in his presence. Richards had an aura beyond that of any cricketer of his generation. Several bowlers could intimidate, but he was the one batsman who could scare the living daylights out of opponents from the moment he entered the arena. He would wait a little for his stage to be cleared, then the languid swagger, the banging of the bat handle with the palm of his hand, the cap – no helmet for Vivian Richards – and the gum.*

I marked my run-up, which was about 20 walking strides (no tape measures or groundsman's paint brushes in those days) and I was bowling from the River Taff end of Sophia Gardens. I was nervous. Bloody nervous. Was I thinking more about Viv Richards than my own job with the ball? Did I have a set thought on what ball I was going to bowl to Viv? A few deep breaths and off I went, past the umpire and let the ball go. It left my hand reasonably well, but came back at me at such a rate that I instinctively ducked for safety. It almost decapitated the umpire, Barrie Meyer, and smashed into the wooden fencing behind me with a 'thwack' that rang around the ground. I looked at Viv, who had taken a few strides down the pitch, chewing his gum as only Viv chewed it, arms wide akimbo, using his bat to gently dab the pitch surface whilst at the same time giving me a look through those big bright eyes that had a message: he was intent on doing it again.

The cricket field can be a lonely place even when you are out there with your teammates. Sure, cricket is a team sport, but essentially it's what you do with the ball against an opponent who is doing his level best to destroy you with his bat. No-one else could help me with my second ball to Viv; I had to work it out myself. I guess I had something in mind when I ran in again looking to bowl as straight a delivery as I could, with possibly some in-swing, in an attempt to keep Viv quiet. I didn't want to give him any room to use those big muscular arms as he had done with my first ball. It was a decent delivery, and it did swing, but it also left Viv's bat with such pace; this time towards mid-off where our diminutive off-spinner, Gwyn Richards, had the misfortune to be fielding. In other words, the poor bugger was directly in the firing line. Gwyn got his hands to it, or rather, the ball smashed into his hands. He stopped it going for four, but it was two, and our off-spinner almost lost two fingers in the process. Mentally, I had to regroup and think about my third delivery.

I tried to bowl the in-swinger again but, at the very last moment, saw Viv take a huge stride down the pitch so let the ball go – with an air of uncertainty – wider than the previous two. Viv connected with a violent swing of his big bat that sent the ball skywards, but off the outside edge, and it flew high towards third man. There, standing on the third man boundary was Malcolm Nash. Shouts of 'catch it!' rang out from every Glamorgan player on that field. I just stood there at the end of my follow-through with my mouth wide open as this missile was heading towards the third man rope. It had 'six' written all over it but somehow Nashy managed to stretch his arms up high into the air and, in a surreal moment in my life, Viv Richards had been caught off only the third ball I had bowled at him in the County Championship.

Viv couldn't believe it and neither could I. The great man was trudging back to the Somerset dressing room as Glamorgan players gathered around me to offer their congratulations. In truth, had it been anyone else but Malcolm Nash, the ball would have gone for six, but Malcolm was one of the tallest players in our side. I dread to think where the ball might have gone had Viv hit it cleanly. Cardiff Castle maybe. But for now, I smiled with utter contentment as I had just dismissed the great Viv Richards.

It was the start of a good day for me and one I will never forget. I managed to pull out an in-swinging yorker to uproot Ian Botham's leg stump to bowl him for just five, and then later, I got revenge on Joel Garner by bowling him as well for 13. We bowled Somerset out for 203 and I finished with decent figures of 19.3 overs 3-51: Viv Richards, Ian Botham and Joel Garner my three unfortunate scalps. The arrival of more rain meant that the match ended as a damp squib of a draw, but I was pleased with my efforts, and was so looking forward to more.

There was no time to savour the overwhelming feeling of satisfaction because of the ridiculous scheduling of professional cricket in those days. Cricketers who had been playing for three days at one end of the country had to pack their bags, jump into cars, and then drive over the speed limit around Britain's motorways, and sometimes off the motorways, to get to the next venue, often past midnight, with the next County Championship match starting the following day.

For Glamorgan that meant Nottinghamshire at Worksop, a town located on the northern edge of Sherwood Forest of Robin Hood fame, known for its coal-mining in the days when Great Britain was the foremost provider of coal to the rest of the world. The car journey would take over four hours, not including a stop for an evening meal in some motorway services, so we would eventually arrive in a place none of us had been before in search of a hotel that we knew only by name. There was no GPS in cars in those days, no mobile phones and therefore no apps, no Google Maps, no short cuts! The way to get anywhere if you were lost was to stop the car, wind down the window and ask a pedestrian where the hell you were and whether they could direct us to our hotel. Often the answer would be along the lines of, 'Oh, you are miles away from there. You'd better turn around and ask someone else!'

We got there in the end at around midnight. Utter madness! The next morning we won the toss and batted – thankfully, because most of us wanted to catch up on sleep in the dressing room.

Even more crazily, after a day of cricket in the far north of the county of Nottinghamshire, we then had to pack up yet again and head back south to Cardiff, (where we had been playing 24 hours earlier) for a Sunday League match against Hampshire. The Sunday League was a one-day competition of 40 overs per side, but it was a popular format even then with spectators who enjoyed the somewhat faster fare on offer.

All the cricketers involved in English county cricket at that time were in the same predicament; an ongoing kaleidoscope of car journeys across the motorways of Britain in the name of professional cricket. It was sheer stupidity when I think back to how some drivers of the cars would be so tired it would be a hazard, not just for us as passengers, but for other motorists on the road. We lost that Sunday League match against Hampshire and went through the procedure once again – pack up the bags and cricket cases, and head north again to resume the three-day County Championship match against Nottinghamshire, who themselves had travelled to Northampton to play their Sunday League match. You would have thought that someone in the corridors of power at Lord's would have caught on to the idea that they were putting cricketers' lives at risk by sending them on high speed car journeys, always at night, to play another game of cricket. Wouldn't it have made sense to have stayed in Worksop on the Saturday night and played our Sunday League match against Nottinghamshire in the middle of the Championship match? Eventually, that would happen, but not during that season.

The match at Worksop was another three-day County Championship match that ended in a draw, because there was insufficient time for a result. My first innings figures were unremarkable: 22-7-36-1, but I somehow managed to enhance my batting reputation, if I had one at all in those days, because I weighed in with the dullest possible innings of 70 – in our second innings – having been sent in as night-watchman. I bored the hell out of the great South African all-rounder, Clive Rice, who was uncomfortably quick, and Dilip Doshi, the Indian spinner, whose left-arm spin bowling was as neat and presentable as his persona on and off the field. I never did manage to improve upon that 70 at Worksop, and it remained my top score in county cricket. Those poor souls at the Worksop Town Ground who had to sit through it for the hours it took me must have wondered why on earth they had bothered to turn up.

Among the spectators at Worksop was a strapping thick-set 67 year old man whom I'll never forget meeting. He was none other than the great Bill Voce, partner to the great Harold Larwood for Notts and for England in the 1932-33 Ashes series when their 'Bodyline' tactics won England the series but created controversy which reached Cabinet level in both countries.

Bill Voce talked to me after my 22 overs in Nottinghamshire's first innings, and asked me about what I was trying to bowl. Was I trying to bowl fast? Was I trying to swing the ball? Did I try and vary my pace? What was my thinking throughout the day? In a technical discussion, Bill Voce suggested that I should modify my action in order to bowl quicker, by bringing my front (right) arm down sharply in the delivery stride, so as to get my bowling (left) arm through quicker. His advice was in stark contrast to the technique that was being coached into me at the time by our player/coach, Tom Cartwright, the former Warwickshire, Somerset and England medium pace bowler. Tom had always said that I must try and keep my right arm as high and as long in the air through my action to keep me upright in my delivery, and to encourage me to stay taller through the crease. Tom's thinking was of a medium-pacer with the idea of swinging the ball. Bill Voce was advising something completely different with the purpose of bowling quicker. I might have been a bit confused after our conversation, but I was privileged to have met one of the greats of English cricket.

After a couple of days at home in Cardiff, we took the short trip across the River Severn to Bristol to take on a Gloucestershire team led by the great South African all-rounder, Mike Procter and including two outstanding Pakistani batsmen, Sadiq Mohammad and the wonderfully gifted Zaheer Abbas. It was the first time I'd played against Zed, already a legendary run-scorer who had made 274 in his second Test against England in 1971 and, the previous season, had topped the national averages in England with 2,554 runs at an average of 75.11, with 11 centuries. Throughout his career Zaheer, who batted in spectacles, was just the most beautifully composed and elegant run-machine, the first Asian to make 100 first-class centuries and the only player to have scored a century and a double-century in a first-class match four times! Furthermore, he finished each of those eight innings not out.

So it was with some trepidation that Glamorgan travelled the short journey to Bristol, but it turned out to be a fortuitous trip. Glamorgan beat Gloucestershire by 143 runs, our first win of the season, a terrific effort against the county they called 'Proctershire' for all that the South African did for them over the years. I was on a hat-trick twice in the match, both times involving the same three players: Zaheer Abbas, John Sullivan (bowled – both times -first ball) and a real character of Gloucestershire County Cricket Club, David Shepherd. 'Shep', who went on to become one of the great personalities as an international umpire, and highly regarded by every player, thwarted me both times on the hat-trick ball but, in the second innings, I did run him out off my own bowling, first ball. Alas, it didn't count as a hat-trick.

Next up was Worcestershire at Swansea, and an extraordinary innings by their New Zealand opening batsman, Glenn Turner, whose 141 not out in a total of 169 is the highest ever percentage of runs in a single innings. No other batsman got into double figures. It was the most phenomenal virtuoso innings I had ever seen, and it amazed the entire Glamorgan team.

Just a week later, Glamorgan travelled to Worcester, with the magnificent Cathedral forming an imposing backdrop to one of

England's most picturesque cricket grounds. From a personal point of view I was enjoying every day, and this three-day match at New Road served to reinforce my thoughts that I was coping with the demands of professional cricket. I took a personal haul of eight wickets in the match, with a five-wicket bag of 5-71 in 23 overs in Worcestershire's second innings, after the batting exploits of our captain, Alan Jones with 106, and John Hopkins, who made a career-best 230, and Glamorgan came away with a resounding win by eight wickets. I trapped Basil D'Oliveira LBW for 34 in the first innings, but the Cape Town-born England all-rounder was undefeated on 156 in the second innings as wickets fell at the other end.

However, it was the one-day formats where we were looking strongest. We won in the Sunday League against Northamptonshire, for whom Pakistan's Mushtaq Mohammad was captain, and they also had the wonderful Indian left-arm spinner, Bishan Bedi. It was our fourth win on Sundays and life was beginning to feel good in this Glamorgan side. Three days later we beat Worcestershire at New Road, this time in the second round of the Gillette Cup, the premier one-day competition played over 60 overs per side. Again, I was satisfied that I had contributed to our cause with figures of 12-2-40-1.

Our Sunday League trip to Worcester in late July was less successful, although I was delighted to get the wicket of D'Oliveira again, but it was bracketed by yet another championship victory, against Hampshire at the United Services Ground, Portsmouth. I took 5 for 58 in their second innings, with an in-swinging yorker dismissing their West Indian opener Gordon Greenidge for 38. His partner, the brilliant South African Barry Richards, batted 11 in both innings – citing illness – but we suspected something else was on his mind as he seemed to have lost all interest in county cricket.

The satisfaction of winning cricket matches, whatever the format, was tangible. It just felt damn good to be a professional cricketer travelling all over the country and playing sport for a living; the remuneration was nothing to write home about, but money was the last thing on my mind in the middle of that summer. Next we travelled to Nuneaton, a quaint little town about 30 miles east of Birmingham, to play Warwickshire. At the same time as Ian

Botham was taking five wickets in his first Test to take England 2-0 up in the Ashes series at Nottingham, I was taking six more wickets for Glamorgan. It was a super game of cricket where we had set Warwickshire 335 to win; they finished 313-8, with their England opener Dennis Amiss 144 not out, and with us pressing for the last two wickets for the win.

Everything was going so well that it felt natural to run in and take wickets. I was hitting the stumps often, getting great players out and I looked forward to the next day of cricket with huge anticipation of improving with every bowling spell. It was not a feeling of invincibility, but just a sense that I was comfortable in this environment. However, in any sport those feelings can dissipate without warning and that is what happened when Essex played Glamorgan at Aberystwyth, the university town on Wales' west coast. It was the last day of July 1977, and the Vicarage Field was jam-packed for the visit of Essex who – in their side – had Graham Gooch; the South African batsman, Kenny McEwan; two England captains in Keith Fletcher and Mike Denness; and the England left-arm quick bowler, John Lever.

Another good day seemed in prospect when I bowled the Essex opening batsman, Matthew Fosh who, the previous year, had toured the West Indies with Young England (along with Mike Gatting and David Gower). Graham Gooch changed that thinking very quickly. At the crease Gooch presented a formidable sight from 22 yards; that massive black moustache that made him look like a Mexican policeman, the high backlift with his huge bat and the stare down the pitch straight at you. What I wasn't prepared for was the way he walked down the pitch with his hands holding his bat aloft behind him. He proceeded to take me apart as he hit me to all parts of Vicarage Field, aptly named that day, because all I could do after every smashing blow was utter a religious profanity, not at Goochie, but into the air as the ball flew into the crowds along the boundary rope. I went for 54 runs in eight overs, my worst figures of the season but, more than the runs conceded, what hurt more was the utter despair I felt at letting my teammates down.

I hit a low that afternoon that I hadn't felt all season. Graham Gooch had given me a hiding as he bludgeoned his way to 80, although it felt like a physical beating as Essex rattled up 234-7. Glamorgan got close with the wonderful batting of Collis King, who hit 66, but who was then bowled by Gooch and our hopes of winning disappeared. We lost by just 15 runs. I took it personally and felt that it was only my bowling that cost us the game. If I had bowled a lot better, then I reckon we should have won. I felt dreadful and apologised to the boys in the dressing room; it was a salutary lesson. Just when I thought that everything was going the way I wanted that season, it took a few minutes for the mental landscape to change complexion. Matters were compounded when we lost our Championship match against Kent at Swansea over the following two days. While I had taken the wicket of Kent's captain, Asif Iqbal, two defeats in three days were a couple of big body blows.

It was hardly the ideal preparation for our next big game, which was the very next day, a quarter-final in the Gillette Cup in Cardiff against Surrey, who had beaten us in a three-day match at Sophia Gardens just a month earlier. Surrey's line-up was strong: John Edrich was captain, Alan Butcher, Younis Ahmed (Pakistan), Graham Roope, Intikhab Alam (Pakistan), Robin Jackman, Geoff Arnold, Pat Pocock and Jack Richards, the wicket-keeper. I don't know why, but there was no love lost between the two sides, and this was the nastiest atmosphere I had experienced in a cricket match. It was the first time that I had heard ugly words exchanged between professional players. Surrey won the toss and batted. John Edrich top-scored with 53, but not before he had got embroiled in a nasty verbal exchange with our wicket-keeper, Eifion Jones, who never took a step backwards in his life, and certainly not on the cricket field. Given the importance of the game, I felt it was just about my best bowling performance of the season as I returned figures of 12-3-33-2, getting the key wickets of Younis Ahmed, bowled for 27, and England's Graham Roope, caught and bowled for 13.

Younis and I had 'words', and it was the first of many occasions where we swapped insults in the middle of the pitch. He called me everything under the sun, sometimes in Urdu, which I obviously didn't understand, but the tone of his voice suggested that he disliked me intensely. The feeling was mutual; I didn't like him and I told him. It was the first time that umpires had got involved and spoke to all of us who took part in this ugly verbal jousting. Surrey were bowled out for 199 in 59.2 overs, and we got the runs in 56 overs with our captain, Alan Jones, making 54, and Collis King hitting a typically belligerent 55. Surrey left the field with heads bowed, and disappeared from Cardiff in a hurry, as Welsh cricket fans cheered for joy around Sophia Gardens. Our spirits were running high that evening, but had I learned something new about professional sport? Was this a part of the game?

We were in the semi-finals and suddenly, our season was all about the Gillette Cup. We were still doing quite well in the Sunday League but we were never going to win it and neither did we have any remaining aspirations in the County Championship. Beating Surrey made us believe we could make it to the final, but we still had lots of cricket to play throughout August. We went south to the coastal seaside resort of Eastbourne to play Sussex – boasting Tony Greig as captain, Javed Miandad, Imran Khan and John Snow – and drew that match. We then lost to Essex on a raging turner of a pitch at Leyton in East London, although I picked up four more wickets. But we won three more Sunday League matches, against Middlesex, Lancashire and then Nottinghamshire – a day before my 24th birthday – as I recorded my best Sunday League figures of 5 for 32 in 6.5 overs. But none of that mattered compared to the Gillette Cup semi-final which was to be played at St. Helen's in Swansea.

Glamorgan's opponents for the semi-final were Leicestershire, led by Ray Illingworth, the former England captain, with a line-up that included: David Gower; Chris Balderstone; the hard-hitting Zimbabwean batsman, Brian Davison; Roger Tolchard the former England wicket-keeper; Jack Birkenshaw, the former England off-spinner; and two nasty fast bowlers in Alan Ward and Ken Higgs, both former England players. The match was broadcast across the UK on BBC 2, with the great Richie Benaud leading the commentary team.

It was the biggest cricket match of my life, but heavy persistent rain meant that no play was possible on the designated match day. It rained again on the second day, but eventually the rain relented and bright sunshine shone on St. Helen's and, maybe, on our captain, Alan Jones. He won the toss and put Leicestershire into bat on a dry pitch, but with a damp outfield that rendered boundaries difficult to come by.

The tension level was raised by an incident involving David Gower and me. Opening the innings, David was on 43 and batting beautifully when our off-spinner, Gwyn Richards, came on to bowl. David drove his third ball uppishly straight at me at extra cover; I dived forward and got my fingers under the ball and claimed the catch. In that split second David Gower just stood there, looking at me. I looked at the umpire, Kenny Palmer, at the bowler's end, and held my arm up high clutching the ball and claiming the catch.

The other umpire, the uncompromising Australian, Bill Alley, who was always red in the face, went puce and just looked at me. David stood there in his crease and I was standing at extra cover when he just asked, "Alan, did you catch that?" I replied immediately, "Yes David, I did." To his credit, David just left the crease and walked past me towards the direction of the dressing rooms. Glamorgan team-mates gathered around to congratulate me on taking the catch, but I was to learn that my claiming that catch completely incensed the Leicestershire captain, Ray Illingworth.

I weighed in with the prized wicket of Brian Davison, LBW for 40, and then got Jack Birkenshaw caught at gully from a dreadful delivery. Suddenly, Leicestershire were in trouble and into bat walked a fuming Ray Illingworth. As soon as he got to the middle, he had an animated conversation with the umpire, Ken Palmer, and gave me looks that suggested I was not going to be on his Christmas card list. I was now bowling from the Mumbles (sea) end of St. Helen's, running away from where the BBC TV commentary box was erected on top of temporary scaffolding. Illingworth took guard and he was also rather red in the face. My first ball went past his outside edge and we all heard a noise. Eifion Jones took 'the catch' and he and three slips and I went up in unison appealing for the umpire to give it out. In that moment when you shout 'howizzzzzzzzthaaaaaat!' at the top of your voice, you are also mentally celebrating taking a wicket, because you believe fervently that the batsman is out. Ray Illingworth just stood there and stared at me. I was in the middle of the pitch staring at him, and then I turned back to the umpire,

Bill Alley, and made a second appeal for the catch. "How-Is-That?" I shouted straight at him to which he shouted back, "NOT OUT!"

I was livid. We all knew that Illingworth had got an edge, and he knew it as well, but for some reason – maybe Bill Alley thought that I hadn't taken the David Gower catch cleanly – my appeal fell on deaf ears.

My second ball to Ray Illingworth was a shocker, a rank long hop that was an excuse for a bouncer, and the former England captain just pulled it away backward of square for four. "That is a poor delivery from Alan Wilkins," said Richie Benaud in the commentary box, "what you might call 'inexperience'."

The day finished with Leicestershire 138-7, with Illingworth 10 not out and a former friend of mine at Loughborough, Peter Booth, making a nuisance of himself with 20 not out. The following day, our third day at St. Helen's for a one-day cup game, Leicestershire had six overs left to bat and they took their score to 172-7. I was happy with my bowling effort of 12-5-34-2, but now it was up to our batsmen to get the runs that would get us into the Gillette Cup final. Our captain, Alan Jones, and fellow opener, John Hopkins, put on 109 for the opening wicket with Hopkins top-scoring with 63 as we got home, 175-5 in 57.3 overs. It was a tense finish – it had been a tension-filled three days in Swansea – but Glamorgan had made it into their first ever cup final. We were going to Lord's, a ground I had never been to before, and now I was going to play there in the Gillette Cup final.

Our opponents in the final were to be Middlesex who, in the other semi-final, had annihilated Somerset at Lord's, bowling them out for just 59. Viv Richards was one of West Indian Wayne Daniels' four wickets and the former England fast bowler, Mike Selvey, took three. Middlesex, on their home ground at Lord's, were going to be the hot favourites to win the final.

Before that, we had to finish our County Championship season at Sophia Gardens where the visitors were Mike Procter's Gloucestershire. We lost the match on the third day, but local media organisations still wanted photographs, interviews and time with each and all of us. The following day was going to be the biggest in Glamorgan's history.

The journey from Cardiff, capital city of Wales, to London was about three hours along the M4 motorway, and a convoy of sponsored cars set off for London on that Friday evening. Could you imagine that happening in the modern game? Driving three hours along motorways the evening before an early morning start to a major one-day cup final? I was with my parents and a cousin, Bob Collier, a former Cambridge University and Wasps rugby player, who lived just outside London. Arriving in London in busy Friday evening traffic was not a lot of fun, neither was the checking-in process at the Clarendon Court Hotel in Maida Vale, where the team was staying. Alan Jones had informed me earlier in the day that I was in the playing XI for the final, so you can imagine my utter shock when, in answer to the receptionist's question for my name, she said, "We do not have a room for Alan Wilkins. Are you sure you have a booking?" Rather perplexed, I replied, "Yes, I do have a booking. I am playing for Glamorgan in the Gillette Cup final at Lord's tomorrow, and this is the official team hotel, so there must be a mistake on the hotel's part, because I am definitely part of the team booking."

"Mr. Wilkins," she said, "your name was down for a room, but it appears that someone has taken it." "May I ask who that person is?" I asked the smiling receptionist. "I am afraid I cannot tell you the person's name Mr. Wilkins, but he checked in a few hours earlier and I believe he may be in the lounge behind you right now."

I turned around and in one of the hotel's reception rooms, off the foyer, a boisterous party was going on with lots of animated conversations, clinking of wine and champagne glasses, and a jolly old knees-up. I had not been invited, nor did I wish to step inside the room, but there were lots of people I recognised, including Wilf Wooller, most of the Glamorgan committee people and the club's chairman, Ossie Wheatley, the former Cambridge University and Glamorgan captain, who stood out due to his height and blonde hair. He caught my eye and must have sensed my discomfort because he was quickly asking me what the problem was. When I explained to him that I did not have a room in the hotel, and that my room had been taken by someone in the room he'd just left, Ossie calmly said, "Oh don't worry, Alan, we'll sort this out."

When the chairman asked the receptionist to put me into a room in the hotel she said with a dead pan face, "We are full, sir, totally full." Now getting rather frustrated, "Surely you must have one single room?" Ossie Wheatley implored. "Not one single room at all, sir. Mr. Wilkins's room was taken by a person earlier this evening, sir."

It was established that my room had been taken by a committee member of the club, using whatever authority he thought he had to scrub my name from the hotel ledger and book himself into the room designated for me. At that point, my cousin came into the foyer since this process was taking time, and I hadn't said my farewell to my family in the waiting car outside the hotel. He knew Ossie Wheatley from Cambridge University days. "Hi Ossie," said Bob, "is there a problem here?" "There appears to be," said our chairman "in that Alan does not have a room at this hotel and he is playing in the final tomorrow." "Well that doesn't sound too good, surely there is a room for Alan if he's playing." "It appears there isn't," our chairman reaffirmed.

I was dumbfounded by the farce taking place in front of me but, sensing my displeasure, my anger and my emotional state, Bob, with a calm assurance, just said, "Alan can stay with us tonight and I will drive him to Lord's in the morning, if that's OK with you Ossie?" The chairman replied, "Bob, how kind of you, that would be marvellous if you could." He turned to me and said, "Alan, are you alright with this? I am sorry about the mix-up, but I am sure you'll be OK for tomorrow." I don't think I said anything. There was no alternative, unless I was going to sleep the night in the foyer of the hotel. "No problem," said Bob, "let's go. What time in the morning does Alan have to be at Lord's?" The chairman said, "Nine in the morning will be fine, Bob, and thank you. See you in the morning, Alan."

There I was, with my bags on the floor beside me, thinking that this was not a good start to the biggest match of my short career to date. Playing in the Gillette Cup final and I had no room in the official team hotel! I would miss conversations between players that evening and the important meeting at breakfast on the morning of the match. I was flabbergasted. Would this have happened with any other county cricket club in the country? Would it have happened to a footballer on the eve of the FA Cup final at Wembley? Somehow,

I doubt it. I felt ridiculous departing from the official team hotel knowing that the team I was playing for the next day were all staying there. Was this how professional cricket was supposed to be? It was nine o'clock in the evening and we had to make our way through London traffic again, and find the A40 to Beaconsfield, which was about 26 miles outside London. The journey took about an hour and it was way past 11 in the evening by the time I got to bed, knowing I had to be up early in the morning to beat the traffic heading back into London.

I didn't sleep well. The events of that evening were on my mind and kept me awake; I was naturally upset and angry with what had happened. How could I have felt any differently? The following morning I was tense, wound up and apprehensive, which was to be expected given that I was due to play at Lord's for the first time in my life, in front of 30,000 people in the biggest match of my cricket career. But I was also apprehensive about the car journey ahead of us to get into London by 9am. We left Beaconsfield just after 7.30am but the A40 road was under construction for most of the journey into London, and soon we were stuck in a traffic jam. We were going nowhere fast. There were no mobile phones to alert anyone at Lord's that I might be late; the journey was one of the most nerve-wracking of my life, because I could sense that we were not going to make Lord's on time. Sure enough, we didn't. It was 9.15am when Bob dropped me off outside the Grace Gate and there were thousands of fans lining up in queues to get into Lord's. I had walked past the Grace Gate in St John's Woods Road on a visit to London before, but now I was running through it and through a throng of stewards, past the Harris Garden which was full of blazers and suits and MCC ties, most of them getting an early start on the champagne, but this was no champagne moment for me. I attempted to sprint past the two stewards at the entrance to the Lord's Pavilion, but they would have nothing of that. They wanted to see a letter or document that proved I was actually a Glamorgan cricketer. Right there and then I didn't feel much like one. After some pleasantries I was directed up the wide stairway to the visitors' changing room. Lord's Pavilion is no ordinary cricket pavilion. It was an overwhelming experience seeing it for the first time, being in it for the first time, albeit late for my job.

As I opened the big wooden door of the visitors' dressing room there wasn't a player in sight and the only person in the dressing room was the Lord's attendant who welcomed me with a smiling face and with the greeting, "Good morning sir, are you playing today?" "I am supposed to be but I got caught up in traffic getting here," I replied whilst hurriedly trying to change into my cricket gear. "You *are* late sir," said the jovial attendant. "The Glamorgan players went over to the Nursery nets at least half an hour ago."

I was a dishevelled mess, mentally and physically, but now I had to get my head straight to concentrate on the day ahead: the 1977 Gillette Cup final. The Nursery End at Lord's is where the space-age media box now stands with the Compton and Edrich Stands on each side, and behind these stands are the MCC cricket nets. I ran out of the dressing room, down the huge staircase and through a doorway into the famous Long Room brushing as politely as I could past MCC members who all seemed to be standing motionless in their own time space gazing either at their morning newspapers, or just into thin air around the beautiful surroundings of this magnificent building. I could hardly take it all in. It wasn't meant to be like this. It was supposed to be a very special moment in my life, but it didn't feel like it. I strode through the Long Room and out onto the steps in front of the Pavilion where the MCC members sit on long benches in their Panama hats, cream summer blazers and striped egg-and-tomato MCC ties, through the little white, wooden picket gate and onto the hallowed turf. The view was spectacular. The grass was so lush and green; it was a veritable carpet. I was half-walking and half-running to get over to the other side of the ground, but it seemed miles away. Eventually I got to the nets and there was the Glamorgan team, using three of the nets, with the Middlesex team using another set of nets. I was just so relieved to be there with the team, but felt so conspicuous by my late arrival. Before I had a chance to say anything to anyone, our player/coach, Tom Cartwright, approached me: "Where the hell have you been? You are late. And you will be fined for this." "Hang on Tom," I pleaded, "I didn't have a room at the hotel last night, and I had to stay outside London at my cousin's home. The traffic getting into London this morning was dreadful. I am sorry but this is not my fault." Tom was furious and he didn't want to know why I did not stay at the hotel the night before. "Get in those bloody nets and start bowling," he ordered. I felt terrible. I went over to Alan Jones and started to explain why I was late. Alan stopped me in mid-sentence and just said quietly: "Alan, don't worry now, just get in the nets and have a bowl. We will talk later."

'Talk later?' I thought, 'but what about? Why did I have to justify my being late when the circumstances were not my fault?' I felt a well of emotion inside me that was in danger of transforming into rage. I had felt humiliated at the hotel the night before, and now felt humiliated in the nets on the morning of the Gillette Cup final. But men don't cry, do they? I was a young man, I was a professional cricketer, and I had to toughen up right there, or I was not going to be in a fit state, mentally, to play.

The walk back from the nets over the ground was just a procession of questions from my teammates asking me what had happened the night before, and why I had been late on this morning of all mornings. I didn't want to talk about it, but I had to explain my circumstances. In the dressing room, I just felt awkward and I was beginning to doubt that I was going to play. Did Alan Jones want to talk to me later because he was going to drop me? Had they changed the team because I did not stay in the official team hotel or because I was late getting to Lord's? Could I have felt worse on my first ever visit to Lord's? The short answer is no.

Just before Alan Jones was due to go out to the middle for the toss, he stood up in the middle of the dressing room to give a short speech in which he announced the team news. He read each name out. Mine was the eleventh and last name to be mentioned, but at least I was playing. I felt a bit better as Alan walked past and gave me a reassuring tap on the shoulder. We all watched the coin toss from the players' balcony, with the crowd noise a heavy murmur in the MCC members' seats but a sea of noise in the popular stands around this iconic ground. Welsh cricket fans had come to London in their thousands and they were singing. It was a wonderful sight and sound. The support from our fans had been outstanding all season and this was their day out, as much as it was ours.

Middlesex captain, Mike Brearley, won the toss on a damp, dull, overcast morning and he put us into bat. This was no surprise. The outfield was damp from overnight rain and in Wayne Daniel, the big, fast West Indian opening bowler, and Mike Selvey, who had played for England against the West Indies in the 1976 Test Series, Middlesex had two of the best opening bowlers in England to open the attack. They also had the England spin duo of Phil Edmonds and John Emburey, with Mike Gatting to bowl his medium pace in the middle.

In difficult conditions, Glamorgan's innings never really got going. John Hopkins made a workmanlike 47 and Mike Llewellyn top-scored with 62, hitting John Emburey for a monumental six that nearly cleared the roof of the Lord's Pavilion, but we struggled and stuttered to end up 177-9 in 60 overs. I had the pads on, but didn't manage to get in, which was par for the course that season. We had feared Wayne Daniel as the main bowling threat, but he didn't take a wicket. Mike Selvey bowled beautifully for his 2 for 22 in 12 overs. The South African-born part-time off-spinner Norman Featherstone took 3 for 17 and Phil Edmonds 2 for 23, and Mike Gatting got on the bowling sheet with a wicket. 177 didn't look nearly enough, but when Malcolm Nash had Mike Brearley caught behind by Eifion Jones off the first ball of the Middlesex reply, a sense of euphoria, mainly of the Welsh variety, engulfed Lord's. The singing under the Lord's Tavern rang out with songs that only Welsh sporting fans sing, and it was as dramatic a stage on which to play cricket as I could have imagined.

In at three walked Clive Radley, one of the most tenacious batsmen in county cricket and often a saviour for Middlesex. This day was no different, but we contributed to his reputation as a dogged player who was difficult to dislodge when Collis King dropped him at slip – on two runs – off Malcolm Nash, at which point the singing gave way to a collective Welsh groan across Lord's. Radley made us pay, as he chipped away all afternoon to eventually lead Middlesex to victory with an unbeaten 85.

That dropped catch apart, I didn't think that we got our act right in the final. We changed our bowling formula on the day and I was called upon to bowl as Glamorgan's sixth bowler, when the match had gone away from us. I thought I should have bowled much earlier than I did, and as I'd done in the earlier rounds of the competition.

My return was a less than impressive six overs for 27 runs and I didn't look like taking a wicket. Middlesex got home in the 56th over and they beat us by five wickets.

After the match, our dressing room was naturally a glum place, but we had a number of visitors who congratulated us on our achievement that season. Losing a final, however, is a horrible feeling and we knew that we had not done ourselves justice on that day in London. For me, it had been an unfortunate day from the moment I walked into an empty Glamorgan dressing room. The rest of the day felt empty, but there was still more intrigue ahead. Where was I going to sleep that night? The team was due to return to the Clarendon Court that evening, because the following morning we were due to travel to Leicester to play Leicestershire in the last Sunday League match of the season.

The evening was a damp squib and alcohol played its part, as it so often does when you're looking to drown your sorrows. My second attempt at checking into the team hotel was more successful than the first; this time, the hotel had a room for me: the committeeman had presumably now checked out and left for Wales. I was informed by the club secretary that the cost of the evening dinner would be covered by Glamorgan, and that because of my unfortunate circumstances the previous evening, I could have a bottle of wine on them. So, let me get that equation right in my head: no room at the hotel with the team before the final, being fined for being late, and now a bottle of wine to soften the blow. A couple of beers did do the trick and I guess I mellowed through the evening, but we all felt flat at losing the way we did.

The following morning there were some sore heads around at breakfast, but we now faced a bus trip of some three hours to Leicester for our last game of the 1977 season. What made matters worse was the presence of the BBC television cameras on that coach, filming our weekend for the programme *Glamorgan's Day Out at Lord's*. It was just as well that one of Glamorgan's former players, Peter Walker, was the presenter and interviewer. Peter was a household name and face on BBC television across the UK, and would become a great friend in the broadcasting profession, but for now, on that coach, he had the difficult task of trying to compile a television programme with a group of hung-over, unwilling cricketers.

Leicestershire were intent on two things that Sunday afternoon: firstly, they wanted revenge for our win over them in the semi-final of the Gillette Cup but, more importantly, they needed to beat us to win the Sunday League title. They achieved both objectives with some ease. We were in no fit state to play cricket and although I bowled decently for figures of 8-3-12-1, we couldn't wait for the match to end to get home.

Before boarding the coach I was handed an envelope by the club secretary. Inside it was an invoice for a bottle of wine at the Clarendon Court Hotel from the previous evening. I couldn't believe it, but there it was. Of course, I had chosen one of the more expensive wines. Now I had to pay for it. A lesson learned. There was no point in crying over it.

There were better times to come, and they would come very soon, because three Glamorgan players – Mike Llewellyn, Gwyn Richards and myself – had been invited to tour Canada to inaugurate the Lord's Taverners Charity in Canada. The Lord's Taverners, founded in 1950 by actors who enjoyed watching games from the Lord's Tavern, is now the official charity for recreational cricket and the UK's leading youth cricket and disability sports charity. Its objective is 'to give young people, particularly those with special needs, a sporting chance'.

It was a wonderful tour. The warmth of hospitality shown by our Canadian hosts was second to none. We played a couple of matches in Toronto – at the magnificent Toronto Cricket, Skating and Curling Club – where I had the privilege of opening the bowling on a matting pitch with the legendary England fast bowler Fred Trueman. He was an amazing character who had stories and jokes for every occasion, and some of the better ones were reserved for new batsmen out in the middle. He was incorrigible, but he could still bowl, even if he did so in my brand new, unworn cricket shoes that had rubber soles, and not spikes. Fred hadn't packed the right cricket boots for bowling on matting, so he just 'borrowed' mine. Fred usually wore boots with steel toe caps which could cope with his notorious 'drag' – the toe of his trailing back leg dragging along the turf – but the toe of my new right boot was ripped apart and the shoes were unusable after Fred had worn them. Fred handed them back to me, muttering the words, "Waste of fookin' time those ballerina shoes, son! You'd better get a proper pair to bowl in!"

Fred formed a comedy double-act with Colin 'Ollie' Milburn, the England opening batsman, who'd lost his left eye and damaged his right in the car accident that had ended his international career in 1969. He was an aggressive, hard-hitting batsman whose Test career was far too short – nine Tests between 1966 and 1969 – but here in Canada, he was Fred's stooge and just marvellous fun. They were hilarious every day of the tour, although I would probably look for another word for the occasions when Ollie took his glass eye out on the dinner table to give his eye socket a wash!

The Lord's Taverners tour took us to various parts of Ontario and onto Montreal in Quebec, where it was starting to get chilly in the evenings. The highlight of the trip was to see the magnificent Niagara Falls. It is breathtakingly beautiful and at the same time a nerve-wracking experience standing there getting soaking wet and watching the sheer volume of water cascading over the falls from The Great Lakes accompanied by the thundering roar that fills the air around you.

And that was the end of the 1977 cricket season. I had experienced half a season with Glamorgan after finishing my studies at Loughborough University, but ended up top of the club's bowling averages with 47 wickets at 23 apiece. I felt I belonged in the company of professional cricketers, even if I couldn't get into the team hotel with my own team for the biggest game of my life, but the trip to Canada ensured that bad memories didn't linger. The winter was ahead and there would be more rugby to look forward to, but rugby was going to cause me some problems – not so much on the rugby pitch, but more on and off the cricket field.

# 4

# Home Truths

*'Nothing in life comes easy. More often than not, achievement comes
at the end of a long period of preparation and hard work, and Alan's
broadcasting career – after his retirement from our great game of
cricket – is the perfect example of this. Alan epitomises what sport
is all about.'*

**Clive Lloyd**

The life of a county cricketer in those years, and for decades
previously, was to play the summer season in England for your
county and, at the end of the six months – around mid-September –
head south to the warmer climes of Australia, South Africa or New
Zealand, away from the British winter, for a cricket job that would
combine coaching and playing. If you were an England cricketer,
you would be looking forward to an overseas tour. I didn't fall into
that category, so I was on the trail for a job.

My first winter – off-season – saw me stay in Wales where I
started a teaching job at Newbridge Comprehensive School in
Monmouthshire. In the 19th century, Newbridge, like so many of
the Welsh valley towns, was at the centre of the coal-mining boom.
That winter, it provided me with an income from teaching physical
education and history at a very good school, formerly Newbridge
Grammar School. I also did an eye-opening short stint at a school in
a town called Nant-y-glo, which is deep in the eastern Welsh valleys.

There it was decided that I should do some cricket coaching, after school hours, in the indoor PE centre.

When I wore my Glamorgan sweater, with its beautiful daffodil emblem, all it did was to arouse the curiosity of the boys I was coaching. None of them recognised the badge as that of Glamorgan CCC, the team which, if they ever had the chance, they should have aspired to play for. I mention this only because Bryan Williams, one of the better fast bowlers I had seen and played with for the Welsh Secondary Schools, and who should have gone on to a first-class career, came from that area.

Teaching was combined with playing rugby for Glamorgan Wanderers – a club on the outskirts of Cardiff – one of 17 teams competing in the Welsh Merit Table. In February 1978, we pulled off an outstanding victory against the mighty Pontypool, at home, in fairly appalling cold, wet conditions. In the final minute, I felt a twinge in the back of my right thigh, and I just could not run. I had pulled a hamstring, the first of many in the years to come. The main priority now was to get fit for the cricket season. While I had no Glamorgan contract, it was an unwritten code that everyone had to report fit for the new season on April 1st.

Physiotherapy and rehabilitation took weeks; I decided that my rugby season had ended, and I was now preparing for the new cricket season. It was a cold, wet start to the 1978 campaign, and many first-class cricket matches were abandoned in those first few weeks. Glamorgan had also signed a new overseas player to replace the West Indian, Collis King. He was Peter Swart, the Zimbabwe-born, Cape Town-based all-rounder, who had forged a good reputation in the Lancashire League and also for Western Province in South Africa's Currie Cup cricket, where he batted middle-order and bowled brisk medium-pace with a slingy action.

Our first proper game of cricket came in the third week of April when Somerset visited Cardiff for a Benson & Hedges Cup match (55 overs per side). Somerset made 196 for 7 in their 55 overs and I had been given a tough time by that man again – IVA Richards – with a brand new bat that looked and sounded like no other bat on display that day. Viv was on his way to a century then, somehow, whether it was misjudgement from him – or maybe I shouldn't sell myself too short on this one – I managed to deliver a beauty that went clean through the Richards attacking off-drive. The ball swung late, back towards his pads, missed them and his bat and it took his off-stump.

I would say that it was the best ball I had ever bowled, mainly because of the player it accounted for, but not just that, it *had* to be something special to get Viv out. My 11 overs cost 44 runs, reasonable enough figures, but that wicket was worth its weight in gold, platinum and silver. It is difficult to describe in words that special feeling, which lasts for about ten seconds, when your best-laid plan – in bowling to one of the game's superstars – suddenly works the way you dreamt it. The instant gratification is tangible. It really is the best feeling in the world.

In reply, Glamorgan were well on course to winning the match at 168-3, but we suddenly started to lose wickets. Despite 61 from Alan Jones, still our captain, and 55 from the debutant Peter Swart, the scores were tied at 196, but because we had lost eight wickets, Somerset were awarded the points because they had lost fewer wickets (seven). The Glamorgan dressing room was a downcast place, in which the numbing silence amongst the players was broken by the spouting of our new overseas signing. It became clear that there was already a personality clash between the outspoken Peter Swart, and our coach, Tom Cartwright, who had given up playing, but was now very much a mentor to the team.

A week later, we had net practice in Cardiff before travelling to New Road to play another B & H Cup match, this time against Worcestershire. I had felt in good shape physically but then, to my horror, I felt a slight twinge in my right hamstring. It was a shock because I had not felt anything for weeks, but now I was under pressure to be fit to play at Worcester. I stopped bowling in the nets and immediately had a leg massage and some treatment from our physiotherapist, a former British Army man, Tudor Jones. He then told me to go for a little jog and let him know how it felt. It actually felt alright, and after bowling a few more balls in the nets, I told Tom Cartwright that I would be fit to play in the match the next day.

Tom was sceptical and said: "You had better be 100 per cent fit for the match tomorrow. If you're not, then I want to know right now, so we can replace you in the team." I reaffirmed that my leg felt fine and that I would be 100 per cent for the match against Worcestershire. We then drove to Worcester, a journey of around two and a half hours.

The following morning, we went through all our usual warm-up exercises on the outfield and I felt perfectly fine; no twinge and no tightness in the hamstring. It helped that we won the toss and batted, but we laboured under grey skies and on a seaming pitch to 131 for 9 in 55 overs. Could you imagine scoring rates like that now, with the proliferation of Twenty20 cricket ?

Worcestershire had a very decent batting top order: Alan Ormrod, the prolific New Zealander, Glenn Turner, Phil Neale, Ted Hemsley, Basil D'Oliveira, and Dipak Patel (who later emigrated and played for New Zealand) and we anticipated the worst. Malcolm Nash bowled beautifully with the new ball, getting a couple of early wickets, but Glenn Turner was still there and looking ominously menacing. I was the fourth bowler used by Alan Jones and the pressure was on to get wickets because we had such a small total to defend.

For my first ball I came off my normal – longer – run-up but, just a few yards from the crease, I pulled up in pain and immediately clutched my right hamstring. I didn't even make it to my delivery stride. To my utmost horror, I knew immediately that my hamstring had twinged, and that I was now definitely not 100 per cent fit to bowl, despite all the fitness tests and my protestations that I would be fit to play in this important match. Alan Jones, who was fielding at mid-off, ran over to me and asked: "Is that your hamstring? Has it gone badly? Can you bowl?"

I knew that I just had to bowl as I'd declared myself fit to play and, without me, the team would be a bowler short. I turned to Alan and replied: "I think I will be alright if I try to bowl off my shorter run-up, not my longer one." The shorter run-up was the 15-yards maximum allowed in the Sunday League, and I had become very comfortable with it mainly because it was a more economical run, and the length of stride was fractionally shorter. In the middle of this conversation I glanced over to the dressing room, where the visitors' window was a large pane of glass looking out onto the field. There in the middle of it was a fuming Glamorgan coach, Tom Cartwright, arms raised to the ceiling in a gesture suggesting that he was not entirely pleased to see me pull-up in my run-up with my very first delivery. I knew that I was in trouble, not so much physically, but more in breach of my promise to the coach, the captain, and the team, that I was fully fit to play in this match. I had to bowl eleven overs with a pulled hamstring – there was no other option – but God knows what I would do if I could not deliver the ball.

The first ball I delivered off the shorter run left my hand as smoothly as any bowler wants the ball to behave, and it swung nicely. The second one did the same. I felt good, and there was minimal discomfort in the back of my thigh. I bowled my eleven overs all in one stint – eleven overs on the trot – and that was basically for two reasons. Firstly, because I felt I could not stop in mid-spell and hope to bowl another, and secondly, it was possibly the best I had bowled since turning professional. I finished with figures of 11-4-17-5, including the wickets of Glenn Turner and Basil D'Oliveira, both caught at slip. The final ball I bowled went through slips at catching height and went for a boundary; it could easily have been 6 for 13. I was elated as much as I was utterly relieved. Remarkably, we bowled Worcestershire out for just 104 and we won the match by 27 runs. I was applauded off the field and given the match ball for my bowling effort, but when I got inside our dressing room, Tom Cartwright completely ignored me. Not a single word of congratulation. Nothing. Not even a glance in my direction. He was deadpan. Tom was a seasoned professional, and one of the finest exponents of seam bowling to have played for England, but he was a no-nonsense professional cricketer. I knew that he was intensely annoyed with the fact that I had pulled-up with a hamstring twinge first ball, and then continued to bowl off a shorter run. In spite of my match-winning figures, Tom saw it as professional insubordination.

The dressing room that day was a good place to be; despite a little discomfort in my hamstring, I knew that I had bowled as good a spell as I could have hoped for, and I would like to think that my eleven overs helped Glamorgan win the match. Hell, we bowled Worcestershire out for just 104, defending a paltry total of 131! The B & H Cup official match adjudicator for the Man of the Match award was MJK Smith, the former England batsman and captain, and a long-time former teammate of Tom's at Warwickshire. I had also met 'MJK' on the Lord's Taverners Tour to Canada the previous September, and he was a most affable person, but I will not forget his short speech to the gathering of crowds outside the dressing room and, of course, to the players of both teams: "Today, we saw a wonderful spell of left-arm swing bowling which enabled Glamorgan to take the game away from Worcestershire and win the match with only a small total to defend. My Benson & Hedges Man of the Match award goes to ... Malcolm Nash."

Nashy was sitting in a towel in the corner of the dressing room with a cigarette in his mouth, and I was sitting opposite him. We had taken nine wickets between us, and had bowled Glamorgan to an unlikely win. But when his name was announced, his mouth gaped open and the cigarette fell into his towel. "What?" he said, "that can't be right! Wilkie is surely the Man of the Match. This shouldn't be me." It was a generous reaction from Nashy, but it was he, not I, who had to go outside, after hurriedly putting on a tracksuit, to collect the B & H Man of the Match medal from MJK Smith. I have to admit that I was hoping it would be my award for having taken 5 for 17, a new B & H Cup Glamorgan record, which was to stand for almost 20 years. But I suspected some conversation had taken place between Tom and MJK. Maybe it was a way of reprimanding me for having confirmed my fitness and then pulling up, but surely my subsequent bowling effort more than made up for that? Even at that point, all I wanted was a pat on the back from Tom, but I got nothing. I was learning quickly that in professional sport there was no room for sentiment, and certainly no room for personal emotions. Was this the way of the 'hard professional' in sport? Had I behaved 'like a proper professional sportsman?' Clearly, in Tom Cartwright's mind, I hadn't, and I was being made to feel like it. It was another salutary lesson during my early cricket career. I just had to take it and move on, but the moment stayed with me as we left New Road.

The rest of the B & H Cup campaign for Glamorgan that season was a real mixture of results in that we beat Hampshire at Swansea with their three big stars – Barry Richards, Gordon Greenidge and Andy Roberts – but barely scraped past the students of the Combined Universities at the Oxford Parks by one solitary run. But this was a very decent team of students: captained by Alastair Hignell

(Gloucestershire) and with outstanding players like Vic Marks (Somerset & England), Ian Greig (Sussex & England) the younger brother of Tony, and Paul Parker (Sussex & England). Peter Swart took the Man of the Match award for an unbeaten 83 and I failed to take a wicket, delivering 11 overs for 36 runs. We failed to make it to the knockout stages of the Cup after losing to Warwickshire at Edgbaston, where Bob Willis ravaged us with a hostile spell of fast bowing, taking 2 for 12 in eight overs.

With four competitions in the county cricket season, teams knew fairly early on what kind of season they were going to have. We were out of the B & H Cup by the first week of June, had won only one Sunday League match from five (with two abandoned without a ball bowled), hadn't yet won a County Championship three-day match, and the Gillette Cup (60 overs knockout competition) hadn't started.

My first Championship appearance was in the fifth match of the season, picking up three top order wickets against Leicestershire at Swansea, all LBW, including the Zimbabwean, Brian Davison. The match tapered out into a draw, as many did under the three-day format unless something spectacular happened from a bowler or batsman, or there was a 'captains' agreement' to try and contrive a result. No, this was not the early beginnings of match-fixing, but accepted standard practice when either the weather or the limited time available under the three-day format made it impossible to get a result. If the first two days were washed out, the captains might agree to forfeit their first innings, creating a single-innings match on the final day. Looking back, it was a scenario ripe for match-fixing, but that term was unknown to cricketers in those days. Discussions often took place in the bar, with the captain then telling the rest of his team what had been agreed between the two captains to try and 'get a result out of the game'.

A typical conversation might have been thus.

Skipper (1): "Hey Skipper (2), we have lost two days of cricket but the forecast is good for tomorrow, so why don't we just call it quits on the first innings, let's forfeit those, and if the weather is fine in the morning, we'll bat and leave you a reasonable target to chase. How does that sound to you?"

Skipper (2) "Sounds good to me, so are we looking at a sort of 240 target in 45 overs, or something close to that?"

Skipper (1): "Yes, I was thinking along those lines. Look, if it is getting unrealistic, just bowl a couple of silly overs so that we can get some cheap runs on the board, and that will give you more time for your chase, OK?"

Skipper (2): "Perfect. Have a good evening and we'll see you in the morning."

Job done. All it needed was the weather to be fine for the third and last day of the match, and we had a game of cricket on our hands. As bizarre at it sounds, it was a way of keeping the interest factor at a premium, and it also kept in consideration the loyal supporters who would turn up in all kinds of weather. In those days, I never once heard the words 'match-fixing', and it simply was not part of any cricketer's mindset or conversation. Or am I being naive to think that?

There was nothing contrived about our next match, which was against Derbyshire at the beautiful Queen's Park cricket ground in the town of Chesterfield, overlooked by the famed Church with the Crooked Spire, a 14th-century landmark which twists 45 degrees and leans almost ten feet from its true centre. This has been attributed to the absence of skilled craftsmen following the Black Death but, whatever the reason, it is a sight to behold.

Glamorgan's performance on those three days in early June in Chesterfield was also fairly twisted and leant towards mediocrity, and possibly the result of the absence of skilled craftsmen. It also owed much, however, to the exquisitely talented South African batsman, Peter Kirsten, who caressed his way to an unbeaten 206, an innings of dexterous fluency. The next top score was just 42, from Derbyshire's captain, the ebullient South African all-rounder Eddie Barlow, as Derbyshire rattled up a first innings score of 341 for 6 declared. I was reasonably happy with my personal bowling effort, bowling 26 overs, getting both openers out and taking 2 for 88. But we capitulated against Derbyshire's bowlers – Mike Hendrick (England, fast medium), Colin Tunnicliffe (left-arm, fast medium) and Geoff Miller (England, off-spinner) – bowled out for 140 and 181, losing the match by an innings and 20 runs.

Leaving what felt like the Black Death behind us in Chesterfield, it was back on the motorways to Wales, a journey of some three to four hours, with a match against Essex the very next day. Keith Fletcher's Essex team was a fun side to play against. They had a team full of eclectic personalities who played the game seriously, but with smiles on their faces; unlike the teams who represented the likes of Leicestershire, Surrey and Yorkshire, for instance, whose approach to the game – I felt – was dour and unattractive. I may be too sweeping in that assessment, but it just felt like a different game against some counties.

Essex plundered us in their first innings for 372 for 7 in 100 overs. In the 1978 season, the TCCB (now called the ECB) experimented with a 100 over limit in the first innings of a County Championship match. I bowled virtually all day, opening with Malcolm Nash and, at the end of a very long day, could bathe my bleeding toes and aching limbs in a hot bath, satisfied with figures of 33-8-96-5: getting five of the top six of Essex's top order, including Fletcher – 59 Tests for England, captain in seven of them – LBW for 29. Glamorgan replied with 301-9 declared, and in an obvious 'captains' agreement' Essex declared their second innings on 103 for 1, leaving Glamorgan 175 to win the match in about 36 overs. That's what made for entertaining finishes on the final day of County Championship matches. In this instance, Glamorgan lost a flurry of wickets to the Essex seamers, John Lever (England, left-arm fast-medium) and Stuart Turner, who reduced us to 75 for 7 in 36.3 overs before time ran out. It was a good game of cricket and from a personal point of view I felt I was becoming a reliable player for Glamorgan.

In sport, though, things change quickly, as I discovered on our trip to Liverpool to play against Lancashire, who had two West Indies greats in their side – Clive Lloyd and Colin Croft. It was a blazing hot day for late June, perfect conditions for me to bring up my first century for Glamorgan. The pity of it was that it came off my bowling, not my bat! On a flat, fast pitch at Aigburth – home of Liverpool Cricket Club – Lancashire's opening batsman, Andy Kennedy, stroked a serene century, but then Clive Lloyd strolled in and bludgeoned us (me, mainly) for a 66-ball undefeated 110. It was the first time I had conceded 100 off my bowling, finishing with figures of 29-6-131-0 and a bruised ego. Clive Lloyd hit the cricket ball murderously hard, to the point where bowlers following through, and the umpire standing at the bowler's end, were in mortal danger when he was batting.

I quickly learnt that the game could bring you down to earth in a matter of just a couple of hours. Lancashire's compulsory declaration gave them a first innings total of 401 for 4 from 100 overs. We replied with 195 all out in 62 overs, but my bruising continued. Colin Croft seemed to take a liking to certain parts of my anatomy – mainly my toes and my throat – hitting them with deadly accuracy, and with a cursory look at his prey before turning back to unleash another missile. Of course, the pounding didn't last long, but my bruised toes certainly did. Rain truncated the match, but not before I enjoyed a quiet conversation with Tom Cartwright in the dining room as the rain kept us indoors. It was the first meaningful conversation I had had with Tom since the Worcestershire impasse, and it was difficult to comprehend his change of disposition towards me. He paid me a compliment when he said that I reminded him of someone because I was always asking questions, always inquiring about something or other, and always making myself heard. When I asked him who that person was, he quietly said: "Mike Brearley ... he asked a lot of questions as well but unlike you, he knew most of the answers." Tom laughed. I laughed. It was Tom's way of making a joke but maybe his way of acquiescing.

Academically, of course, Mike Brearley was light years ahead of me, but it was a moment when I felt Tom Cartwright and I had patched up whatever needed repairing after the New Road hamstring incident.

Chesterfield was again on our schedule as we headed north to play Derbyshire in a Sunday League match, which was reduced to ten overs a side because of rain. There was little science to these ten over matches, often referred to as 'ten-over slogs' by most players. We lost to Eddie Barlow's team, but not before I bowled him with a beauty of an in-swinging yorker that ripped out his middle stump. That ball had more significance then I realised at the time as, after the match, Eddie Barlow took me aside and asked what I was going to do in the winter once the 1978 English cricket season was over.

Replying that I had no plans at all, he replied: "Do you want to play the winter of 1978-79 in South Africa? I know that you would do well out there on those faster, bouncy wickets in the Transvaal and I know a club who would love to have you with them. Oh, and by the way, well bowled today!"

I told Eddie that I would be interested in going out to South Africa and he simply said: "Leave it with me. You'll be hearing from my friends over there. This is a great opportunity for you. You will enjoy yourself. It's a great country."

I wasn't expecting the next conversation. Tom Cartwright had seen me talking privately with Eddie Barlow and he asked me what it was all about. "What did Eddie Barlow want with you, Wilkie?" inquired our coach. "Tom, he just asked if I wanted to go to South Africa in the winter for a coaching and playing job in the Transvaal." Quickly, Tom's reply to this was as direct as it was emphatic. "You are *not* going to South Africa. You are a Glamorgan player and you will *not* be going anywhere near South Africa!"

I knew exactly what the issue was with Tom and South Africa. It explained why he had such a fractious relationship with the outspoken Peter Swart, and a love-hate relationship with another South African in the Glamorgan side, Rodney Ontong. Tom had been a key figure in the whole Basil D'Oliveira affair in 1968.

When D'Oliveira, a 'coloured' South African who had qualified for England, was excluded from the England team to tour South Africa in the winter of 1968-69, in spite of scoring 158 not out in the final Test against Australia, the selectors were accused of succumbing to political pressure from South Africa, whose Prime Minister B J Vorster had already said a team including D'Oliveira was not acceptable.

Tom was selected and when he dropped out with an injury, D'Oliveira was chosen to replace him and the tour cancelled. It was a vital stage in the turning of opinion against *apartheid* and the growth of the sporting boycott that steadily isolated South Africa. They did play, and heavily beat, Australia in 1969-70, but after that did not play international cricket for 22 years.

This was the background to Tom's disaffection with South Africa, and his objection to the possibility of my going to the country for the forthcoming winter, now only a matter of six weeks away. The conversation between us did not augur well for the remainder of the season. I said: "Tom, I am not contracted by Glamorgan for the entire year, so when it comes to the end of the season, I will make up my own mind whether or not I decide to go to South Africa."

Tom's reply was terse: "We will see about that!" But the seed of curiosity had been sown in my head by Eddie Barlow. Another consideration was that it would be work for me through the winter months as a professional cricketer in South Africa. I had not made any decision, because I had yet to hear from the people in South Africa but I was clear on one issue – that I would decide myself if I was to travel to South Africa. I would not be under contract with Glamorgan, and in my mind they could not stop me from going. I knew that this was not what Tom wanted to hear. It was clear that I had again incensed Tom Cartwright, and that it would be a rocky few weeks ahead.

There was a lot of cricket still to be played, and Glamorgan welcomed the touring New Zealanders to St. Helen's in Swansea, where we almost pulled off a win. Glamorgan made 198 – with Lance Cairns taking 5 for 58 – and New Zealand replied with 235 for 8 declared. My bowling figures were 19-4-49-3, getting the wickets of their captain, Mark Burgess (50 Test caps), John Parker (36 Test caps) and Bev Congdon (61 Test caps): all three caught behind by our wicket-keeper, Eifion Jones. We made 263 for 8 declared in the second innings – Lance Cairns 5 for 87 – leaving NZ a target of 227 to win. We had them at 98 for 7 in 53.4 overs before time ran out. I chipped in with 2 for 37, getting John Parker again – caught behind – and their wicket-keeper, Jock Edwards. What pleased me more than anything else was the fact that I was not allowing myself to be distracted by the South Africa issue. The best way of keeping my nose clean was to keep taking wickets, and that was my intention for the rest of the season.

Whilst we lost the three-day County Championship match to Middlesex at St. Helen's – succumbing to the superior bowling firepower of Wayne Daniel, Mike Selvey and John Emburey – we pulled off a convincing win in the Sunday League match by seven wickets. I was again in the wickets, taking 4 for 16 in seven overs, in a spell that contributed in no small measure to our win.

The following week, we beat a strong Sussex side – with Imran Khan and Kepler Wessels – on their home ground at Hastings. A week after that we pulled off an unlikely win over Warwickshire at their HQ, Edgbaston, in another 'ten-over slog', after rain had kept both teams in the dressing rooms until after 5 pm. Warwickshire won the toss, put us in and we scrambled to 54 for 7 in our ten overs. We didn't think we had enough but when Alan Jones entrusted the ten overs we were to bowl to Tony Cordle and me, the outcome was a personal triumph – 5 for 23 in my five overs – including the prized wicket of Alvin Kallicharran. If the same match was played today, then five bowlers would have to bowl two overs each. In those days, two could bowl five each.

**Warwickshire v Glamorgan**        **Edgbaston**        **30 July 1978**

**Result:** Glamorgan won by 2 runs

### Glamorgan innings

| | | | |
|---|---|---|---|
| *A Jones | c Maynard | b Brown | 19 |
| MJ Llewellyn | run out | | 8 |
| MA Nash | run out | | 0 |
| AE Cordle | c Whitehouse | b Brown | 0 |
| RC Ontong | lbw | b Brown | 0 |
| +EW Jones | | b Brown | 8 |
| G Richards | not out | | 6 |
| JA Hopkins | | b Brown | 0 |
| DA Francis | not out | | 2 |
| **Total** | | **(10 overs)** | **54-7** |

| **Bowling** | **O** | **M** | **R** | **W** |
|---|---|---|---|---|
| Brown | 5 | 0 | 16 | 5 |
| Rouse | 5 | 0 | 27 | 0 |

### Warwickshire innings

| | | | |
|---|---|---|---|
| DL Amiss | | b Cordle | 13 |
| AI Kallicharran | | b Wilkins | 13 |
| KD Smith | c EW Jones | b Wilkins | 12 |
| *J Whitehouse | c EW Jones | b Cordle | 0 |
| SJ Rouse | | b Wilkins | 3 |

| | | | | |
|---|---|---|---|---:|
| PR Oliver | retired hurt | | | 5 |
| TA Lloyd | not out | | | 2 |
| EE Hemmings | | | b Wilkins | 0 |
| +C Maynard | | | b Wilkins | 0 |
| DJ Brown | not out | | | 0 |
| **Total** | | | **(10 overs)** | **52-7** |

| **Bowling** | **O** | **M** | **R** | **W** |
|---|---|---|---|---|
| Cordle | 5 | 0 | 25 | 2 |
| Wilkins | 5 | 0 | 23 | 5 |

The Kallicharran dismissal gave me a lot of pleasure, as it would have any young cricketer bowling to a player of his calibre but, more importantly, Glamorgan were on a bit of a roll in the Sunday League. Well, I thought so, but as I've mentioned previously, things change quickly in sport, and so it proved as the season entered the home stretch. We lost on the next three Sundays, against Northamptonshire, who had Allan Lamb and Sarfraz Nawaz in their team, Nottinghamshire with Clive Rice in theirs, and Surrey at The Oval, a match which landed me at the centre of an unsavoury incident.

Surrey were hosting Glamorgan for four days on the third weekend of August, a three-day County Championship match on the Saturday, Monday and Tuesday, with the completely unrelated Sunday League (40 overs) match in between, played on two pitches at The Kennington Oval, one of the great Test grounds. On the Saturday, Surrey hit us all around The Oval scoring 403 for 5 in 100 overs, with Alan Butcher (one Test, v India in 1979) scoring a superb 176, and Surrey's captain, Roger Knight, 119. I took 2 for 45 in nine overs, bowling John Edrich (77 Tests for England) for just 9. The Oval was a huge playing area in those days, and we chased that little red ball all over it, all day long.

There was no love lost between Surrey and Glamorgan in those days and you could feel the animosity between the two sides. Knight was one of the game's most upstanding and decent gentlemen, but some of his team members had the uncanny knack of getting under the skin of the opposition. Not only Younis Ahmed, but also David Smith, Robin Jackman and wicket-keeper Jack Richards – probably because they were all damn good cricketers and they played the game hard.

The Sunday was a beautifully warm day and a very good crowd turned up. They were getting rowdier by the hour, alcohol consumption compounded by the strong afternoon sun. Glamorgan scored a very useful 222 for 3 in the allocated 40 overs, with Peter Swart top-scoring with an undefeated 85, and Alan Jones also undefeated on 75.

We felt we could defend that total but Surrey batted well, with good contributions from Graham Roope (21 England caps), Intikhab Alam (Pakistan) and Monty Lynch (three ODIs for England). We could feel the game slipping away from us, as Monty was playing so well and guiding Surrey home. I still hadn't bowled at this point, so still had my eight overs to go. Our off-spinner, Gwyn Richards, was bowling to Monty, who missed it and the ball hit our stand-in wicket-keeper, John Hopkins, who picked it up and threw it back to Gwyn, known as Spitzy because of his hopeless ability to swim. Spitzy had turned towards the umpire and was inquiring about something, when John shouted to warn Gwyn that the ball was about to land on his head. He protected himself with his arms above his head, but the ball ricocheted off his arm and trickled away towards cover. No-one did anything much, because we all believed the ball was dead, having gone through to the wicket-keeper. But then, to our surprise, the non-striker – Robin Jackman – called for a run. "Come on, Monty, there's a run there!" Monty answered the call and they crossed for the single. Alan Jones was incensed, and complained bitterly to the umpires that the ball should have been declared dead, and that Surrey should not have taken the liberty of a single. His argument was overruled, and the run added to the Surrey total. Off the last ball of Gwyn Richards's over they took another single, meaning that Robin Jackman was the non-striker at the Pavilion End. It was now that Alan Jones decided to call me to bowl my first over of the match.

I was at the end of my run-up mark, and Alan was still in conversation with me, setting the field with arm gestures and hand waving and making sure that everyone was in the right place for my first over. Then he dropped a bombshell. "Wilks, I want you to run up as normal, but I don't want you to bowl the ball, I don't want you to let it go. I want you to whip the bails off without warning Jackman at all!"

"Alan!" I protested, "I can't do that, very first ball. At least let me warn Jackers that he is taking liberties by backing up too far."

"No!" Alan was furious, and I had never seen him as wound-up as this at any time in my time at the club. Alan Jones is one of the game's nicest fellows and certainly it would take an awful lot to upset him, but he was upset right there at that moment, and he wanted me to 'Mankad' Robin Jackman, running him out at the non-striker's end, without any warning whatsoever.

"Alan, come on, we can't do this," I pleaded. I was the youngest player in the side. Malcolm Nash had finished his eight overs at the top of the innings and so, here I was, in the middle of a packed Oval, and about to 'do the dirty' on one of Surrey's favourite cricketers.

Alan Jones came back at me with a threatening tone: "If you don't do what I tell you, Wilks, you will be fined and dropped from the side." I had no choice. The field was set, and Alan Jones walked away to take his place at mid-off. I was at the end of my run-up and I gave Alan one last glance with a look on my face that was pleading for this not to happen. He just had a stone face and nodded for me to do it.

I ran in and got into my delivery stride, brought my bowling arm over and didn't let the ball go. Robin Jackman was yards down the pitch, backing up way too far: this was the moment I was dreading. In that moment, everything seemed to happen in slow motion. I looked at Jackers, who'd stopped about three yards down the pitch and was looking back at me. He was stranded. I looked at the umpire, a very nice fellow called Tom Wilson – not a former player – who was a rookie umpire on the first-class circuit, and he had a look of utter horror on his face.

Jackers snarled at me: "Don't you f***ing dare do what I think you're going to do!"

"Jackers!" I said back to him, "I'm under captain's orders! I have to."

I whipped the bails off and Robin Jackman was run out for one. I had 'Mankaded' Robin Jackman, one of Surrey's favourite sons, at

The Oval in front of his home crowd. Jackers was spitting blood at me.

"You f***ing prick, Wilks, I will kill you for this. You have just made the biggest f***ing mistake in your f***ing life."

"Jackers, I'm sorry," I said. What else could I say?

He came back to me with: "And you miserable little bas***d, you've forgotten that you're batting in the morning, so you're going to get it right between the eyes from me tomorrow!"

He was right. I hadn't even thought about the three-day match that was to resume on the Monday morning, and I knew that I was going to resume our first innings with only two wickets remaining.

At that moment, however, The Oval was a cauldron of booing from the Surrey fans who were calling me everything under the sun. The match was eventually won by Surrey, off the final ball of the innings, with Monty Lynch unbeaten on 45. But now, with the match at an end, we all had to walk off the ground and into the pavilion. I noticed a large contingent of police who'd just assembled on the playing area in front of the pavilion. A few of them formed a ring around me as I walked off. The members were shouting at me, and I could hear the chanting of 'Cheat! Cheat! Cheat! Cheat!' as I ran up the stairs into the safety of the dressing room. It was not a pleasant experience.

Once in our dressing room, and with all of us sitting down, there was silence. For one thing, we had lost the match after scoring 222 in 40 overs, and that was extremely disappointing in itself. The atmosphere lightened when Peter Swart just burst into laughter, coughing and spluttering as he always did, and just howling at what had just happened.

"Wilkie, you beauty! Couldn't have done it better myself!" It broke the ice. Soon there was a lot of laughter in the Glamorgan dressing room, but it quickly silenced when a Surrey official burst into the room accompanied by a policeman.

"Is there an Alan Wilkins here, please?" I just looked at this man in a suit and wearing the Surrey County Cricket Club tie, standing in the doorway, and held my arm aloft. "Yes, I am Alan Wilkins," I answered with a slightly apologetic tone to my voice.

"Well Sir, if I were you, for your own safety, I would remain in this dressing room for as long as you can, until we can disperse the mob outside, who are not very happy with what you did out there to Mr. Jackman!" came the stern words from the Surrey official.

"Thank you," I replied rather meekly. I felt terrible. Why did it have to be *me* to 'Mankad' Robin Jackman? Why couldn't it have been the senior bowler, Malcolm Nash? Alan came up to me and patted me on the back, and told me not to worry about it. I said: "I'm batting against him in the morning, Alan! Have you forgotten?"

"Don't worry, you'll be OK!" said my understanding captain.

The Glamorgan team waited in that visitors' dressing room for what seemed like hours. Eventually, another official knocked on the door and said we could begin "to leave The Oval, but be careful as you go, especially Mr. Wilkins!"

We got into our cars and drove back to our team hotel. I was glad it was all over, but I wasn't really looking forward to the next morning and batting against Robin Jackman.

I wasn't quite sure what to expect when we got to The Oval the following morning but I did know that Robin Jackman was not going to let me forget what I had done to him. It wasn't long before I walked in to bat, last man in for Glamorgan at 188 for 9; we struggled in reply to Surrey's 403 for 5, but it was Pat Pocock, the England off-spinner, and Intikhab Alam, the Pakistan leg-spinner, who had done the damage.

I was at the non-striker's end, and that's when the Surrey 'fun' started. Jackers hadn't been bowling because the spinners had taken eight wickets between them, but he most certainly wanted a crack at me. He was at the end of his long run, one of the longest run-ups in English cricket, and he just stared at me. He was going to bowl at Alan Lewis Jones, one of Glamorgan's young talented batsmen, and I was the non-striker, the last man in. Jackman ran in, and I just watched him approach the crease. He had a beautiful bowling action and he was a superb exponent of fast-medium seam bowling. Only this time, he didn't let the ball go.

Of course, I was backing up, but my bat had not left the crease. Jackers just held the ball next to the stumps and said: "Make sure you don't f***ing back up too far ... and hurry up down that end!"

Sure enough, I did get down the other end and, sure enough, the next delivery from Jackers was short and fast. I just ducked and got out of the way of it, but then came the verbal barrage. In fairness, Jackers wore a smile on his face throughout this little episode because he knew that I was unlikely to keep him out for long. But somehow I did. So much so, that Roger Knight, the Surrey captain, rested Jackers and handed the ball back to Intikhab Alam.

Glamorgan's last wicket partnership managed to get the 200 onto the scoreboard and I was on 17 when Intikhab fired a fast delivery straight at my toes. It was quicker than anything else he had bowled, and it hit me straight in front. Wilkins out, LBW, for 17. Glamorgan all out for 205. I guess I derived a little pleasure in not falling to Jackers and was relieved that there were chuckles when I came in to bat – there always were – and a prevailing sense of fun, albeit at my expense. Glamorgan had to follow on, and we made 343 all out in the second innings, leaving Surrey to score 148 to win, which they duly did.

Not a great weekend in London, beaten by Surrey in both games and not the best way to celebrate my birthday, August 22nd.

Years after this incident, Robin Jackman and I not only played against each other numerous times, but we got to know each other as friends and, of course, Robin went on to become an outstanding cricket broadcaster, based in Cape Town. We have shared many a good evening recalling the events at The Oval and the way Jackers tells the story is pure gold in entertainment value. He was a champion bowler for Surrey and England, and I was so glad that he never allowed the nastiness of that 'Mankad' incident to spoil what has become a good friendship. Robin Jackman is a dear friend, and for that I have to thank him, but it could have transpired so differently.

The term Mankad originated from the great Indian all-rounder, Vinoo Mankad, an opening batsman and slow left-arm orthodox bowler who played 44 tests for India. In 1956 he scored 231 against New Zealand in Chennai (then Madras) and together with Pankaj Roy established the world record opening partnership of 413 runs which stood for 52 years. His score was a Test record for India at the time and would remain so until it was broken by Sunil Gavaskar in

1983. Mankad caused controversy on the 1947-48 India tour of Australia when he ran out Australia's opening batsman, Bill Brown, in the second Test in Sydney whilst he was backing up. Mankad had done the same thing to Brown in the match against an Australian XI earlier on the tour, but it was this incident that infuriated the Australian media, and the action became known as 'Mankading'.

Ironically, Don Bradman – in his autobiography – supported the action of Vinoo Mankad, explaining that it was the batsman who should have been within his crease at the time otherwise he was gaining an unfair advantage. More recently, Sunil Gavaskar has made it very clear that he feels the term 'Mankading' should be dropped altogether, as it doesn't reflect well on one of India's greatest cricketers, and even suggests that the term be changed to 'Browning' because it was Bill Brown who was seeking to derive an advantage at the non-striker's end. It is an emotive subject both in name and in deed.

The 1978 season was drawing to a close. I was not selected for the next two County Championship matches, but I was picked for the Sunday League match against Kent at Maidstone, and the final Championship match of the season against Hampshire at the County Ground, Southampton. I was chuffed to have Gordon Greenidge caught and bowled for 0, and pick up two more wickets, including the Hampshire captain, Richard Gilliat, taking 3 for 55 from 23 overs, but Hampshire beat us by 55 runs, with Greenidge scoring 133 in the second innings.

Controversy, it seemed, was never far away in those last few weeks of that season. It escalated again when, having spoken on the telephone to the people in South Africa and been offered a six-month contract to coach and play, I informed Tom Cartwright that I had decided that I would be going to South Africa.

My air ticket was booked and I was going to spend the winter of 1978-79 in South Africa at a club called Springs High School Old Boys, based on the East Rand of what was then called the Transvaal, about 50 kilometres east of Johannesburg. I would be coaching in schools, following a line of Glamorgan players who had been appointed at Springs HSOB in past years: Don Shepherd, Jim Pressdee, Malcolm Nash and Alan Jones.

I was both excited and slightly apprehensive. I have to admit that I was not totally *au fait* with the politics of South Africa, but Eddie Barlow had convinced me that this was a good move for my career to play on the hard grounds of the Transvaal. Tom Cartwright was vehemently against my going to South Africa, and he couldn't have made his feelings any clearer. He didn't want me to go, but I certainly was. September 16th, 1978 was my departure date from London Heathrow, on Lux Air, via Luxembourg, to Johannesburg. My cricket travels were about to take off, and it was going to be one giant step into the unknown.

# 5

# High Hopes on the Highveld

*'I have known Alan for most of my adult life. Our paths first crossed when we were both playing 2nd XI cricket for our respective counties. Alan was a young tearaway left-arm fast bowler who played for Glamorgan and I opened the batting for Sussex. We were both desperate to break into the top flight of county cricket. We had some feisty encounters and I can remember one at Hove when the "red mist" descended and Alan was less than complimentary about my batting! Since those days we have become good friends and I always enjoy working with Alan in the commentary box. He is an excellent broadcaster and a pleasure to work with.'*

**Kepler Wessels**

Heaven knows what I looked like when I walked out of arrivals at what was then called Jan Smuts Airport, Johannesburg (now Oliver Tambo Airport), but I didn't feel too well after a long flight. I had been seated, for the most part, down at the very back of the plane, next to a good friend of mine with whom I had played that summer – Neal Radford – a Johannesburg-born cricketer, who would go on to play for England. 'Radders' had introduced me to cheap South African red wine on the flight and, given that we were seated in the last section of the plane, with the section of seats in front of us being a *smoking* section – yes, I flew so long ago, that the plane had smoking sections in it – and given that I was neither a red wine drinker, nor a smoker, I felt absolutely dreadful when I was greeted by the small group who had come from Springs to meet me.

"Welcome to South Africa, Alan," said Bobbie Gouldie, headmaster of Springs Boys' High School, one of the schools where I would be coaching over the next six months.

"We are delighted to have you with us and we're looking forward to your being part of Springs Boys' High School, and Springs High School Old Boys. Everyone is looking forward to meeting you!"

The accents were so strong and so different to anything I had heard before, although I knew Peter Swart, Rodney Ontong and Eddie Barlow. But the welcome I received at the airport was genuinely warm. We walked a fair distance to the open parking area and I remember looking up at the skies above me and thinking how wonderfully azure blue they were, but then looking down at the bare grassy areas around us and thinking how remarkably red the colour of the soil was.

The only semblance of familiarity was my cricket coffin – professional cricketers used rectangular-shaped cases to carry their equipment, hence the often-used 'coffin' – which had my name emblazoned across the front: 'Alan H Wilkins, Glamorgan CCC' with the county's daffodil emblem painted below my name. I just stared at my case as it was being loaded into the boot of the car and suddenly I felt a long way from Wales, my family and my friends. Had I made the right decision to travel to South Africa? What was ahead of me? Was I right to defy Tom Cartwright? My head was full of conflicting thoughts, but this was no time to be a student. It was time to grow up fast. This was the real world, even if I was at the other end of it.

I realise that I had gone to South Africa in defiance of the Gleneagles Agreement – a sporting boycott of South Africa – which had been agreed by the Commonwealth Heads of Government at their summit in Scotland on June 15th, 1977. The Gleneagles Agreement was the first international action in the global campaign to isolate South Africa from world sport and was set up to cease contact and competition between Commonwealth nations and the sporting organisations, teams and individuals from South Africa. Agreed some six months before a parallel United Nations boycott, it was powerful, effective and its success probably led the way to sanctions in cultural and economic areas.

However, cricket – at an individual level – remained a 'grey area' and the voice inside my head was telling me to see the country for myself and make my own mind up. While the political world almost unanimously agreed to isolate South Africa, many sportsmen and sportswomen did not see the difference between human rights abuses in South Africa and those in other countries – asking why, if they could compete against totalitarian regimes such as the Soviet Union and other communist states, or countries run by brutal dictators, could they not compete against *apartheid* South Africa? Attitudes were polarised, with one side advocating 'don't mix politics with sport' (and I guess that was the underlying tenet in my thinking), while the other said 'no normal sport in an abnormal society'.

Cricket tours stopped after the Australian tour to South Africa in 1970 but, somehow, the South African Cricket Union kept interest alive in the domestic cricket competitions which eventually led to drastic measures, such as the advent of the rebel cricket tours in the early 1980s and a rebel New Zealand rugby team – the Cavaliers – in 1985-86. The rebel cricket tours were the governing body's means – probably with the tacit support of the South African government – of undermining the international sports boycott, and were implemented because the years of isolation were beginning to expose a waning interest in the sport.

At a lower level, county cricketers of my ilk went about our business with a distinct air of uncertainty because there was no directive from the game's governing body in England (then, the Test & County Cricket Board, the TCCB) to dissuade individuals from visiting South Africa. A few years later, George Mann, the chairman of the TCCB, is reported to have said in October 1981: "We do not object to, and are legally unable to prevent, individuals from making their own arrangements to coach or develop their careers in other countries, including South Africa."

After my first visit to South Africa from September 1978 to March 1979, of course I could see the inequalities in lifestyle between black and white people and naturally there were many instances where I knew that the country's political system was unjust. But I was earning about R200 a month which barely kept me going for the time I was there, and in all this time, there were numerous British multi-

75

national companies, including some of the biggest corporations such as Barclays Bank, Cadbury Schweppes, Pilkington, BP, Unilever and Boots trading in the country with billions of rands on their balance sheets.

In a naïve admission, I would postulate that the mindset of a journeyman county cricketer like myself knew little about the hardcore politics that, on the one hand, tried to ban sporting ties with the country and yet, on the other, allowed some of the world's biggest companies to continue trading there. The inconsistency was, to me and many others, enormous. So vast in fact, that individuals in my walk of life (the out-of-season cricket coach/player) happily travelled to South Africa to enjoy the tough competition and perfect weather, largely oblivious to what was happening in townships, often just miles from where we lived or played our cricket, or in the boardrooms of banks, oil companies, building companies, insurance and investment companies. Was it naïve of us to go to South Africa with heads of Commonwealth governments saying we shouldn't when, at the same time, those same countries continued to trade in South Africa, with many of their blue chip companies – via subsidiaries – listed on the Johannesburg Stock Exchange? I assure you that not many county cricketers could have answered that question in the late '70s and early '80s.

The drive from Jan Smuts Airport to the mining city of Springs was about an hour along the R22, going east. I was astonished by the sheer vastness of the country. It was a sprawling red landscape, flat for miles as far as the eye could see, but punctuated by the strangest-looking things that protruded sporadically from this rolling flatness, which were bright yellow in colour. Some were flat, like massive, inverted baking trays, others were steep, like gigantic, inverted flower pots. This was my first lesson.

"Alan, what you are looking at," said Bobby Gouldie, "is the reason that this country has wealth. Those are the gold mining dumps from many years of mining, that go back to 1884 when gold was first discovered here. There's still gold in those dumps, which will be recycled for more gold, but all around you, there is a different kind of wealth in the soil that is just as important."

Bob Gouldie was an articulate and intelligent man who was happy to answer many of my questions as I took in this vast wilderness of a foreign landscape around me. "Bob," I said, "I cannot get over how red the soil is." "Yes," said Bob and, with a more considered tone, added, "Alan, once you have been here a little while, the soil becomes a part of you. It will never leave you. That I promise." Those words never left me; they were spoken in all seriousness and as a way of saying that in whatever capacity, this country would have a considerable impression upon my life.

The mood was lightened by the news that we were not going to my accommodation – which had not yet been decided, so I had no idea where I was going to live for the next six months – but would call in at the Springs High School Old Boys Club to meet a few people and introduce me to the members of the club for whom I would play my cricket in the months ahead.

It wasn't the prettiest place. The sprawling city of Springs had been founded on the discovery of rich seams of coal and gold back in 1904. Located 50 kilometres (31 miles) east of Johannesburg, and 72 kilometres (45 miles) southeast of Pretoria, and sitting at a height of 1,628 metres (5,340 feet) above sea level, this mining and industrial centre on the East Rand of the Transvaal (now Gauteng) would be my home for the next six months. Back in the late 1930s, there had been as many as eight gold mines in and around Springs, making it the largest single gold-producing area in the world.

We drove past a big rugby stadium – the Pam Brink Stadium – that once staged one of the most infamous brawls in British Lions rugby history. The 1968 Lions played Eastern Transvaal in an ugly affair later known as the 'Battle of Springs', culminating in the sending-off of one of Cardiff Rugby Club's most prominent front-row forwards, John 'Tess' O'Shea. I was given the history of the match as we slowed to look at the stadium.

I knew who John O'Shea was, of course, because he played his rugby for Cardiff RFC and was a good friend of my father Haydn.

The initial idea of visiting South Africa had been instigated by my father, who was secretary of Cardiff RFC and assistant manager when they were the first Welsh club to tour South Africa in 1967. I remember seeing him off from Cardiff railway station when I was in my first year of grammar school, in May 1967. I also remember thinking that he was away from home for what seemed an eternity, whilst my mother, Anne, was left to look after me, my sister Marian, and my brother Howard, single-handedly.

When my father returned home after a month in South Africa, he sowed the initial seed in my head that I should also visit the country. "Son, you have to go there one day. You won't like all of it, but it is a wonderful country, and I think you would enjoy the sport especially." This was a pivotal moment in my life as, from that day onwards, I was determined – and felt duty bound – to follow my dad's advice and visit this amazing place, which now took on mystical qualities – a holy grail – for me. My dad's words from all those years before were now swirling around in my head as the car stopped for me to look at this rugby stadium in Springs, some eleven years after he had toured the country.

We drove through an industrial area, with factories on both sides of the road, although the main roads through Springs were lined rather pleasantly by perfectly manicured palm trees in between the lampposts. Across a couple of railway tracks, with oncoming trains as long as you could see, blasting their shrill horns, with trucks full of coal, heading to the bigger cities and ports. We eventually pulled into the car park of the Springs High School Old Boys Club (SHSOB). It was midday and I was a bit on the tired side, still feeling groggy from too much red wine on the long flight, but I was hungry and needed lunch.

There was a game of cricket going on, with spectators watching from deckchairs around the boundary. I was quickly introduced to what seemed like dozens of people, then ushered into the clubhouse, where the bar was occupied by a number of club members, all of whom wanted to buy me my first drink.

"What are you having?" asked this enormous man in front of me, "beer, whisky, cane?" "Actually, I would like a sparkling water, if that's alright," was my reply, setting off a guffaw of laughter around the bar. "You're going to have to do better than that, 'Pro' because we don't serve water in this bar!" he replied.

'Pro' was to be my name for the next six months because I was the new professional cricketer from 'England', and this was the start of my steep learning curve in Springs. The big man introduced himself. "I'm Eric de Vries ... and I'm going to buy you your first beer in this club!" There was no option. "Sure, I'll have whatever you suggest."

78

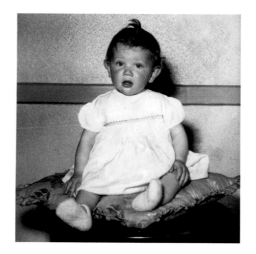

Above left: A life in sport awaits.

Above right: My sister, Marian, and me. She loved this photo and so do I.

Right: On my first bike, aged about three, in Rhiwbina, a suburb of Cardiff. It was a wonderful place to grow up.

The Wilkins brothers on a visit to London's St. James' Park when I was around nine years of age and Howard was seven.

The Wilkins family: Haydn, Anne, Marian, Howard and yours truly, holding a football.

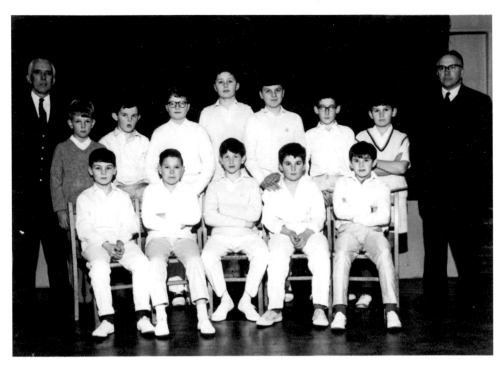

Captain of Rhiwbina Junior School cricket team, aged 11 (front row, centre).

Boy amongst men. Just turned 16 years of age and playing for Cardiff Cricket Club's 1st XI in 1969. Many of the clubs boasted professionals; sitting next to me was George Shaw, who played for Glamorgan, as did Tanzanian-born John Solanky (back row, top right). I learned a lot about the game playing for Cardiff CC.

Whitchurch High School's 1st XV. Sitting (front row, third right) between two of my best friends during my early sporting years. On my left, Keith 'Rhys' Price, and on my right, Hilary 'Chimpo' Roberts. Our team captain (front row, centre) was Gareth 'Gordon' Morgan, and our rugby master 'Big Tim' Harries sitting next to him. Also in the team was the 'other' Gareth Edwards, (back row, fifth left) and, on his left, Terry Charles, son of the great footballer John Charles. I loved those rugby days at Whitchurch High.

Loughborough College's RFC Freshers XV 1973-74 (front row, second left), and some of the most enjoyable rugby I have ever played, with my great pal and roommate, Baron Bedford (right of the captain). Phil Serrell (next to Baron) is now enjoying fame as a BBC television antiques broadcaster and Andy Wyman (back row, fifth left) is now a rugby commentator on BBC radio. Rugby coach and PE lecturer, Rod Thorpe (back row, far left), was an inspiration throughout my Loughborough years.

DAILY EXPRESS Friday September 2 1977

EXPRESS SPECIAL ON THE BIG DAY FOR WELSH CRICKET

# It's a dream

## Unknown Wilkins swings to glory

### By Jim Hill

WHEN Wales's daffodil army invades Lord's tomorrow, there will be a pertinent parallel to the unexpected arrival of Glamorgan at a Gillette Cup final.

It comes in the very presence of Alan Wilkins, a 23-year-old graduate of Loughborough University.

At the start of the season Glamorgan had emerged from a winter of internal discontent, which followed their most unsuccessful summer, with only vague hopes for improvement.

Cardiff - born Wilkins, recently released from his own crisis of final exams, was then just a fringe seamer, who had played only a few holiday games during the disasters of '76 without convincing anyone that ambition was matched by ability.

Yet tomorrow they reach an undreamed peak of peak of togetherness against Middlesex . . . the no-hope county and one of the most inexperienced bowlers to play in a Lord's cup final.

Said Wilkins: "It is like a dream. I have never been to Lord's before — not even to watch. It will not really dawn on me until I am there. That's when the butterflies will start.

"The most that left-arm medium-pacer W I L K I N S expected from this season was steady progress towards a first-team place.

"Now he is an established member of a young Glamorgan side who produced the season's biggest upset when outplaying favourites Leicester in the semi-final.

### Cheaply

Wilkins made his breakthrough on June 15 when Tony Cordle was unfit for the championship game against Somerset in Cardiff.

Included in his three wickets was West Indian wonder bat Viv Richards, cheaply dismissed, and Wilkins was there to stay.

A budding fly-half who hopes to make his mark with Cardiff, cricket remains his abiding passion—with an England cap the ultimate ambition.

Glamorgan bowler Alan Wilkins . . . now graduating from University to cup honours

Making the headlines before the Gillette Cup final at Lord's. Disappointingly I didn't make them afterwards.

On the balcony at Lord's during the final, with (R to L) Rodney Ontong, Tom Cartwright, Eifion Jones (sitting) and Les Spence, Glamorgan CCC president.

One of my proudest moments - IVA Richards, bowled AH Wilkins for 85 - Cardiff, April 1978.

# WELSH WIZARD WRECKS WORCS

**Glamorgan 131 for 9,
Worcestershire 104 all out**

A DEVASTATING career best five for 17 by 24-year-old seamer Alan Wilkins earned Glamorgan a dramatic 27-run Benson & Hedges cup victory in a low scoring struggle at Worcester.

*by W. G. WANKLYN*

Most county cricketers would scour the newspaper sports pages for scores from around the country. On good days some of the headlines made pleasant reading, but the bad days wouldn't make the scrapbook.

C Lloyd LBW b A Wilkins 32, in Glamorgan's 1979 Sunday League win over Lancashire.

Left: With Fred Trueman, one of England's greats, who visited Springs in 1978. I still don't know why 'Fiery Fred' came to Springs, but he managed to have a bowl in the nets and entertained us afterwards as only he could do.

Right: 'Alan Wilkins ... one of the best-dressed cricketers on the field of play, with never a hair out of place!' Alan Jones, former Glamorgan captain, circa 1978.

Runner-up to Mike Procter and Sarfraz Nawaz in the monthly competition run by *The Sun* for 'Demon Bowlers' (hitting the stumps), with Viv Richards unsurprisingly heading the list of 'Big Hitters' (sixes) on both occasions.

Watching the match at the County Ground, Bristol, between Gloucestershire and the West Indies, July 1980, with (R to L), Tony Brown (Secretary-Manager), Brian Brain, Mike Procter, and on the far bench, Viv Richards and Malcolm Marshall.

Left-arm over medium-fast. Some days were better than others.

Gloucestershire captain, Mike Procter, waiting patiently for my chat with the West Indies wicket-keeper, Deryck Murray, to end during the tour match at Bristol, July 1980.

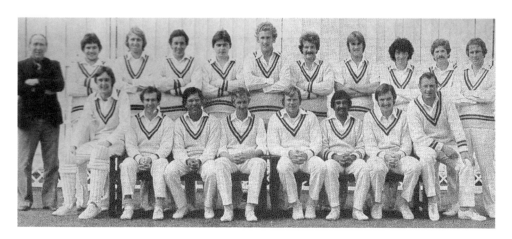

Gloucestershire CCC 1981.

Standing (L to R): Bert Avery (scorer); Ian Broome; David Surridge; John Childs; Tony Wright; Chris Broad; David Partridge; Steve Windaybank; Phil Bainbridge; Alan Wilkins; Martin Stovold.

Seated (L to R): Andy Brassington; Andy Stovold; Zaheer Abbas; Brian Brain; Mike Procter (captain); Sadiq Mohammad; David Graveney; Graham Wiltshire (coach).

# Lancs destroyed by 8-wicket Wilkins

### By MIKE STEVENSON at Old Trafford

## Scoreboard

**LANCASHIRE.——First innings**

| | |
|---|---|
| A. Kennedy c A. W. Stovold b Childs | 44 |
| G. Fowler lbw b Wilkins | 11 |
| I. Cockbain b Wilkins | 2 |
| *C. H. Lloyd b Whitney | 39 |
| D. Lloyd b Wilkins | 23 |
| D. P. Hughes c A. W. Stovold b Wilkins | 8 |
| J. Simmons b Wilkins | 4 |
| †C. J. Scott c Broad b Wilkins | 11 |
| P. J. W. Allott v Hignell b Wilkins | 0 |
| M. A. Holding c & b Wilkins | 32 |
| P. G. Lee not out | 2 |
| Extras (b1, lb1, w2, nb2) | 6 |
| **Total (67·5 overs)** | **182** |

**Fall of wickets:** 1-20, 2-35, 3-88, 4-109, 5-119, 6-127, 7-138, 8-138, 9-164.

**Bonus Pts:** Lancs 1, Gloucs 4.

**Bowling:** Whitney 21-8-62-1; Wilkins 26·5-10-57-8; Bainbridge 7-4-20-0; Broad 9-4-20-0; Childs 4-9-17-1.

## Super show

*. . . from Alan Wilkins with career-best figures*

Career best figures of 26-10-57-8 for Gloucestershire v Lancashire at Old Trafford, September 1981.

Overseas professional coach with Pretoria Boys High School 1st XI, 1981-82, with cricket master and wonderful bon viveur, Charles Mulvenna. Ever smiling, ever helpful, the boys loved him.

Glamorgan CCC, 1983 season. Standing (L-R): Geoff Holmes (died 2009, aged 51); Alan Wilkins; Winston Davis; Rodney Ontong; Alan Lewis Jones; Charles Rowe; Arthur Francis. Sitting (L-R): Eifion Jones; Barry Lloyd (died 2016, aged 63); Mike Selvey (capt.); Alan Jones; John Hopkins.

In 2014, during the Indian Tour to England and 33 years after the photo of my bowling action had been taken, Star Sports India used it in comparison to that of fearsome Australian left-arm bowler Mitchell Johnson. The main difference was about 20 miles per hour – at least – plus 552 international wickets!

Top right: With my first mentor in radio cricket commentary, the great broadcaster, Charles Fortune, Johannesburg 1986.

Right: Receiving the award for the SAB Radio Sports Journalist of the Year 1986-87, from Peter Savory, South African Breweries' marketing director.

Bottom: The 1986 SAB Sports Award winners in Radio and TV came from all walks of life and were some of the finest writers and broadcasters I have known.

On duty at the National Stadium, Cardiff Arms Park, in 1987-88, my first year with BBC Wales television sport.

With Ryan Giggs, the 1996 BBC Wales Sports Personality of the Year winner, and the great John Charles, who presented the award.

With two great Springboks in Cardiff: Jannie Engelbrecht, tour manager, and Francois Pienaar, captain, of the 1994 South Africa rugby tour to Britain and Ireland.

With Susie, enjoying another yarn from our good friend Lynn Davies, CBE, the 1964 Olympic long jump gold medallist. Lynn's photo album is never too far away, and his stories are priceless.

The Russian-built Ilyushin II-76, a massive aeroplane used by the Soviet Air Force in war operations in Afghanistan in the '70s and '80s. Between 1996 and 1998 it was our mode of transport around India for commentators and crew, everyone except Geoff Boycott.

With Robin Jackman at his home in Cape Town in 2001. The Mankad incident is never forgotten, and always an excuse for a celebratory glass of wine between us.

Flanked by a 'A Few Good Men' on the 2002 Indian Cricket Tour to England. The television promotional trailer was filmed at Trent Bridge, Nottingham, with (L to R), Navjot Singh Sidhu, Sunny Gavaskar, Ravi Shastri, Harsha Bhogle and Geoffrey Boycott. The ESPN Star Sports commentary box was one of the most memorable I have been fortunate to be a part of.

On tour in India with Singapore Cricket Club in October 2002.

On commentary duty at the Bangabandhu National Stadium, Dhaka, in 2002, for the Bangladesh v West Indies Test and ODI series, with (L to R), Tony Cozier – the voice of West Indies cricket, Gordon Greenidge, Arun Lal, and Ian Bishop.

Only Tony Greig could have organized a private trip around the eastern seaboard of Sri Lanka in a military helicopter, where we saw the aftermath of the unimaginable horror of the 2004 Indian Ocean earthquake and tsunami.

With Dad and Howard, circa 1996. Notice the identical grips on the beer glasses! 'Like father like sons'.

Mum's 80th birthday celebration with my sister, Marian, and brother, Howard, October 2006.

Eric turned to the barman: "Saul, give the Pro a Castle … and make sure his glass is never empty!"

Saul was black: tall, immaculately dressed, and had a warm, engaging smile. "Welcome to the club, Sir," he beamed as he placed a bottle of beer and a glass in front of me. He was wearing black trousers and he and his three colleagues alongside him on the other side of the bar all wore smart maroon-coloured jackets with matching bow ties and white shirts. It struck me then that all four barmen were black South Africans; everyone on my side of the bar was a white South African. There were no women in the bar. This was the Springs High School Old Boys' Club Men's Bar. No women allowed. No blacks allowed. "Thank You, Saul," I replied, as I stretched out to shake his hand across the bar. "I guess I will be seeing quite a lot of you in the next few months." Saul smiled and then his colleagues all came up to where I was sitting and each in turn offered their hand in a welcome handshake.

If I thought that Eric was a big man, I quickly had to recalibrate my thoughts when Eric introduced me to his younger brother, Leonard, affectionately known as 'Little Boet' (Eric's Little Brother). "Pro, this is Leonard, he's my little brother," said a loudly laughing Eric. Leonard was a veritable man mountain with hands like shovels and he towered over everyone. "Howzit Pro?" was Leonard's opening hello, but spoken in a warm, gentle way and in a much lighter voice than I had anticipated. "Don't worry," said the reassuring follow-up lines, "you're in good hands with the de Vries brothers, we'll look after you."

I had been told about the de Vries brothers by Eddie Barlow. They were legends in Springs. Everyone in the sporting world, certainly in South Africa I was told, knew Eric and Leonard de Vries. I was invited to sit on one of the tall bar stools that formed a ring around the big wooden bar, with a foot rest perfectly placed and an elbow rest also strategically built for a long stay in this establishment. After a couple of cold Castle lagers, that in my recollection were no more than 28 cents a bottle, I was soon introduced to a drink called 'cane and coke'. I should have known better but, there I was, propped up on a bar stool between two of the biggest men I had known, two of the friendliest people I could have hoped to have met on my first day in Springs.

A couple of hours later I passed out. All I remember is being helped off my bar stool, bundled into a car and waved off by the smiling de Vries brothers. To this day I cannot remember where I was taken, but I do recall sleeping for the next 24 hours. Wales was a distant country behind me and now I had to make my mark in this foreign land.

The next few days were taken up meeting people in both a professional and social capacity. My cricket coaching schedule was given to me; I would be coaching every afternoon of the week, and sometimes on Saturday mornings. Springs Boys' High School was the secondary school and then there were the primary schools: Strubenvale, Selcourt and Pinegrove. All the schools were in fairly affluent areas of Springs where the inhabitants were Caucasian. There were no black teachers and neither did I coach a black schoolboy of any age in my first six months in Springs.

As well as coaching youngsters throughout the week, I had coaching duties two evenings a week at Springs HSOB, and then league cricket was played on virtually every weekend on Saturdays and Sundays. Springs HSOB played in what was then called the North-Eastern Transvaal Cricket League, which incorporated three clubs from the East Rand: Springs HSOB, Benoni and ERPM Boksburg.

The three East Rand clubs would then travel to Pretoria to play against the Pretoria clubs such as Pretoria High School Old Boys, CBC Old Boys (Christian Brothers College), Harlequins, Berea Park, *Oostelikes* (the Afrikaans word for 'Easterns'), South African Defence Force, South African Police, and Pretoria University (known as 'Tukkies').

None of these clubs had any black cricketers. League cricket in Transvaal in 1978 was played exclusively by whites, although I'd heard that there were Indian and 'coloured' leagues in Cape Town. That was the stark reality of *apartheid* South Africa; there was segregation in the country and I was seeing it for myself at first-hand. That was important to me: that I would be able to formulate my own thoughts and opinions on South Africa. I had not gone to the country for a king's ransom – far from it – I had a very basic remuneration which never seemed to stretch far enough by the end of each month, but I had accommodation – with a young couple and their baby boy – and a car. The car was the stuff of folklore. It was no Mercedes, but an old Volkswagen Beetle that had been driven by previous cricket professionals on their visits to Springs in years gone by. My life was in that car; cricket bags, cricket equipment, change of clothes, you name it, and it was in there. The air-conditioning was a handle on the door panel; on some days the heat was stifling.

I missed family and friends so much in those days because there was no internet, there were no mobile phones, and international calls back to the United Kingdom cost a lot of money, so I probably made no more than a dozen calls home in the six months I was there. I did write letters home every week, though, sometimes twice a week and I also kept a diary.

There were many days when the feeling of loneliness engulfed me and I questioned my decision to leave behind my *fiancée*, Dot, who had moved from London to south Wales to take up a teaching job and to be near me. I'd met Dot in my first year at Loughborough and, since she was in the year above me and had left to go teaching, whereas I had one more year at Loughborough to complete my Bachelor of Education, we'd spent three years together at university.

I questioned my decision to leave home and to act against the wishes of Glamorgan, but sport makes a person selfish and, in sport, we make selfish decisions because the journey we make is largely our own. I would argue that pursuing a journey to achieve excellence in professional sport leads to the person thinking almost exclusively of themselves, to the detriment of others in their lives. I had certainly made that call with respect to Dot, and I was, in time, going to suffer the consequences for making that decision.

Towards the Christmas break I was taken to the Kruger Park Game Reserve in the Eastern Transvaal, about a six hour drive from Springs, and had one of the most enjoyable weeks of my life in one of the world's great game reserves. There were four of us on that trip; we saw the Big Five – lion, elephant, buffalo, leopard and rhinoceros – drank copious amounts of alcohol around the *braaivleis* (Afrikaans for barbecue) and talked for hours on end around the camp fire. It was an extraordinary experience.

Even before I had set foot in South Africa I had set my heart on visiting Cape Town. For one thing, Peter Swart, my Glamorgan teammate lived there, and he had offered his home as accommodation for the Christmas break. The drive down from the Highveld of the Transvaal (6,000 feet above sea level) to Cape Town took about 15 hours with a stop overnight; I was fortunate that one of my Springs HSOB pals had decided to drive down to the Cape for his Christmas break as well. His BMW 528i went like a flying machine along the straightest roads I had ever seen. Out of the Transvaal, through Orange Free State (now called the Free State) and through the amazing semi-desert landscape of the Great Karoo before descending upon the lush green valleys of the northern part of the Western Province.

Table Mountain in Cape Town is one of the most mesmerising sights on Mother Earth. You simply cannot take your gaze from the magnificent piece of gigantic granite rock that ascends some 3,558 feet above sea level, standing majestically over the city of Cape Town. Nestling in the foothills of this wonderful landmark was the famous District Six area of the city, where Basil D'Oliveira had been born and played his cricket in the 'coloured' cricket leagues of Cape Town. I am glad I saw it in 1978 because, alas, it has since been redeveloped into a modern housing complex, consigning to history one of Cape Town's most important urban areas.

Newlands Cricket Ground was also the most picturesque cricket ground I had ever seen, and it was absolutely packed for the annual New Year Castle Currie Cup match between Western Province and Transvaal. Peter Kirsten stroked a sublime century for Western Province in a line-up that was skippered by Hylton Ackerman (who had been born in Springs), Kirsten, Allan Lamb, Peter Swart and, in Denys Hobson, one of the finest leg-spinners in the world.

In reply, the great Graeme Pollock dominated for Transvaal with an imposing 233, the first time I had seen him bat. He was tall and had an extraordinary presence as soon as he strode out of the old pavilion onto the Newlands turf, with his long strides and his gaze fixed upon the pitch he would occupy for the next day and a half.

The partisan Western Province crowd gave him a welcome that was a mix of adulation for arguably South Africa's greatest batsman, and a tinge of derision from the locals because he was playing for Transvaal, not everyone's favourite cricket team in the Cape. Pollock was originally from Port Elizabeth, the coastal city on South Africa's Eastern Cape, and played his first few years for Eastern Province, but the lure of Johannesburg, both from a cricketing and a business perspective, was an incentive for the great man to move up to the Highveld from the sleepy city of Port Elizabeth.

At the crease, Graeme Pollock was a colossus, with an extra cover drive that pierced the most testing fields set for him, and a pull shot of such ferocity, should anyone pitch it short to him, that the ball left his bat like a gunshot. I couldn't take my eyes off him. The game ended in a draw, but it was three days of the most intense cricket I had seen, compared to County Championship cricket.

I am a daft romantic at heart, and I have to admit that I cried unashamedly when I had to leave Cape Town. I had fallen in love with the place and did not want to leave but the honeymoon with the Cape was over and it was time to return to the Highveld and Springs.

It wasn't just the stark difference in the landscape between Western Province and the Transvaal, but also the attitudes of the people that had a marked contrast. I felt that the Cape had a more liberal attitude towards everything. During my time in Cape Town I befriended Omar Henry, one of the leading domestic cricketers in the country. Omar was a 'Cape coloured' who was born in Stellenbosch and was loved in the Western Cape. One of the great features of the Newlands cricket crowd was the vociferous and knowledgeable section occupied by the 'Cape coloured community. Henry would go on to become the first non-white player in the modern era to play cricket for South Africa, playing three Tests and three One-Day Internationals, making his ODI debut against Sri Lanka in March 1992, and his Test debut against India in November 1992. Omar was a left-arm spinner who took 434 first-class wickets but, more importantly, he did much to break down the colour barrier in sport in the 1970s and 1980s. He also went on to become South Africa's chairman of selectors.

Back in Springs I had another opportunity to see Graeme Pollock bat. This time it was the Datsun Shield one-day (60 overs) final between Transvaal and Natal at The Wanderers in February 1979. Pollock smashed a century off a Natal attack that included Mike Procter and the giant Vince van der Bijl, and the rest of the home batting was formidable with the likes of Henry Fotheringham, Jimmy Cook and Clive Rice. Natal were bowled out for 235, in reply to Transvaal's 311-5 from 60 overs. It was a memorable occasion with not a spare seat in the Bull Ring, the colloquially-named Wanderers Stadium, on a blazing hot day; a pair of sunburnt shoulders, a reminder that I had sat out in the harsh Highveld sun all day long.

My first six months in Springs coincided with one of the worst droughts the country had experienced. The poor farmers were praying for rain: literally. Prayers would be held on a daily basis for the rains that would nourish the parched earth. For so many people it was a harsh environment. For the majority of the population, the political laws at that time made it even more untenable.

As the month of March approached I was mentally and physically ready to return to Britain and to my next season of county cricket with Glamorgan. I would take back with me a kaleidoscope of thoughts from six months in South Africa, and I was uncertain as to how I would be welcomed back by Tom Cartwright, Glamorgan's coach. I was fit and raring to get started for the 1979 season, but very soon I would realise that Tom and I were not on the same wavelength. The same applied to my relationship with Dot. I returned to Cardiff to resume our life together but clearly things had changed. For one thing, Dot had met someone just weeks before I returned, but what could I have expected? I had left behind a young woman whilst I flew to the other end of the world. How could things possibly be the same? It would take time, so would my cricket. The next few months would prove to be a turbulent time in my cricket career when emotions would get the better of me.

# 6

# The Parting of Ways

*'I first met Alan when he was playing for Glamorgan against Somerset and I had a very bad day – I'd been rolled over by Alan – but I didn't mind because he was one of the nicest guys I would ever compete against and, also, when I went to Glamorgan in my latter years in county cricket, he was a great help, giving me all the advice I needed to be an honorary Welshman!'*

**Sir Vivian Richards**

Glamorgan had a new captain for the 1979 season, Robin Hobbs. The former Essex and England leg-spinner had been out of first-class cricket for four years, playing for the minor county Suffolk, but Tom Cartwright had persuaded him to take over from the stalwart Alan Jones, who'd stood down. Robin Hobbs was a very affable man and he could still bowl very decent leg-spin. In his first-class career he took over 1,000 wickets, played seven Tests for England and, in an extraordinary batting display one afternoon in Chelmsford, he blasted the 1975 touring Australians for one of the fastest hundreds in history, from just 45 balls in 44 minutes, hitting twelve fours and seven sixes!

The new season began promisingly with the short trip to Oxford University where I took 5 for 25 in 16 overs, and then a resounding win in the B & H Cup over Worcestershire in Cardiff, where I was happy with my 2 for 34 in nine overs; with Robin Hobbs taking a magnificent diving catch in the covers to give me the wicket of my old adversary Younis Ahmed, who had moved from Surrey. The pity of it was that Younis had hit the ball so hard it almost dislocated our new captain's thumb.

"Hobbsy," I said, "I owe you for that one!" as our captain clutched his mangled thumb. "Too bloody right you do!" he said, as he went off to have the thumb examined and X-rayed. Fortunately, there was no break or dislocation, and we headed to Southampton for our first County Championship match against Hampshire.

It was the first week of May and it was bitterly cold; it had actually snowed over southern Britain, especially in the Southampton area, not exactly ideal for playing cricket. We had also read about Hampshire's new overseas signing, a young fast bowler from Barbados by the name of Malcolm Marshall. He had made his Test debut against India at Bangalore in December 1978 and while Chetan Chauhan was the only wicket he took, the Hampshire scout at the ground had seen enough to sign him for the 1979 English season. This was to be his debut match in England.

We won the toss and put Hampshire into bat; I had never been so cold on the cricket field and it was made worse by Gordon Greenidge pounding us with his flashing blade for a typically belligerent 81. Getting your freezing hands in the way of a brand new cricket ball hit by the West Indies great was not a bundle of fun and it was with some relief when Peter Swart trapped him LBW. It was a truncated first day because of the bad weather and Hampshire closed on 179-3. I had opened the bowling with our Barbados-born, but home-based medium-fast bowler, Tony Cordle, and had bowled reasonably well to take my 100th first-class wicket when I got their opener, John Rice, LBW for 10.

Hampshire resumed their first innings on the second – still very cold – day, and I again found some decent rhythm to take a couple more Hampshire wickets, when Malcolm Marshall came in at number eight with the score 212 for 6. He looked a million dollars as he strode out to the middle with a typical West Indian swagger, his shirt collar turned up against the back of his neck, and every item of his clothing and equipment looking immaculate. He looked a bit bigger than the photographs published in the British newspapers that morning, with headlines like 'Hampshire Sign West Indies Fast

Bowling Sensation' and 'Glamorgan First Up for Marshall' but he was wearing about three long-sleeved woollen sweaters, as a defence against the horribly cold weather.

I had just taken my third wicket and had four balls to go to complete the over. At the non-striker's end was the Hampshire bowling all-rounder, Michael Taylor, a typical English county cricketer, whose career spanned 16 years, playing over 600 games for Hampshire and before that, Nottinghamshire.

"What's he like, your new guy, Malcolm Marshall?" I asked Mike Taylor, as Hampshire's new signing approached the cut square. "He's a nice lad, hasn't said a lot, but he's quite sharp," came the reply with a little laugh at the end of it. "Mind you, he's only bowled off a few paces in the indoor nets, but he was quick enough!"

"Have you seen him bat?" I asked. "Nah, not much, but he's come with quite a reputation as a promising all-rounder. Anyway, you're going to see for yourself aren't you? You're the first bloke to bowl at him in England," said the smiling Taylor. Did he know something that we didn't? His grin suggested he did.

My first ball to Malcolm Marshall swung late, went clean through his bat and pad as he came forward to play the ball, which missed his off-stump by a 'coat of paint'. I followed through with arms aloft and muttered something to myself along the lines of 'bloody hell ... that was close!' The second ball had the same shape, a little in-swing, but this time he made contact and got off the mark with an edge down to third man. As I followed through, and as he cantered past me for the single, there was a brief eye-to-eye exchange; nothing more than that. Mike Taylor got a single off the next ball which meant that my last ball of the over was to Marshall. Despite the bitterly cold weather, the dark red Duke English-made cricket ball was swinging nicely. I ran in and the ball swung again. Malcolm came forward, drove at the ball, and missed. It crashed into his off-stump which went flying back (must have been the soft ground!) and that was my fourth wicket of the innings.

My teammates gathered around me in celebration and I turned to Mike Taylor. "Well, he looked the part, Mike!" I said half-jokingly and half seriously. With a little audible snigger before his reply, Mike retorted, "Yeah, he'll be pissed off with that, because he told us he loves batting!" I quickly interjected, "Too bad he missed it then, isn't it?"

As quick as a flash, Mike replied, "Yeah, he loves batting ... but not half as much as he loves bowling quick!" He was beside himself laughing with a knowing nod of his head suggesting that I would be a target (an easy one, I might add) for Malcolm Marshall when he bowled to us, but that wasn't in my thoughts right then as we bowled Hampshire out for 237 and I recorded my most successful first-class figures of 32-10-79-6.

Cricket is a great game when you take wickets or score runs, and the dressing room was a good place to be after you had performed. It was as if you had earned your right to sit with the professionals who had played many more years than you. As tradition permitted, I led Glamorgan off the field for having taken my six wickets and I was on a natural high.

The focus very quickly turned to Malcolm Marshall, because no-one in England had seen him. As our two opening batsmen, Alan Jones and John Hopkins, walked out to the middle, the rest of the Glamorgan team gathered on the balcony of the old Southampton pavilion. We all wanted to see how quick the new Hampshire signing was. For years Hampshire had been able to call upon the services of the great Antiguan, Andy Roberts, a marvellous fast bowler who, for most of his county career, had terrified opposition batsmen.

Malcolm Marshall stood at the end of his run-up, surveying his field. He didn't have to look around too far, because they were all behind the stumps! Slips, gullies, short-legs, you name it he had them waiting for Glamorgan's batsmen to fall. I think he might have had a cover point, or even a mid-off, but no-one else in front of square. His run-up was beautiful. Quick-stepping, quick-striding and seemingly gliding over the turf, and then the devilishly quick arm action that catapulted the ball around 90 miles an hour; he was fast but the added problem for batsmen was that he could swing the ball either way and get it to deviate off the seam with venom.

Glamorgan struggled from the outset, and we were soon 86 for 6, but it wasn't Marshall who was causing the damage. It was the guy bowling the other end, Keith Stevenson, who ran in and picked up five wickets before Marshall had taken his first. We finished the second day on 133 for 7, but somehow Marshall had not taken a wicket. That was to change on the third and final day.

The final day of this County Championship match was destined for a tame draw but not before Malcolm Marshall had had his turn to bowl to me. Given that we were seven wickets down overnight, and with me occupying the number 11 spot – I always believed I was better than a number 11! – I was a bit leisurely about my preparation on that final day. In fact, I was in the lavatory reading the morning newspapers about my bowling exploits and basking in my own glory, when I was disturbed by a hammering on the door.

"Wilkie, get out of there! You're in!" Bellowed the voice on the other side of the door.

"What?" I shouted, "I can't be! They've only just walked out there!"

In a nervous frenzy, trying to get my clothes on before opening the lavatory door, I half stumbled out of the toilet to see a gathering of teammates and Tom Cartwright, our coach. He was not happy at all. "Get your bloody pads on and get out there!" he blasted at me.

It seemed to take an age to get dressed and padded up. Marshall had bowled our overnight batsman, Eifion Jones, first ball of the morning and, with his third ball, he'd bowled our skipper, Robin Hobbs. So, at 135 for 9, I was last man in. I was a dishevelled mess as I left our dressing room and walked out of the grand Victorian pavilion through the wrought-iron gate and onto the outfield. I could see the Hampshire team in a group out in the middle, but Trevor Jesty, one of their top all-rounders (490 first-class matches, 35 centuries, 585 wickets and 10 ODIs for England), was near the boundary as I walked towards him on my way to the middle to face Malcolm Marshall.

"I have been bloody ages, Trevor, haven't I? I was in the toilet," I spurted nervously. "I can't believe that I haven't been timed out to be honest."

I should have been timed out. I had been more than the five minutes or so allowed for an incoming batsman, but Trevor gave me the reason I hadn't been, with a line that I have never forgotten.

"Wilks, yes you were going to be timed out, but we asked the umpires not to do that. 'Macca' (Malcolm Marshall) really wanted to bowl to you ... and we wouldn't have missed this for the world!" I walked past Trevor Jesty, and he was still laughing when I saw the faces of all the Hampshire players out in the middle as a kind of reception committee.

I tried desperately not to look at Malcolm Marshall, but he was standing near the stumps at the bowler's end and he was making all kinds of gestures organising fielding positions. I asked for my guard and, in looking up at the umpire, I caught Malcolm's eye. Eyeball to eyeball. He smiled, shook his head, chuckled to himself and then walked back to his mark. Every Hampshire player was standing around me: slips, gullies and a couple of fielders in close directly in front of me.

Malcolm stood at the end of his run, flicking the ball up in the air from his hand and generally making this a rather unpleasant wait. Then he started his run-up. In he came, fast-steps, unbelievably fast arm and a red flash went past me! I missed it, or more pertinently, the ball missed me. Then, in an involuntary moment of nervous fumbling and fidgeting around at the crease, feeling more than a little self-conscious, to my utter horror I realised that I had walked out to face Malcolm Marshall without the most important piece of protective equipment for a male cricketer. In my desperate haste to get dressed and padded up, I had forgotten to put on my protective box. Was I out of my mind?

I had to signal to the Glamorgan dressing room for my box to be brought out, an action which brought howls of laughter from the Hampshire players, and even Malcolm was laughing as I clumsily attached it to my person.

I have no idea how I played the second ball I faced from him, but it squirted through the slip cordon for two. I was off the mark, but I had to face him again. The next ball was my last, as it reared off the pitch towards my throat and, with eyes shut, I fended it off towards one of the many gullies in waiting. It was Mike Taylor who caught it and, grinning widely, said: "Well done Wilkie, did you enjoy that? I told you he liked bowling quick!"

Hampshire sensed our discomfort at facing Marshall. They batted and declared their second innings on 117 for 6, leaving us

216 to win. Malcolm steamed in with even better rhythm than the first innings, taking 4 for 23 in 15.3 overs, as Glamorgan were bowled out for exactly 100 in 50 overs. It was pedestrian scoring, but Marshall was hostile and most of the time unplayable. I had the dubious honour of being last man out, and Malcolm had the pleasure of seeing me fend off a brute of a ball from in front of my nose, straight into the hands of Trevor Jesty at silly point. Nought first ball! We lost the match by 116 runs and, in the process, we had also witnessed at first-hand the start of the county career of one of the greatest fast bowlers the game would see. One last gesture from the great Barbadian: as I trudged off having made a duck, he came up to me and shook my hand with one arm around my shoulders and a broad, warm smile on his face. "Well bowled, man!" he said to me as he gestured with his left arm the action of my bowling. "Thanks Malcolm," I replied, "and I hope you have a great year ahead here at Hampshire."

Malcolm Marshall was a wonderful cricketer and person; terrifying to face from 22 yards, but an extraordinarily decent human being with genuine feelings for his fellow players and for opponents. His death from cancer in 1999 at the tender age of 41 was a tragic loss deeply felt by cricketers worldwide. It was a privilege to have met him, and to have been on the same field as him. RIP Malcolm Marshall.

In a cold, wet (and remember it snowed in Southampton) start to the season, I felt good about my bowling. We drove that evening from Southampton to Taunton to play a B & H Cup match the very next day against Somerset, who were without Viv Richards, as he was with the West Indies preparing for the World Cup that was to be played in England that summer. But Somerset still had Joel Garner and Ian Botham. They beat us but I came away with 3 for 23 in my 11 overs, including Botham LBW for 0.

Rain washed out so much cricket in those early weeks, but the summer picked up the first week of June as we headed north to Trent Bridge to play Nottinghamshire. It was during this match that I had an angry exchange of words with Tom Cartwright in our dressing room and our captain, Robin Hobbs, had to intervene. The argument came out of nowhere, but maybe it was inevitable since I had gone to South Africa against Tom's wishes.

Maybe it was also because Nottinghamshire had Richard Hadlee and Clive Rice in their side and we were on the receiving end of a magnificent spell of bowling from Hadlee, who took 7 for 28 in 15 overs in the second innings, to set up a comfortable win for the home side. It was when my good friend, Rodney Ontong, came back into the dressing room after getting out: caught Rice bowled Hadlee for 1. In a gesture of encouragement, I said to Rodney, "Bad luck, Rod, that looked like a hell of a ball to keep out." It was nothing more than a comment from one mate to another in the confines of the dressing room, but it ignited a verbal attack from Tom: "Wilkie, shut up! What the hell do you know about batting?"

I was taken completely by surprise and felt the emotion surging up inside me. Tom was right in the sense in that I didn't know a hell of a lot about batting, but I turned to him and said: "With respect, Tom, I'm not talking to you, I'm talking to Rodney, and it's got nothing to do with you what I say to him, whether it's about batting or anything else for that matter."

He quickly retorted: "Little boys should be seen, and not heard, now just shut up!"

That got me going. "What is the matter with you?" I said. "You have absolutely no right to talk to me like that. I have an opinion just like everyone has in this dressing room, and if I want to express it, I bloody well will do so. You will not talk to me like that!"

Tom muttered something about 'college boys being full of themselves' and how my opinion counted for nothing. It was hurtful and it made me angry. We exchanged some more insults and ended up with my saying to our captain that Tom needed a reality check, and that if he had such little regard for me as a player and as a person, I might as well leave the ground and go home. I threatened to leave and get a train back from Nottingham to Cardiff.

No-one doubted Tom's acumen as a medium pace bowler for whom the mechanics and skills were second nature, but man-management was not his strong suit. I was not the only young player in that Glamorgan team who felt that way about his lack of empathy with a team that needed collective responsibility, a group of young players who needed more encouragement, not the autocratic style which Tom brought to the club which, I felt was archaic and not suited to this team. I stood my ground against Tom and I was soon to pay for it.

This heated exchange was extinguished by Alan Jones and Robin Hobbs, both of whom advised me to 'cool down' and say nothing more. Nottinghamshire beat us easily but once again, I had allowed emotions to get the better of me. Or had I done the right thing by standing up for myself? Was I out of order for voicing my opinion against that of the coach in this professional cricket team? Who was in the wrong? I didn't think I was, but clearly, the hierarchy at Glamorgan didn't agree.

The very next day we had to play Derbyshire in a B & H Cup match in Cardiff. John Wright, the obdurate New Zealand left-hand opening batsman, scored a flawless century which sealed our defeat and our exit from that competition. Our next match, against Warwickshire at Swansea in the County Championship was, in retrospect, the turning point in my relationship with Glamorgan.

The squad of 12 or 13 players had gone through all the pre-match warm-up routines on the outfield at St. Helen's. With half an hour to go to the start of play, we were in the Dressing room for the final team chat, a cup of tea, and the final preparations for going out to field, since we'd lost the toss. No-one had spoken to me at this stage so I assumed I was in the playing XI, but only when the team started to walk out of the dressing room was I told by Robin Hobbs that I was not in the team.

The team walked out to take the field and I was left standing in the dressing room in my full cricket apparel and bowling boots. The club chairman, Ossie Wheatley, came in and began to talk to me. I think I might have got my words in first because I was fuming.

"Ossie, what the hell is going on? Why have I been left out of this side? I am bowling well, I have taken plenty of wickets and there has to be a reason. It's Tom, isn't it?"

Ossie Wheatley had a very calm manner about him, and clearly his explanation was designed to assuage me. "Alan," he said, "I will not deny that Tom has spoken to me about you and that confrontation you had with him at Trent Bridge, and we believe that for your own good it is right to give you a rest, because we feel you are getting too emotional about your cricket."

I completely disagreed with his viewpoint. I was in good form, taking wickets, and only a month before, had recorded my best bowling figures for Glamorgan. We had a frank discussion, but it wasn't going to get me back into the side. In fact I was not selected for the next ten County Championship matches, and would play in only five of the remaining 11 Sunday League matches, during which time I took 4-31 against Middlesex at Lord's and had Man of the Match figures of 8-5-13-2 against Lancashire at Cardiff, getting Lancashire's West Indian captain, Clive Lloyd LBW for 32, and David 'Bumble' Lloyd bowled for 0. Some bright lights on the otherwise dark horizon.

Being out of favour with the 1st XI meant that I played a good deal of cricket for the club's 2nd XI. It proved to be a lot of fun, with our captain, Kevin Lyons, who did an excellent job of developing young players in professional cricket.

One 2nd XI Championship match stands out, and it involved the South African-born opening batsman, Chris 'Kippy' Smith, who was in the Glamorgan team as a last-minute replacement for the trip to the seaside town of Bournemouth to play against the Hampshire 2nd XI. Kippy was playing club cricket in Swansea that summer and was desperate to secure a professional contract with a county, preferably Glamorgan. The match in the last week of June at Dean Park proved to be a career-breaker for Chris Smith.

Not opening, but batting at number five in our first innings, Chris got a big nick first ball he faced from their opening bowler, and the Hampshire team all went up in unison for the catch behind. Everyone heard the nick, even we did back on the players' balcony in the dressing room, but the one man who clearly didn't hear anything was the umpire, who said "Not Out!" The Hampshire boys – Paul Terry, Mark Nicholas, Bobby Parks – were clearly unhappy, but Kippy just kept his head down, prodded the pitch with the end of his bat, took guard again from the umpire – now the most unpopular man in Bournemouth – and carried on batting. He made 124 not out. The match ended in a draw, but it was the conversation that Kippy had at the end of the match with the Hampshire coach, Peter Sainsbury, a former Hampshire player, who inquired about Kippy's playing intentions for the future that remains in the memory. The line that

Kippy uses is a true story: "Well, thank you for your interest, and I know I played OK today after that first ball let-off, but seriously, it is my younger brother who you should see batting. He is a fantastic player now, and he will be a hell of a better player than me in the future."

The upshot of this conversation is that Hampshire did their homework better than Glamorgan did. Kippy had told both clubs that he and his younger brother would soon qualify for British passports, through their father's side of the family, and that they could be considered as 'home-grown' players rather than overseas signings. Hampshire eventually went on to sign Chris Smith, who went on to play 269 first-class matches for them, scoring over 18,000 runs at an average of 44, and with 47 first-class centuries. He also went on to play eight Tests for England.

Not content with one Smith, Hampshire duly acknowledged Chris's recommendation that they should sign his younger brother and, as his elder brother predicted, he would be the better player. Robin appeared in 426 first-class matches scoring over 26,000 runs at an average of 41, with 61 first-class centuries. He went on to play 62 Test matches for England at an average of 43, and 71 ODIs with a highest ODI score of 167 not out against Australia at Edgbaston in 1993. That was the England ODI record which stood for 23 years until Alex Hales blasted 171 against Pakistan at Trent Bridge in August 2015 as England amassed the highest ODI total of all time: 444-3.

Robin Smith was indeed a fantastic player. Glamorgan missed out on two wonderful cricketers and two outstanding clubmen. Had he been around in those days, Chris might have got a first-ball duck, we'll never know.

When I was eventually selected for the Championship team in early August after two months out of the side, it was against Hampshire in Cardiff. Hampshire had their two West Indian superstars – Gordon Greenidge and Malcolm Marshall – missing but, in a rain-affected drawn game, I guess I made my point to the club's management in the best possible way, by taking 5 for 91 in 37 overs.

A month after being left out of the team that played Warwickshire at Swansea, I was called up by the management to be twelfth man in the County Championship match against Gloucestershire in Cardiff. This would be the seventh consecutive Championship match that I had missed, and it had not gone unnoticed by the captain of the visiting team in that second week of July.

No-one wants to be twelfth man. You are basically a drinks-carrier and a general dogsbody for the eleven players out on the field. You are there in the dressing room and with the team, but really, you are no more than an extra on a film-set. And it is a lousy film.

It was during this match at Sophia Gardens in Cardiff that I offloaded some of my emotional baggage to some of the Gloucestershire players. I knew their opening batsman, Andy Stovold, from my Loughborough days – he was a year above me – and Gloucestershire had a reputation as one of the most congenial sides in England. When Glamorgan were out in the field, I was sitting up on the balcony in the old Sophia Gardens cricket pavilion, with the Gloucestershire players alongside me in the adjoining dressing room. Brian Brain, a formidable fast-medium bowler who had started his career with Worcestershire, approached me with the stealth of a secret agent.

"Wilks," he whispered, "what's happening? Why are you not playing? You've missed lots of cricket haven't you? 'Stov' told me you weren't happy here anymore. Is this the case?"

I answered him in a whisper as well: "Yes, Brian, I am not happy at all. Sitting on my arse for weeks on end is not my idea of being a professional cricketer. I want to play, but clearly, I am not in their plans."

"Great!" said Brian, "that's what we wanted to hear." He lit a cigarette and exhaled the first billow of smoke. At the same time, he whispered, "there's someone who wants to talk to you ... in our dressing room ... 'Proccie'. Will you talk to him?"

'Proccie' was the magnificent South African all-rounder Mike Procter, who had been at Gloucestershire for years. Proccie was a physically imposing sportsman: broad in the shoulder, arms like Popeye, a glowing tan and a shock of long blond hair. He was sitting on a table in the middle of the Gloucestershire dressing room, gazing out at the cricket. Gloucestershire were batting but he wasn't padded up yet. It was a surreal moment: here I was being ushered into the inner sanctum of the Gloucestershire dressing room to meet the King of Gloucestershire cricket. Proccie wasn't given to small chat. He cut straight to the chase.

"Howzit Wilks?" he asked in his broad South African accent. "The guys tell me you're not happy here." He had an aura around him that was tangible; a towering presence who commanded respect – and he was just sitting casually on a table.

"Hi captain," I spluttered! I didn't feel I was suitably qualified to call him 'Proccie' and I was slightly nervous standing in front of him. "Yes, I am pissed off, because I've missed a month of cricket, and I feel I should be in the [Glamorgan] side."

He looked at me for a moment, looked ahead at the cricket, and then fixed his eyes on me once again. "Well, why don't you consider playing for us? We would like you to play for Gloucestershire. You know a few of the guys and we need a medium-fast bowler who can bowl first-change behind Brainy and me. Have a think about it and let me know, but I would like you to come over to us next season and play for Gloucestershire."

'Brainy' was Brian Brain and he was standing just a few feet away from me. I felt a million dollars right there at that moment. For weeks on end, I had been out of the Glamorgan side and been accused of being too emotional about my cricket, and now here was one of the game's greatest cricketers asking if I would play for his team the following season. Mike Procter asked me to play for Gloucestershire and that was like a bell ringing inside my head. Brainy winked at me and said, "It'll be great for us to have you bowling with me and Proc, and it'll be great for you to play in this team."

I turned to Proccie and just said: "Thank you, captain. I honestly wasn't prepared for that, but obviously it is a hell of a proposition for me to consider." I didn't really know what to say. I was still a Glamorgan player, even though I had not been in the side for a month or more, and I was the Glamorgan twelfth man for a home match in Cardiff, so I felt a little uneasy but, at the same time, absolutely thrilled that another county was making me a firm offer to play for them. In a strange sort of way, I was also 'taking the emotion out of my thinking' by contemplating a move away from the county of my birth.

The thought of playing for Gloucestershire the following season appealed immensely. Mike Procter and Brian Brain was as successful an opening fast bowling partnership as any in the country, and I was asked to bowl first-change behind them, which suited me and the way I regarded myself as a bowler. I was also told that I would have to work hard on my batting (that was an understatement) because Gloucestershire would need me to bat in a higher position than I did for Glamorgan, which was usually 9, 10 or 11.

Gloucestershire's overseas players were Mike Procter, and the two Pakistani batsmen, Zaheer Abbas and Sadiq Mohammad. I was also good friends with a number of their team, so the proposition from Mike Procter sat comfortably with me.

I was left out of the next match against Warwickshire at Edgbaston but, for some inexplicable reason, was selected to play against the touring Indian team at St. Helen's. On this 1979 India tour to England, the captain was Srinivas Venkataraghavan. They had lost the first Test to England, by an innings and 83 runs at Edgbaston, then lost to Gloucestershire. So that came to Wales in need of a win as they prepared for the second Test.

The weather in Swansea for their visit was just perfect. They won the toss and batted, opening with Sunil Gavaskar and Anshuman Gaekwad. Our opening attack featured two left arm medium pacers: the very tall Andy Mack, who had joined Glamorgan from Surrey, and me. With the score on 27, I got one past Sunny Gavaskar, not past his outside edge, but inexplicably, behind his legs. The ball swung late, an out-swinger to the right-handed Gavaskar but, in a moment of extremely rare misjudgement from Sunny, he walked across his stumps, the ball took out his leg stump, and I was suddenly flavour of the month for bowling the great Sunil Gavaskar for 15. Sunny and I talk about that dismissal to this day and he has always pulled my leg about bowling him around his legs. He says he was still taking guard!

With that mischievous smile of his, he refers to "that scary pace that made him move out of the way of the ball!" I still don't know how I managed to bowl Sunny Gavaskar around his legs, but treasure the fact that I did.

It was a strange feeling; I had not been in the Glamorgan side for about seven weeks and, here I was, bowling against the formidable Indian tourists. Of course, you are naturally elated when you bowl someone of the calibre of Sunny Gavaskar, but at that moment I didn't know how I should celebrate getting his wicket.

I also managed to pick up the wicket of Mohinder Amarnath, caught at slip for 14, and finished with first innings figures of 17-3-58-2. India made 332-4 declared with centuries from Gaekwad and Gundappa Viswanath. 'Vishy' was wonderful to watch: wristy, artistic and elegant.

When we batted we were undone by the beguiling spin of Bishan Bedi, who took six wickets in each inning as we were dismissed for 122 and, following on, 317. But I enjoyed batting in our second innings, scoring 43 before Bedi had me caught and bowled. The ground is small and I took the liberty of trying to hit their spinners out of the ground, a ploy which worked up to a point. I managed to hit Chandrasekhar and Venkat for sixes and did the same to Bedi with an ungainly heave which flew over the boundary towards mid-wicket. It was a horrible shot but Bedi stood on the pitch, caught my eye, and applauded with his hands in front of his face. For the next ball I thought I would try and repeat it, and hit him over the rugby grandstand at the Mumbles Sea End of St. Helen's, but the execution didn't quite match the plan. It was as if Bedi had the ball on a piece of string. I lunged towards the ball as it landed, but in the next instant it simply was not there. All I managed to do was to hit it like a schoolboy straight back to the open hands of Bedi. Caught and bowled for 43. Bedi smiling; me walking back to the pavilion.

At least we made India bat again to beat us, and it was a memorable experience to be on the same field as the likes of Gavaskar, Kapil Dev, Bedi, Viswanath, Mohinder Amarnath, Chandrasekhar and Venkataraghavan. In those days, touring teams played matches against the counties, who would usually field their strongest XIs, but the tradition has gone. Nowadays, they play maybe one or two matches against counties and then head straight into a three-match Test series, or a five-match ODI series. It is another sign of how tradition has made way for the commercial aspect of the game.

**Glamorgan v Indians    St. Helen's, Swansea    25,26,27 July 1979**

**Result: Indians won by 7 wickets**

**Indians 1st innings**

| | | | |
|---|---|---|---|
| SM Gavaskar | | b Wilkins | 15 |
| AD Gaekwad | c Lloyd | b Perry | 109 |
| M Amarnath | c Lloyd | b Wilkins | 14 |
| GR Viswanath | c & b Perry | | 112 |
| Yajurvindra Singh | not out | | 36 |
| BP Patel | not out | | 27 |
| **Total** | | **(92 Overs)** | **332-4 dec** |

DNB: N Kapil Dev, +SC Khanna, *S Venkataraghavan, BS Bedi, BS Chandrasekhar.
FoW: 1-27, 2-64, 3-262, 4-271.

| Bowling | O | M | R | W |
|---|---|---|---|---|
| Mack | 14 | 2 | 50 | 0 |
| Wilkins | 17 | 3 | 58 | 2 |
| Swart | 8 | 1 | 30 | 0 |
| Parvez Mir | 4 | 0 | 21 | 0 |
| Perry | 23 | 7 | 69 | 2 |
| Lloyd | 14 | 3 | 38 | 0 |
| Holmes | 12 | 2 | 47 | 0 |

**Glamorgan 1st innings**

| | | | |
|---|---|---|---|
| *A Jones | c Khanna | b Kapil Dev | 15 |
| JA Hopkins | c Kapil Dev | b Bedi | 55 |
| BJ Lloyd | lbw | b Kapil Dev | 11 |
| Parvez Mir | c Gaekwad | b Bedi | 10 |
| PD Swart | | b Bedi | 0 |
| DA Francis | c Khanna | b Bedi | 0 |
| GC Holmes | st Khanna | b Bedi | 6 |
| +EW Jones | c Khanna | b Venkataraghavan | 5 |
| AH Wilkins | c Yajurvindra Singh | b Venkataraghavan | 2 |
| NJ Perry | not out | | 2 |
| AJ Mack | | b Bedi | 4 |
| **Total** | | **(45.2 overs)** | **122** |

| Bowling | O | M | R | W |
|---|---|---|---|---|
| Kapil Dev | 15 | 4 | 48 | 2 |
| Amarnath | 5 | 2 | 10 | 0 |
| Bedi | 13.2 | 4 | 28 | 6 |
| Chandrasekhar | 6 | 4 | 2 | 0 |
| Venkataraghavan | 2 | 1 | 5 | 2 |
| Yajurvindra Singh | 4 | 0 | 17 | 0 |

**Glamorgan 2nd innings (following on)**

| | | | |
|---|---|---|---:|
| *A Jones | c & b Bedi | | 55 |
| JA Hopkins | st Khanna | b Bedi | 47 |
| BJ Lloyd | lbw | b Venkataraghavan | 16 |
| Parvez Mir | c Gavaskar | b Bedi | 6 |
| PD Swart | c Gaekwad | b Chandrasekhar | 60 |
| DA Francis | c Bedi | b Venkataraghavan | 49 |
| GC Holmes | | b Bedi | 4 |
| +EW Jones | st Khanna | b Bedi | 4 |
| AH Wilkins | c & b Bedi | | 43 |
| NJ Perry | not out | | 5 |
| AJ Mack | st Khanna | b Venkataraghavan | 18 |
| **Total** | | **(96 overs)** | **317** |

FoW: 1-98, 2-112, 3-117, 4-218, 5-223, 6-227, 7-235, 8-292, 9-294, 10-317.

| **Bowling** | **O** | **M** | **R** | **W** |
|---|---|---|---|---|
| Kapil Dev | 11 | 2 | 37 | 0 |
| Bedi | 38 | 13 | 83 | 6 |
| Chandrasekhar | 19 | 1 | 72 | 1 |
| Venkataraghavan | 23 | 6 | 99 | 3 |
| Yajurvindra Singh | 5 | 2 | 16 | 0 |

**Indians 2nd innings (target: 108 runs)**

| | | | |
|---|---|---|---:|
| SM Gavaskar | not out | | 34 |
| AD Gaekwad | c A Jones | b Perry | 12 |
| N Kapil Dev | c Hopkins | b Perry | 16 |
| Yajurvindra Singh | c Mack | b Perry | 5 |
| BP Patel | not out | | 36 |
| **Total** | | **(24.3 overs)** | **110-3** |

| **Bowling** | **O** | **M** | **R** | **W** |
|---|---|---|---|---|
| Mack | 2 | 0 | 9 | 0 |
| Wilkins | 2 | 0 | 17 | 0 |
| Perry | 10.3 | 3 | 51 | 3 |
| Lloyd | 10 | 1 | 26 | 0 |

The rest of the season, which is remembered most for the West Indies winning the second World Cup and Sunil Gavaskar's sensational fourth-innings 221 as India chased, and just failed to reach 438 at The Oval, was a roller-coaster of emotion. I was in and out of the side, but at the back of my mind, all the while, was the conversation I'd had with Mike Procter in Cardiff.

Things came to a head between Tom Cartwright and me at the end of the final match of the season when we were thrashed by Worcestershire at New Road. Turner annihilated our bowling with a superb knock of 135. He hit me to all parts of that picturesque cricket ground, which left a nasty taste in the mouth, but not nearly as bitter as that which followed the conversation between Tom and me on the steps outside the New Road pavilion. We had a heated discussion about where I felt I had been let down by Tom, and he told me in no uncertain terms where he felt I had gone wrong. The exchange laid bare the feelings that had simmered below the surface for most of the season.

The season had ended and I felt that my relationship with Tom, and therefore Glamorgan was also over. A watershed point had been reached. My playing contract with Glamorgan was also up, and the thought of joining Gloucestershire under Mike Procter's captaincy became a burning priority. I had the next six months in South Africa to prepare for it and I had one more important date before heading off to South Africa – my marriage to Dot – which took place on September 22nd, and we were then to embark upon a six-month adventure honeymoon in South Africa.

Everything is easier in hindsight, but I knew at the time that the marriage wasn't right. I remember vividly speaking to my parents before the wedding, confiding in them that my heart was not in it. "What will Dot's parents say if I decide to call it off now?" I asked. My parents urged me to be bold and make the right decision and that if I didn't feel like going through with the wedding, then I *had* to tell Dot immediately. I didn't and we got married, and we then flew out to South Africa, where the next six months would lead to a deterioration in our relationship. It would be no honeymoon.

# 7

# Over the Bridge to Bristol

*'I first met Alan in Johannesburg during South Africa's period of cricket isolation. He immediately displayed a passion and love for the great game of cricket, both as a player and broadcaster. Alan's a lovely guy, always warm and friendly, and he was very well received in South Africa.'*

**Dr. Ali Bacher**

Leaving Britain for the second winter in a row was a more comfortable process. I knew what I was going back to in Springs, and felt I needed to be away to gather my thoughts and work out my return to county cricket the following summer. The writing was clearly on the wall for me at Glamorgan. The pity is that I knew that Tom Cartwright and I maintained a healthy respect for each other, and that we basically got on well, but I believe fervently that it was initially the South Africa issue that vexed him. After all, it was a deeply emotive issue. I now wanted to move to Gloucestershire, but it was not a straightforward decision as all my life I'd cherished ambitions to play for the county of my birth. For the first few months back in South Africa I didn't want to think about my cricketing future. All I did was immerse myself in playing decent cricket in the North-Eastern Transvaal League and coaching full-time in the various schools around Springs.

Once we got past Christmas it was time for letter-writing, and informing Glamorgan of my decision. These were hand-written letters from the heart – once again, too much emotion involved –

but I had made up my mind that I wanted a clean start with Gloucestershire. It was not the straightforward process it might have seemed. For one thing, it was TCCB policy that a player registered with the county of his birth had to be deregistered by that county before he could have discussions with another county. The procedure was an elongated one. Emails would have shortened it, but this was the age of the pen and air mail letters. Everything took time.

In fairness to Glamorgan there was no obstruction from them, and early in 1980 the way was paved for me to contact Gloucestershire. It might all seem a bit formal but it was the correct procedure, and rightly so. Eventually, the written offer of a three-year contract with Gloucestershire came from the club's secretary-manager, Tony Brown, a former captain and fine all-rounder. The rest of my stay in South Africa was geared to making myself as fit as I could for the new season with my new county team.

My home was still in Cardiff, so the first couple of weeks found me doing the hour's drive across the Severn Bridge for pre-season training and warm-up matches with Gloucestershire. Within days, Dot and I had found a newly-built apartment on the outskirts of Bristol, on the old road to the beautiful city of Bath. Dot had been desperate to leave South Africa and the last six months had been a stern examination of our marriage. I don't think that either of us knew how the next six months would pan out between us. The Gloucestershire players were a friendly bunch and I felt good in the new playing and working environment. There were the usual photograph sessions to start the new season and interviews with local radio, television and the press.

What struck me from the start was that the enormous County Ground in Bristol was cold and windswept with the nets located on a far corner of the ground, exposed to the elements. Trying to warm up for a net session in early April was a challenge. But soon the smell of cut grass made me think of summer and the new cricket season. I was ready for my debut for Gloucestershire.

My first game for my new team was against Oxford University at The Parks, a comfortable win in which I took 4 for 12 in ten overs. But reality set in with my championship debut which was, ironically, at Worcester, where I had mentally 'signed off' with Glamorgan six months earlier.

Gloucestershire were at full strength with Mike Procter captain and our other overseas players, Pakistan's top order batsmen Zaheer Abbas and Sadiq Mohammad. Rain truncated the match but not before Glenn Turner had hit an imposing 228 not out. He was always a problem for me; it was as if his bat was wider than anyone else's, and he certainly enjoyed facing me. I bowled 18 overs and took 1 for 81, with a large number of fours from Turner's bat. Days like that induce doubt. Am I good enough? Why can't I produce something better than this? How is this going to go down with my new teammates? It didn't get much better when I conceded 40 runs in my eight overs in our first Sunday League match against Northamptonshire at Bristol. We lost by 14 runs. Early days, but it was a less than auspicious start.

Early season mental frailties were tested when, in spite of bowling in the Sunday League, I was left out of the next four County Championship matches. But, by the end of the season, I had played in 16 of the 20 Championship matches and all 16 Sunday League games, where I picked up 18 wickets in 109 overs with an economy rate of 3.97. The numbers were acceptable, but could always have been better. Doubting your ability is part of the challenge of playing professional sport. You train hard, have high ambitions and work hard for your spoils. When those rewards, in the form of wickets or runs, don't materialise and your place is under scrutiny, you feel at your most vulnerable and question whether you're good enough.

Mike Procter was one of the greatest all-rounders the game has seen, a fabulous cricketer who led by example. He bowled fast, hostile in-swingers off a long, intimidating run, belted the ball miles with immense power when he batted, and took wickets with off-spin when he felt a change in bowling was needed. He also caught everything at slip. But he was taciturn for the most part. I cannot recall having an in-depth conversation with him at any time in my first year at the club. Our early matches in the 55-over B & H Cup were cases in point.

How ironic that Glamorgan should be early visitors to Bristol. They had made some outstanding signings – the brilliant Pakistan batsman Javed Miandad and Barbadian fast bowler Ezra Moseley. They were now captained by Malcolm Nash, a gifted left-arm new-ball bowler who did not have pace, but could trap the best batsmen in the world with prodigious swing. Nashy was something of a strange personality. He was a genuinely talented cricketer, but I found him no help when I started at Glamorgan. He never once offered advice on how to swing the ball, something that I had to work on. The one man who did help me in learning about left-arm swing bowling was John Lever. When Gloucestershire played against Essex in a County Championship match, 'JK' kindly took time out to show me his different grips on the ball, his slower ball delivery and various other nuances. That an opponent gave me advice while a teammate offered nothing illustrated the insecurities of professional cricketers, who protected their patch with a zealous fervour.

Our 'attack' against Glamorgan was not quite as fearsome as it might have been. Procter was playing, but only as a batsman, prevented from bowling by knee pains resulting from years of fast bowling. Brian Brain was also injured. We did well enough, even with our diluted bowling, to restrict Glamorgan to 228 for 8 in their 55 overs, but fell just short in a dramatic finish, ending on 227 for 8. I was there at the end, with David Graveney, and although we put on a few quick runs for the ninth wicket, we couldn't get the two runs to give us the win. My former teammates had come to my new club and given me a reminder that maybe the grass is not always greener on the other side.

Four days later we had Procter and Brain fit again, which was just as well against opponents who fielded Imran Khan and Kepler Wessels, but went down narrowly again by nine runs. Brian Brain bowled beautifully and finished with figures of 11-6-9-1, having Wessels caught by Sadiq Mohammad at slip, but bowling first-change I felt I let the side down. Their Sri Lankan opener Gehan Mendis, an awkward customer with or without a bat in his hands, carved me to all parts of Hove and I ended with 2 for 55 from my 11. I got Mendis eventually – but not before he had smashed a century – and also trapped Paul Parker LBW for 4, but when you lose an important one-day match by just nine runs, you naturally scrutinise your own contribution, and I felt that my expensive bowling that day cost Gloucestershire the match, even though Mike Procter himself went for 48 in his 11 overs.

Three days later we welcomed Essex to Bristol. Essex, skippered by former England captain, Keith Fletcher, also included Graham Gooch, Mike Denness, the South African Ken McEwan and England left-arm quickie, John Lever, and got off to a flying start. Brain was injured again, so I shared the new ball with Procter on a cold morning. Proccie always ensured he had the wind at his back, or the downhill run-up, which was any captain's prerogative, so I bowled up the slope. I didn't mind, since I preferred to bowl up rather than down a slope as it helped my delivery stride and kept me more upright as I delivered the ball. Unfortunately I immediately found myself bowling into a stiff headwind, and it was called Graham Gooch. It was alarming to see the great big Mexican bandit's moustache coming at you, and that's what Gooch did to me from the outset of the match: he walked down the pitch, with his big bat high in the air behind him, and he set about subjugating me from the first ball I bowled at him. Biffing my deliveries to both sides of the ground showed that I was bowling both sides of the wicket, but he had a wonderful eye and the most marvellous hands and was a fearsome prospect to bowl at.

During the lunch break, with Essex still batting, I felt a bit sorry for myself. Once again the seeds of doubt were rattling around in my head. Being belted around the ground by somebody like Gooch was a huge and painful body blow to my confidence, like being caught on the ropes and taking a pounding from a heavyweight boxer. Five minutes before the restart Mike Procter called for silence in the dressing room and simply said: "Right, let's get this job done. That was a sloppy start, so let's go and do the job properly."

As he spoke he put his right leg up on the chair in front of him and wrapped an enormous black brace with straps that had to be tightened on every side around his troublesome knee. I looked at this and thought: "Here's our skipper, bowling virtually off one leg and I am whining to myself about my wayward bowling." He turned to me as we left the dressing room. "Wilks, are you OK? Are you struggling or what?" He was looking straight at me as he rolled his trousers down over his heavily protected knee. "No Skipper, I am fine. Let's go." I replied, and knew immediately that this was his way of telling me that he expected a much better effort from me after lunch.

It worked. I was thankful to our medium-pacer, Phil Bainbridge, for bowling Graham Gooch for 62 and he, and another of our medium-paced attack, David Partridge, took two wickets apiece to remove the Essex top order. It helped me take 4 for 55 in my 11 overs, as we bowled Essex out for 224 in 54 overs. In reply, all our big guns failed to fire – Sadiq Mohammad 28, Chris Broad 11, Zaheer Abbas 12, Mike Procter 13 – but we got there through a fine partnership from the Stovold brothers, my former Loughborough colleagues. Andy made an unbeaten Man-of-the-Match 73, and his younger brother Martin contributed 32, to see us over the line.

Tragically, Martin Stovold died at the tender age of 56 on May 11th, 2012, after a long illness. He was a universally-liked schoolmaster at Cheltenham College, and had been one of the early coaches of the great South African all-rounder, Jacques Kallis, in Cape Town, where he lived and coached for many years.

Gloucestershire had won the B & H Cup in 1977, beating Kent in the Lord's final, just a couple of months before the Gillette Cup final in which Glamorgan and I lost to Middlesex. Three years later, Gloucestershire were stopped in our tracks in our last B & H Cup outing, losing to the Minor Counties in the quaint west country town of Chippenham. Minor Counties rarely beat the Championship teams, but this was one day when they did. The New Zealand all-rounder Lance Cairns scored 54 in their total of 212 for 8 in 55 overs. I took 2 for 35 in 11 overs. In reply, Gloucestershire looked to be in command, but we then lost Sadiq for 42, Zaheer for 26 and Procter for 45. I went in at nine with the score 151-7, needing 62 runs to win. I played my best innings yet for Gloucestershire, responding to Mike Procter's emphasis on my contributing runs from the lower order, putting on 51 with Partridge before Cairns had me LBW for 27 with his slower leg-cutter. I still felt that we would get over the line, but we went down by three runs, a defeat which ended our B & H campaign. The defeat really hurt. We left the picturesque cricket ground that evening to the sound of the home side celebrating in the bar.

For Gloucestershire's Championship match at Taunton, Somerset did not have Viv, since the West Indies were on tour, but had replaced him with Sunil Gavaskar, who was making his debut for them. On a hot, sunny day, Somerset won the toss and batted. The pitches at Taunton always had a reputation for being flat and excellent for batting; this one was no exception. Gavaskar was batting beautifully and, on his way to a century on his debut for Somerset, until somehow – on 75 – he edged my slanting delivery low to Sadiq Mohammad, who had good hands at slip or gully. With Sunny Gavaskar gone and Viv not playing, we looked set for a good afternoon but Ian Botham had other ideas. He went berserk, with the most extraordinary onslaught.

Botham and Peter Denning took Somerset from 119-3 to 429-4: a partnership of 310 between lunch and tea. Botham smashed 228 with 27 fours and 10 sixes! It was a bewildering experience, as my bowling figures testified. At lunch, with Gavaskar out, my figures were 12-4-30-1. By tea, Botham's pyrotechnics had converted them to 18-4-112-1. I had conceded 82 runs in six overs. More than that, it felt as if we had been physically beaten up. No-one was spared: Procter and Brain had also been in the firing line. Somerset's score from their 100 overs was 536 for 4. And Viv Richards wasn't even playing!

To make matters worse, after being pounded all day Saturday by Botham, we had to drive in convoy up to Manchester for a Sunday League match, before returning to Taunton on the Sunday night to resume the Championship match against Somerset. Whoever compiled the fixtures must have had a peculiar sense of humour, and clearly cannot have been a cricketer.

The final word on that Botham innings came from our scorer, Bert Avery, while travelling up to Manchester. It was Brian Brain's sponsored car and Bert was sitting in the front passenger seat, with me and David Partridge in the back. We were sore in the body, the back, the feet and the head after that pummeling and not a lot was said apart from the occasional "bloody 'ell ... how did he hit it there?" comment from all three bowlers in that car going up the motorway that evening. Bert opened his immaculate scorebook and said: "They scored 536 in 100 overs against us today, and 350 of those runs are sitting in this car going to Manchester!" I thought Brian was going to hit him, but it broke the ice and we all had a good laugh.

For the record, we lost to Lancashire but on Monday and Tuesday had the pleasure of watching Zaheer Abbas scoring a beautiful 173 and Alastair Hignell making a century as we followed on, but saved the game. Somerset used 11 bowlers, including Sunny, on the Tuesday.

In July Clive Lloyd's West Indies team, complete with its terrifying line-up of fast bowlers – Michael Holding, Andy Roberts, Joel Garner, Malcolm Marshall and Colin Croft – came to Bristol, where we fielded a full-strength team.

**Gloucestershire v West Indians**    **Ashley Down**    **2,3,4 July 1980**
                                     **Ground, Bristol**

**Result: West Indians won by 58 runs**

**West Indians 1st innings**

| | | | |
|---|---|---|---|
| CG Greenidge | c Zaheer Abbas | b Wilkins | 42 |
| DL Haynes | c & b Procter | | 12 |
| SFAF Bacchus | c Brassington | b Brain | 9 |
| AI Kallicharran | | b Wilkins | 15 |
| *CH Lloyd | lbw | b Procter | 10 |
| CL King | lbw | b Procter | 0 |
| +DL Murray | c Procter | b Brain | 64 |
| Dr. Parry | lbw | b Wilkins | 0 |
| AME Roberts | c Hignell | b Wilkins | 0 |
| J Garner | c Broad | b Graveney | 104 |
| MA Holding | not out | | 10 |
| **Total** | | **(87.1 overs)** | **278** |

FoW: 1-20, 2-59, 3-70, 4-92, 5-92, 6-100, 7-100, 8-100, 9-229, 10-278.

| **Bowling** | **O** | **M** | **R** | **W** |
|---|---|---|---|---|
| Brain | 25 | 3 | 95 | 2 |
| Procter | 18 | 4 | 51 | 3 |
| Wilkins | 19 | 5 | 51 | 4 |
| Bainbridge | 6 | 2 | 11 | 0 |
| Graveney | 18.1 | 4 | 43 | 1 |
| Sadiq Mohammad | 1 | 0 | 15 | 0 |

**Gloucestershire 1st innings**

| | | | |
|---|---|---|---|
| BC Broad | lbw | b Roberts | 2 |
| Sadiq Mohammad | c & b King | | 76 |
| Zaheer Abbas | c King | b Holding | 0 |
| AW Stovold | c Murray | b Holding | 7 |
| *MJ Procter | | b Garner | 7 |
| AJ Hignell | c Greenidge | b Roberts | 2 |
| P Bainbridge | lbw | b Garner | 0 |
| DA Graveney | c Bacchus | b King | 50 |
| AH Wilkins | | b King | 6 |
| +AJ Brassington | not out | | 8 |
| BM Brain | c Greenidge | b King | 0 |
| **Total** | | **(61 overs)** | **183** |

FoW: 1-12, 2-13, 3-29, 4-62, 5-65, 6-66, 7-141, 8-165, 9-183, 10-183.

| Bowling | O | M | R | W |
|---|---|---|---|---|
| Roberts | 17 | 4 | 41 | 2 |
| Holding | 16 | 5 | 37 | 2 |
| Garner | 13 | 6 | 34 | 2 |
| King | 15 | 3 | 46 | 4 |

**West Indians 2nd innings**

| | | | |
|---|---|---|---|
| CG Greenidge | c Hignell | b Brain | 4 |
| DL Haynes | | b Bainbridge | 32 |
| SFAF Bacchus | c Brassington | b Broad | 69 |
| AI Kallicharran | | b Wilkins | 5 |
| CL King | lbw | b Wilkins | 2 |
| +DL Murray | | b Broad | 24 |
| AME Roberts | c Bainbridge | b Graveney | 3 |
| J Garner | c Procter | b Graveney | 0 |
| MA Holding | st Brassington | b Graveney | 6 |
| Dr. Parry | not out | | 1 |
| *CH Lloyd | c Brassington | b Graveney | 0 |
| **Total** | | **(50.4 overs)** | **161** |

FoW: 1-8, 2-69, 3-76, 4-78, 5-139, 6-144, 7-144, 8-156, 9-160, 10-161.

| Bowling | O | M | R | W |
|---|---|---|---|---|
| Brain | 10 | 0 | 52 | 1 |
| Procter | 8 | 1 | 23 | 0 |
| Wilkins | 9 | 3 | 20 | 2 |
| Bainbridge | 7 | 2 | 25 | 1 |
| Graveney | 8.4 | 3 | 12 | 4 |
| Broad | 8 | 4 | 14 | 2 |

**Gloucestershire 2nd innings (target: 257 runs)**

| | | | |
|---|---|---|---|
| BC Broad | c Murray | b Roberts | 4 |
| Sadiq Mohammad | | b Garner | 27 |
| Zaheer Abbas | c Haynes | b Holding | 33 |
| AW Stovold | | b Roberts | 25 |
| *MJ Procter | lbw | b Roberts | 28 |
| AJ Hignell | lbw | b Holding | 1 |
| P Bainbridge | | b Holding | 1 |
| DA Graveney | not out | | 15 |
| AH Wilkins | c Murray | b Garner | 44 |
| +AJ Brassington | | b Garner | 0 |
| BM Brain | c Greenidge | b Garner | 12 |
| **Total** | | **(59.1 overs)** | **198** |

FoW: 1-46, 2-71, 3-112, 4-113, 5-119, 6-121, 7-180, 8-180, 9-198, 10-198.

| **Bowling** | **O** | **M** | **R** | **W** |
|---|---|---|---|---|
| Roberts | 11 | 0 | 44 | 3 |
| Holding | 17 | 5 | 55 | 3 |
| Garner | 14.1 | 5 | 31 | 4 |
| Parry | 17 | 1 | 60 | 0 |

It was a memorable three days in warm, sunny weather in front of a full house at the County Ground. We had the West Indies in all kinds of trouble at 100-8, when Joel Garner walked in. 'Big Bird' changed the entire complexion of the day's cricket by scoring his first and only century in first-class cricket, and it had to be against us! Without Joel Garner and his batting heroics, who knows what might have happened. I was happy with my effort in taking 4 for 51 in 19 overs – including Greenidge and Kallicharran – and Ted Dexter, Chairman of England Selectors, was there to see it. I have no idea who he was looking at that day. For all I know he had come for a game of golf and one of the County Ground lunches which were reckoned the best in England, but at least he congratulated me and said: "Well done, a fine bowling display, Alex, keep it going!"

An abiding memory of that game is being the non-striker when Michael Holding was bowling from the Pavilion End. His run up was almost back to the boundary edge, but it was his giant leap into the delivery stride that was simply unbelievable. I swear he could have been an Olympic long jumper, so long and imposing was this leap before he unleashed his 90 mph missiles. And you couldn't hear him running. He was frighteningly fast, beautiful to watch and even better from the safety of the non-striker's end!

After bowling the West Indies out for 161 in their second innings, we thought we had a chance of chasing down 257 to win, but Clive Lloyd had other ideas, and was in no mood to grant us any favours. I walked in at 121 for 7 and, to this day, still don't know how I managed to top score with 44, but I enjoyed – if that's the right word against that bowling – every minute of being out there. It was exhilarating and terrifying at the same time. I also won't forget Faoud Bacchus giving me words of encouragement as I was about to face Michael Holding. There was no-one in front of square on either side of the wicket and behind me was a fan of slip fielders. "Watch the ball in his hand, man, watch him and concentrate, you'll be OK!" said Faoud, crouching beside me at short leg.

I barely got out a "thank you" to him before Holding began his run-up. It was an extraordinary experience. I have a vague, flashing memory of a red object flying past my nose and thudding into the gloves of Deryck Murray. It barely registered, but I knew it had gone past me at around 90 miles an hour. This is when you realise that adrenalin is brown!

The second ball connected with my bat, rather than me hitting it, and somehow flashed past gully for four. "Bloody hell!" I thought, "I'm not sure if I should be doing that!"

Faoud Bacchus once again offered me advice: "Shot! Well played." But then he smiled, and there was something about the smile. I guess Mikey didn't enjoy being hit for four. The next one went past my nose again, and I had the distinctly uncomfortable feeling that this experience wouldn't last too long. Except that it did, and God knows how. Clive Lloyd even took some slips out, mainly because the ball was finding the edge of my bat and flying off for four. With a half century very much in my thoughts – and it was a mistake to look at the scoreboard – Clive Lloyd brought back Joel Garner for another spell with the words, "Come on Bird, let's finish this."

It didn't last long. Joel bowled me his throat ball, which I could only fend off and edge through to the keeper Deryck Murray, and my little cameo with the bat was over. It was fun while it lasted and being top scorer gave me bragging rights in the dressing room. More importantly, it also helped restore some much-needed personal confidence. Negotiating the territory between the lows and highs of the game was the key to success in playing professional cricket.

Every August, Gloucestershire play a festival on the beautiful ground at Cheltenham College, one of England's best-known public schools. The 1980 season produced a clean sweep of three Championship victories for Gloucestershire; against Hampshire, in which I took 5-50, Worcestershire and Middlesex, plus Sunday League wins over Hampshire and Middlesex.

Middlesex were the form side that summer, winning the Championship and the Gillette Cup. They had a formidable bowling side spearheaded by the West Indian, Wayne Daniel, and the giant South African, Vincent van der Bijl. In another test of my batting technique and bravery I had to face them both on a greenish pitch and, with David Graveney, bat to save the follow-on. Somehow we managed to do that. It's amazing how you can score runs even with your eyes closed!

But this was Mike Procter's week. His all-round performances showed why we were often called 'Proctershire'. He hit a brilliant – match-winning – 134 not out against Wayne Daniel and Vince van der Bijl then, against Worcestershire, not only hit a quick fire 73 in our first innings, but took 7-16 in their first innings and 7-60 in the second; firstly bowling pace and then off-spin. He was an irrepressible cricketer who, on his day, had no peer.

As the season wound down another trip to Hove brought my second five-wicket haul – 5 for 76 in 24 overs – in a draw against Sussex. Looking back at my first season with Gloucestershire, I was reasonably pleased with 52 first-class wickets at an average of 23.94 from 393 overs in 19 matches. In one-day matches I bowled 160 overs and took 27 wickets at 24.11 with an economy rate of 4.04. Reasonable, yet I always felt that I had left something out on the park. Quite what that was I'm not sure. I was torn between feeling that I had more to give and suspecting that I had already given the best I'd got. Somewhere in between was where mental battles became a fight for confidence. The players who won those inner battles were the ones who went on to higher honours. You had to be mentally tough. That was the basis for being a professional sportsman. I became worried if I'd had a bad spell of bowling, or if I had finished the day with poor figures. Did Ian Botham ever worry about anything he did on the cricket field? This is not to compare myself with England's great all-rounder, but to make the point that a strong mind and solid belief in oneself was half the battle.

I felt I had made a solid contribution to Gloucestershire, but there was always room to improve. I had also decided to stay at home for the winter and not fly off to distant climes such as South Africa. Instead I looked forward to playing rugby again and working at the County Ground for Gloucestershire's new sponsorship and marketing department, secure employment in the winter months and a welcome break from playing cricket. I also realised that if my marriage to Dot was to continue then I had to put more into it, and think less about myself and my cricket career. Dot had also become settled in her life in Bristol; she had taken on a position with the *Bristol Evening Post* newspaper and seemed as happy as I'd seen her in years. In time to come, I came to realise that I wasn't the reason for her new-found happiness. Someone else was.

# 8

# Christmas in Calcutta

*'Alan is easily one of the most recognisable faces across south-east Asia when it comes to sports television. Be it cricket, tennis, golf or rugby he's one of the best broadcasters in the business, and easily one of the funniest people I have worked with! I wish the Welshman well. Way to go "Wilkinson"... that's how he is known in my part of the world!'*

**Ravi Shastri**

Looking for sponsorship opportunities for the club and its players under the guidance of Chris Coley, a very able businessman, made for a rewarding off-season. I was also thrilled to join Bristol RFC. Mercifully, the dreaded hamstring injury did not recur and the regular rugby training, even if most sessions were held on cold, wet, miserable wintry evenings, was a good way of keeping fit with the following summer in mind.

But I was not to spend the whole of the winter at home. In December, around the time when everyone was horrified by the murder of John Lennon in New York, I received a telephone call which, although I did not know it at the time, would change my working life.

"Is that Alan?" said the man at the other end of the line in a beautifully cultured English accent. A voice full of authority but at the same time so warm and friendly. "Yes, it's Alan Wilkins here, who is this please?" I replied. "Jolly good," said the man, "then I have the correct number and I hope for everyone's sake I have the right man."

"Which man were you looking for?" I asked a little apprehensively. "I hoped it would be Alan Wilkins the Gloucestershire cricketer," said the man. "How rude of me," he continued, "allow me to introduce myself. Alan, this is Geoffrey Howard and you may or may not have heard of me, but I was wondering what you were doing for Christmas?"

Geoffrey Howard had played three first-class matches for Middlesex in 1930 as an amateur, but he earned his place in cricket history as an enlightened administrator and popular tour manager. He had been secretary of Lancashire (1949-1965) and Surrey (1965-1975) and managed three MCC touring teams: to India, Pakistan and Ceylon (now Sri Lanka) in 1951-52, the Ashes-winning tour of Australia in 1954-55 and the 'A' tour of Pakistan in 1955-56, when he had to quell the crisis which followed several of the touring team drenching umpire Idris Begh with water.

"Well, Mr. Howard," I said, "I plan on having Christmas here at home but not quite sure what I'll be doing for New Year's Eve," adding a little laugh as I said it.

"Please call me Geoffrey," said the gentleman, "and let me ask how would you like to spend some time over Christmas and New Year playing cricket in India?"

"Playing cricket in India?" I repeated his sentence. "Yes, there is a very big cricket match taking place in Calcutta and I am the tour manager for the team which is being captained by the England captain, Mike Brearley, and we were wondering if you would be available to come with us?"

I nearly swallowed the phone. "Of course, Geoffrey, please just tell me the dates, what I need to do and where I have to be."

"Wonderful, Alan, it will be a great experience for you – have you been to India before?"

"No, not at all, Geoffrey."

"Then this will be your first time and what a great place to start. Calcutta. It is a five-day cricket match in Eden Gardens to celebrate the Golden Jubilee of the Cricket Association of Bengal. You will be playing for the Cricket Association of Bengal Overseas XI against the Indian Board President's XI, and we're putting together a pretty good side. I'll post you instructions with flight itinerary and dates, but you will be spending New Year in Calcutta. Marvellous, Alan, and thank you for accepting my invitation."

"Thank You, Geoffrey," was all I could utter. I was trembling with excitement.

Sure enough, the letter came with all the details of my first trip to India. I was to fly out from London Heathrow on December 27th on Air India to Bombay (now Mumbai) and then take a connecting flight to Calcutta (now Kolkata). In his personally-typed letter, Geoffrey wrote: 'This is a Special Jubilee match to celebrate the Golden Jubilee of the Cricket Association of Bengal. Why am I involved? Simply because I took a side there in 1956-57 for their Silver Jubilee. Play will be from December 30th to January 4th with January 2nd as a rest day. I will check with Air India in London but you should consult your doctor for health advice. Mike Brearley suggests that you might arrange an anti-hepatitis inoculation. I am delighted that you can make it. Best Wishes, Geoffrey."

Payment for the trip was 1000 rupees, or £125 with a further 200 rupees per day to cover hotel expenses at The Oberoi Grand in Calcutta.

It all sounded so exciting – at least to me it did – but to my wife it was just another instance of Alan doing his own thing. This time it was jetting off to India just two days after Christmas and not spending New Year's Eve with her family. I know that Dot's parents were disappointed that I chose to go to India but how could I have turned down this opportunity? I did not ask if other players were taking their wives to India, but just accepted the invitation to see a part of the world I knew nothing about. To Dot it was simply another decision I had taken without consulting her.

I had no idea what to expect in India, although I knew it was going to be a lot warmer than the cold winter days on which I'd been playing rugby. It was also three months since I'd bowled a cricket ball in earnest, but I wasn't worrying about that: I was on a jet, flying from London, and I was going to be playing cricket in India on the last two days of 1980, and welcoming the New Year in the city of Calcutta.

Nothing could have prepared me for the noise and congestion from the moment I walked into the airport terminal building. It was chaos! Even more congested was the drive from the airport to the hotel. It seemed there were only two types of cars on India's roads: tiny little Fiat taxis and the car I was travelling in – a big, heavy Ambassador. It was an extraordinary experience getting through all that traffic, but once we had drawn up to the hotel and walked inside this magnificent building, a veil of tranquility came down and shut out the noise and turmoil outside.

The majestic grandeur of The Oberoi Grand was a far cry from the hotels I was used to on the county circuit. Our team, officially named the 'Cricket Association of Bengal Overseas XI' was led by Mike Brearley, the current captain of England. It was a decent collection of cricketers:

Mike Brearley, Middlesex & England (captain)
Wayne Larkins, Northamptonshire & England
Roger Knight, Surrey
Alan Butcher, Surrey & England
Frank Hayes, Lancashire & England
Roger Tolchard, Leicestershire & England (wicket-keeper)
Jack Simmons, Lancashire
Ray East, Essex
John Lever, Essex & England
Alan Wilkins, Gloucestershire
Simon Hughes, Middlesex

The 'Indian Board President's XI' picked to play against us over five days at the famous Eden Gardens ground wasn't the worst either, considering that the full Indian team was touring Australia at that time, under the captaincy of Sunny Gavaskar. It was:

Pranab Roy
Arun Lal
Anshuman Gaekwad
Surinder Amarnath
Brijesh Patel

Madan Lal
Deepak Chopra
Sambaran Banerjee (wicket-keeper)
Barun Burman
Srinivas Venkataraghavan (captain)
Sunil Valson

The reception from our hosts was formal but warm and friendly. There were numerous official functions to attend, dignitaries to meet and many speeches and introductions on the evening before the match. I will also never forget our tour around Calcutta, with police escorts carving a clear path through the traffic – human and motorised – so that our vehicles could move a bit quicker. I was overwhelmed by the sheer size of Calcutta, its sprawling roads and buildings, and its mass of humanity moving in all directions about its daily business and chores. The landmark buildings such as the Indian Museum, the Marble Palace, the National Library, the Raj Bhavan (Government House) and the Victoria Memorial Hall, modelled on the Taj Mahal, were also spectacular.

Our police guide stopped the car and beckoned us to take a look at the Howrah Bridge across the Hooghly River, on which there were thousands of people in a constant stream of traffic in cars, on bicycles, mopeds and on foot. I don't think he intended us to take photographs of the one thing that wasn't moving: a dead female body floating in the river just yards below us. Who was this unfortunate soul? How did she come to lose her life in such a ghastly way, floating in the waters of the Hooghly River, and who did she leave behind? How many more people would end their life like this? These were questions our police guide could not answer. Just a shrug of the shoulders as if to say: 'That's life in this part of the world.' It was time to move on and get back to the safety of The Oberoi Grand and a team meeting in the famous Chowringhee Bar.

The sun shone hard and bright onto the vast playing area of Eden Gardens, and the huge wooden stands and concrete seats surrounding the plush grass gave the impression of a coliseum in which these pale-skinned county cricketers were soon to be tested to the full. It was a bad toss to lose, especially since some of the team was already suffering stomach bugs. To use Ramachandra Guha's delightful title, we were in *A Corner of a Foreign Field* and – boy – did we soon know it!

John Lever led our pace attack, supported by two uncapped bowlers: Simon Hughes and myself. We quickly discovered that the batsmen in the Board President's XI liked to play a shot at just about every ball, and we chased that red ball all over Eden Gardens. Surinder Amarnath blasted an impressive 144, and Madan Lal stroked his way to an undefeated 119, with Anshuman Gaekwad adding 54. They declared their first innings on 445-7 in 122 overs but, out there in the field, it felt more like 1,000 overs. I was pleased with the 20 overs I bowled – figures of 20-6-37-1 – which were more than acceptable in the circumstances, but the soreness in the limbs and joints the day after was palpable.

Remember, none of us had bowled since mid-September. It didn't help when Alan Butcher misjudged a catch on the boundary and the ball went right through his hands, hit him flush in the eye, and cut his head just above his right eye.

In reply, we were bowled out for 274, Frank Hayes top-scoring with 88, Jack Simmons hitting a half-century and I stuck around a bit at the end with 16 not out, which clearly annoyed the home bowlers. Suddenly I was fending off all kinds of hostile bowling, especially from the left-arm quickie, Sunil Valson, who I swear threw his faster ball, and once or twice didn't bother to land it either; his beamer was fairly intimidating.

With a first innings lead of 171, the Board President's XI piled on the runs in the second innings with Pranab Roy hitting 160 in their total of 302-7 declared. Somehow, I managed to get through 26 overs taking 2 for 60 but, by the time they declared, every bone in my body was aching.

Set an improbable 474 to win the match, we were bowled out for 254 with John Lever showing defiance by top-scoring with 73. He always reckoned he could bat. All bowlers do. Remember he scored an important 53 in his debut Test match for England against India in Delhi in December 1976, as well as taking 7-46 and match figures of 10 for 70, as England beat India by an Innings and 25 runs.

We were well beaten by 219 runs but it had been a wonderful experience playing in front of a sizeable crowd on one of the world's iconic grounds. There was a memorable New Year's Eve dinner in The Oberoi Grand, at the end of which we were introduced to India's Prime Minister, Indira Gandhi, who'd landed on Eden Gardens in an Indian Army helicopter. Some of us were invited to play in another match in Bombay, but politely declined; our aching bodies made the decision for us.

It was a memorable first visit to India, and one I will never forget. As well as the dozens of leather handbags that Jack Simmons had bought in the Calcutta markets, we all took back indelible images and memories from 'Incredible India'. I, for one, vowed to return to see more of the country, although that would take another 16 years.

The delightful Geoffrey Howard was there at Calcutta Airport to see us off, and make sure that we got on the plane for London. "Alan, is everything alright? Have you got everything? Have you had a good time?" Geoffrey asked, with his warm welcoming smile. "Yes, Geoffrey, I have had the most amazing time in India. I cannot thank you enough. Thank you, Geoffrey."

"No, Alan, thank you for playing for us. I am so pleased you came; best of luck for the coming season. I'll see you in the summer." He was a delightful man.

It was the first week of 1981 and I was already mentally preparing for my second season with Gloucestershire. India had been a welcome departure from the cold winter in Britain. I wish I had agreed to play in the other match in Bombay but in all reality my body was in bits after five days on Eden Gardens. I also needed a garden salad with a couple of slices of British ham to restore the ph balance in my stomach. Everything in India had been a new experience.

# 9

# Reality Check

*'As captain of Gloucestershire, in the twilight of my career, it was a pleasure to welcome Wilko to the team. Even on flat wickets, Wilko was likely to make a breakthrough with his sharp left-arm deliveries: in modern players' jargon he bowled "a heavy ball". If he'd used the in-swinger more consistently – to right-handers – he would probably have been an international candidate.*

*He's great company, a good friend and someone who I always look forward to having a beer with.'*

**Mike Procter**

These vivid memories of India served as an incentive for the year ahead; the travel bug was now with me and I craved for more. The reality was that my travel in those early months of 1981 was confined to coach trips – with Bristol RFC – across the Severn Bridge to play against various Welsh rugby clubs and that in itself was a new experience. I was certainly reminded how hard Welsh rugby was; there was no hiding place on those rugby pitches in Wales, and certainly not for a Welshman playing for an English club.

The 1981 summer in England has gone into history for 'Botham's Ashes', but for us at Gloucestershire it showcased the extraordinary batting skills of Pakistan's Zaheer Abbas, whose insatiable appetite for run-scoring was astonishing. His presence in our side was a privilege for all of us fortunate enough to share the same changing room.

We would have to wait for mid-summer for Zaheer's exploits because the month of May was all but washed out with incessant rain; over half a dozen matches in different competitions were abandoned, more often than not without a single ball bowled. We did manage a win in the B & H Cup at New Road against Worcestershire, where I picked up 4-35 in my 11 overs, but our match against Kim Hughes' touring Australians was reduced to just one day: at least we got out onto the park for a bowl. For some reason, Mike Procter gave me the new ball to share with Brian Brain, coming on himself as first change. I got through 29 overs in a decent spell, taking 3-65, getting the wickets of Kim Hughes, LBW for 7; Allan Border, caught behind for 24, and Dirk Wellham, LBW for 2. And that was it. But rain in the summer is part of British life. It's why, after all the rained-out days year after year, the All England Lawn Tennis Club has installed a roof on the famous Centre Court at Wimbledon and Court No 1 is scheduled to have its roof completed for the 2019 Championships.

Gloucestershire lost heavily to Nottinghamshire in the first week of June, but we bounced back immediately by beating Yorkshire at Bristol, my spirits buoyed by taking six wickets in the match with a first innings spell of 4-40 in 19 overs. Not such good news was the persistent knee injury to our skipper, Mike Procter, who was unfit to play in two matches against West Country rivals Somerset, at Bath.

Somerset had their 'big three' lined up – Richards, Garner and Botham – and with Procter resigned to watching from the old wooden clubhouse, at the delightful Recreation Ground in the centre of Bath, we were effectively two short. The next four days of cricket, however, left an indelible impression on everybody involved.

First, Zaheer Abbas stroked a flawless unbeaten 215 all day Saturday as we declared at 361-4 in 103 overs. It was a batting master-class that not even the great Joel Garner could ruin; he didn't take a wicket in his 26 overs, but his contribution would come later.

The Sunday League match was played on a hot, sunny day and we had a full house with people enjoying the first really warm day of the summer. Somerset batted first, and we thought we had worked out a plan to bowl to the great Viv Richards. David 'Grav' Graveney, who was acting captain, and I decided that I should bowl a leg-side line to Viv, a full length, no room outside the off-stump and five fielders on the leg-side. Viv, as always, was looking ominously dangerous and I was feeling a little apprehensive when a couple of swinging leg-side deliveries were dispatched amongst the deckchairs towards mid-wicket and backward square. Grav then moved another fielder over to the leg side, which meant even more pressure on me to bowl the right line.

With Viv quickly onto 21 and looking to score big in this 40-over match, I somehow got one to swing, not into his pads – as was the plan – but away towards first slip, which was vacant. The ball found the edge of Viv's flailing bat and Andy Stovold took a great catch diving low to his right. Viv gone for 21; me feeling pleased with myself, but those precious moments of exhilaration of having the greatest player in the world caught behind didn't last for long. In the huddle of players with the usual back-slapping – we hadn't heard of high fives in those days – Grav just blurted: "What the hell was that all about?" I knew exactly what he meant. We had agreed a predominantly leg-side field for Viv, and I then slipped in an away-swinger, definitely not part of the strategy. My personal celebration suddenly became a rather muted affair.

It meant nothing that Viv had nodded in acknowledgement, as only he did, that it wasn't that bad a delivery. That was like getting approval from God for showing best behaviour towards other human beings. No, my acting captain was unhappy that I had not bowled according to instructions. Elation with the game could, and did, so easily make way for feelings of deflation. We lost the Sunday League match even though Mike Procter did play, and hit a typically belligerent 91 not out. Joel Garner took 4-21 in eight overs and we lost by 20 runs. I was expensive, conceding 56 runs in my eight overs, and the gloss of getting Viv Richards out was not as gleaming as I would have liked.

Off with the Sunday League hat, and back to the Championship with Somerset beginning their first innings in reply to our 361-4 declared. Without Procter we looked a bit thin on fire-power, but surprised ourselves by reducing Somerset to 164-7, with Viv gone for 2, bowled by Phil Bainbridge, who also got Ian Botham for 41. But the complexion of Somerset's innings would soon change. Firstly, Brian Brain pulled-up with a leg injury and he left the field after bowling 14 overs, which meant that Gloucestershire's 'attack' was Phil Bainbridge, Alan Wilkins and Chris Broad with his very occasional seamers. It wasn't exactly heavy artillery. In walked Joel 'Big Bird' Garner with Somerset struggling. Joel, as we knew from the previous season, could bat a bit so Phil Bainbridge made the outrageous decision to bounce him with a series of short-pitched deliveries that he clearly didn't like. 'Bains' just muttered something like, "Well, we know he's going to bounce us when we bat in the second innings, so let's give it to him first!"

After 'Bains' had rattled Joel Garner with his short stuff, he threw the ball to me and said, "Right Wilks, you give it to him as well!" This was like a pair of pea-shooters trying to cause physical pain to one of the most feared fast bowlers of our generation. We hadn't pre-meditated this ridiculous succession of short balls to 'Big Bird', but proceeded with it, and it did cause some damage ... to Joel's bat, which cracked when one of my short deliveries hit the splice.

Joel was not amused. Apparently, he loved that particular bat, and he didn't have another in his bag. What followed next was outrageous. With play now stopped because Joel's bat was broken, Zaheer Abbas ran up said, "Joel, I have some good bats in my bag. Do you want me to get them for you, so you can use one of mine?"

Phil Bainbridge and I were aghast. Zaheer's bats were made to his personal specifications by Gunn & Moore, and they had a longer blade than a normal bat; perfect for Joel. We were bowling our guts out, and here was Zaheer offering to help Joel continue batting with decent equipment.

It was difficult for both Bains and me. We had to show respect to Zed, both as one of the game's great players and a teammate, but at the same time we had to make it clear we were not amused. Harsh words were spoken, but not towards the opposition. It was not a great example of team-building, but the emotions of the moment were raw.

Play resumed and Joel weathered whatever pitiful storm we could muster, batting on to get 90 before I yorked him. They finished on 316. We had done a decent job, but knew that we would be on the receiving end in our second innings.

When we returned to the pavilion we found that Mike Procter was clearly not amused. He took Bains and me aside and told us that we were totally out of order and utterly disrespectful towards Zed. We had to take our medicine from Proccie, but it didn't feel right.

Zaheer then proceeded to do what he did best, and let his bat do the talking. He batted just as elegantly as he had in the first innings, adding an unbeaten 150 to his unbeaten 215, with Alastair Hignell not out at the other end in both innings. We declared our second innings on 303-4, leaving Somerset 349 to win. I managed to get Viv caught at gully by David Graveney for 37, Ian Botham was bowled by Bains for just 1, and Somerset were reduced to 200 with nine wickets down. We thought we had the job done with plenty of overs to go, but Brian Rose, the Somerset captain, and Peter Roebuck – both normally opening batsmen, and both batting with injuries – came in at 10 and 11; they hung on to the bitter end at 245-9 to save a draw. There were lessons to be learnt from an incident-packed and emotional four days in the city of Bath.

With Mike Procter struggling to bowl due to his ongoing knee injuries, and Brian Brain also injured, Gloucestershire announced the signing of a new quick bowler. We hadn't heard of him, but he soon made an impression. Mike Whitney, a strapping left-arm fast bowler from New South Wales, was a welcome addition to our flagging resources. He made his debut against the touring Sri Lankans – who would be raised to full Test status a month later – on an inhospitably cold three days in Bristol. Whitney had plenty of pace and plenty to say, giving the freezing Sri Lankans something to think about on their way back to the pavilion, which they doubtless found more hospitable than facing Whitney's verbal volleys in horribly cold conditions. Zaheer skippered us, but it was our other Pakistani batsman, Sadiq Mohammad, who got runs in the match: an unbeaten 203. The game petered out into a draw, but we knew that Mike Whitney was a much-needed signing.

The summer warmed up, and so did the heat emanating from Zaheer's beautiful bat. Wherever he played, a century inevitably followed: 101 not out against Hampshire in Southampton; two (135 not out and 128) against Northamptonshire at Northampton, where India's great all-rounder Kapil Dev was leading the attack for the home side; 145 against Sussex at Hove; 159 against my former county, Glamorgan, at Bristol; 136 not out against Kent at Cheltenham; and 103 not out against Worcestershire at New Road.

Given my numbers in first-class cricket as a batsman, it is probably better that the idea of what it was like to have fabulously-gifted Zaheer Abbas in our Gloucestershire side should come from one of our batsmen. My teammate and good friend, Alastair Hignell – who played cricket for Gloucestershire (1974-83) and rugby union for England (1975-79) – had the privilege of batting alongside 'Zed' many times during the 1981 season, and recalled him vividly in *Wisden*'s *Cricketer Magazine* article, 'The Art of Z':

> *When Zaheer was at the crease, the whole thing looked ridiculously simple. Upright and elegant, he was equally at ease off front foot or back, but such were his reflexes that he quite often switched from one to the other mid-shot. Stylish and graceful, he never seemed to hurry a stroke or offer a false one. At the top of a backlift with more twirls than a cheerleader's baton he seemed to pause for a fraction of a second before bringing the bat crashing down at the last moment to send the ball scorching away to the boundary.*

My season fluctuated between the good, the bad and the ugly, reinforcing my view of this as a profession of mental peaks and troughs. In and out of the side, a good spell here or there, interspersed with a load of trash. You wondered how on earth you were capable of delivering the cricket ball so well one day, and so badly the next.

The denouement of my 1981 season came in the penultimate championship match against Lancashire – at Old Trafford – led by Clive Lloyd and with Michael Holding in the team.

This was an occasion where the ball did everything that I hoped it would do. It swung and it seamed and it brought me the reward of my career-best bowling figures in first-class cricket.

**Lancashire v Gloucestershire    Old Trafford      9,10,11 September 1981.**

**Match Drawn**

**Lancashire 1st innings**

| | | | |
|---|---|---|---:|
| A Kennedy | c AW Stovold | b Childs | 44 |
| G Fowler | lbw | b Wilkins | 11 |
| I Cockbain | | b Wilkins | 2 |
| *CH Lloyd | | b Whitney | 39 |
| D Lloyd | | b Wilkins | 23 |
| DP Hughes | c AW Stovold | b Wilkins | 8 |
| J Simmons | | b Wilkins | 4 |
| +CJ Scott | c Broad | b Wilkins | 11 |
| PJW Allott | c Hignell | b Wilkins | 0 |
| MA Holding | c Broad | b Wilkins | 32 |
| PG Lee | not out | | 2 |
| **Total** | | **(67.5 overs)** | **182** |

| **Bowling** | **O** | **M** | **R** | **W** |
|---|---|---|---|---|
| Whitney | 21 | 8 | 62 | 1 |
| Wilkins | 26.5 | 10 | 57 | 8 |
| Bainbridge | 7 | 4 | 20 | 0 |
| Broad | 9 | 4 | 20 | 0 |
| Childs | 4 | 0 | 17 | 1 |

**Gloucestershire 1st innings**

| | | | |
|---|---|---|---:|
| BC Broad | c Scott | b Holding | 25 |
| +AW Stovold | lbw | b Lee | 43 |
| P Bainbridge | lbw | b Holding | 9 |
| Zaheer Abbas | c Scott | b Lee | 17 |
| AJ Hignell | not out | | 80 |
| MW Stovold | | b Holding | 1 |
| SJ Windaybank | | b Holding | 6 |
| *DA Graveney | c Kennedy | b Allott | 14 |
| JH Childs | c & b Simmons | | 17 |
| AH Wilkins | | b Holding | 1 |
| MR Whitney | | b Holding | 0 |
| **Total** | | **(82.1 overs)** | **219** |

| **Bowling** | **O** | **M** | **R** | **W** |
|---|---|---|---|---|
| Holding | 30.1 | 7 | 74 | 6 |
| Allott | 15 | 2 | 47 | 1 |
| Lee | 24 | 5 | 69 | 2 |
| Hughes | 9 | 1 | 19 | 0 |
| Simmons | 4 | 3 | 4 | 1 |

**Lancashire 2nd innings**

| | | | |
|---|---|---|---:|
| A Kennedy | | b Whitney | 2 |
| G Fowler | lbw | b Wilkins | 2 |
| I Cockbain | run out | | 85 |
| DP Hughes | | b Bainbridge | 27 |
| *CH Lloyd | c Hignell | b Bainbridge | 14 |
| D Lloyd | | b Whitney | 40 |
| J Simmons | c Hignell | b Childs | 26 |
| +CJ Scott | | b Whitney | 4 |
| PJW Allott | not out | | 14 |
| **Total** | | **(102 overs)** | **230-8 dec** |

| Bowling | O | M | R | W |
|---|---|---|---|---|
| Whitney | 26 | 5 | 74 | 3 |
| Wilkins | 31 | 10 | 62 | 1 |
| Bainbridge | 16 | 8 | 29 | 2 |
| Broad | 11 | 5 | 19 | 0 |
| Childs | 15 | 5 | 25 | 1 |
| Graveney | 3 | 1 | 5 | 0 |

**Gloucestershire 2nd innings (target: 194 runs)**

| | | |
|---|---|---:|
| BC Broad | not out | 41 |
| +AW Stovold | not out | 12 |
| **Total** | | **63-0** |

I was still mentally digesting this career best performance when the offer came through of another six months of playing and coaching in South Africa, this time in Pretoria. For various reasons, both personal and professional, I needed to get out of Britain for the winter; my head was a mess and I could think of no better place than the warm, sunny climes of the Highveld in South Africa to get away from it all. It was time to reflect on what had happened over the past five or six months with Gloucestershire, and whether or not I was improving as a cricketer. It was also time to assess my marriage to Dot, which had completely broken down by the middle of the season. Dot had found happiness elsewhere, and there was no way that she would contemplate leaving her contented life in Bristol for another six months in South Africa with me.

Throughout the 1981 season David Graveney had been especially kind towards me. At one point in the season I confided everything to Grav and told him that my marriage was in bits, that Dot and I were no longer together and that with my decision to spend another six months in South Africa, we were to all intents and purposes splitting up for good. Grav had put his arm around me, literally and metaphorically, a few times during the season. I was so grateful for this, but knew that I had to get my life in order. I knew that I was not going to be able to retrieve my marriage – it had broken down months before I cared to admit it – but I had to try and salvage the part of my life that I had some control over: my cricket career. It would resume in Pretoria.

For the record, my second season with Gloucestershire hardly set the world alight. I played 21 first-class matches in which I bowled 630 overs, 146 of them maidens, and had taken 52 wickets at 36.68 runs apiece. Economy rate was acceptable at 3.00 runs per over, but it was an ordinary return for the efforts of bowling 630 overs – only once taking five wickets in an innings and that was the 8 for 57 against Lancashire at Old Trafford. In List A matches, I bowled 106 overs and took 17 wickets at 27.70 with an economy rate of 4.44 and a best bowling return of 4 for 35. The numbers weren't good enough, but neither was my psychological apparatus. In layman's terms, I needed Pretoria to get my head right.

# 10

# The Jacaranda City

'The Welshman who became a first-class cricketer, who lived and played in South Africa during apartheid, to forging an international career as a sports commentator, Wilko's story is as varied and engaging as it is challenging at times. The many robust conversations we have had about sport, politics, people, culture, character and hard choices have without doubt provided me with another narrative about cricket and life. The experiences he has gone through and his take on moments that have changed the face of sport and athletes' careers always has me hooked.'

**Melanie Jones**

After two seasons with Gloucestershire, I felt I had made progress as a cricketer and I was ready for a new challenge in South Africa. My new club was the Pretoria High School Old Boys, who played in the Northern Transvaal Premier League, and I would coach at Pretoria Boys High School, a renowned cricket and rugby nursery.

I was the third British cricket professional to coach at Pretoria Boys High. The previous two were Geoffrey Boycott and Bob Willis, so I felt I had fairly large shoes to fill. I needn't have worried. I soon learnt about Boycott's penchant for not showering, or sharing a drink and dressing room banter, after a full day's cricket with PHSOB, but going straight home to his apartment. He scored plenty of runs in Pretoria but, as was his nature in those years, led a loner's life and did not mix with the club's cricketers. In Geoffrey's defence, the drinking culture of South African clubs was not his thing, preferring time spent in the middle to time in the bar. He is now much more affable, and a good friend, but his closest friendship in his formative years was with his cricket bat. At that time he allowed his bat to do the talking but, since retiring, has become an outstanding, authoritative voice in radio and television commentary boxes all over the world.

Bob Willis was a different kind of personality altogether and, by all accounts, thoroughly enjoyed socialising on the Highveld after bowling on the flat pitches of Pretoria. The first six months in Pretoria were amongst the most rewarding of my times as a cricketer and as a coach. It was a privilege to be welcomed so warmly at Pretoria Boys High. I spent hours talking to two wonderful members of staff: Charles Mulvenna and Paul Somerville, both dedicated to teaching and to enhancing the lives of young people through cricket. 'Uncle' Charles has since passed on to the great cricket club in Heaven, and richly deserves his place there. He had the Irishman's gift of the gab, could sell sand to Arabs and loved a tipple at the end of a day's cricket. Pretoria High's was one of most enchanting of all school pavilions, and also a bit different; a fully-stocked bar had been built on the second floor! With photographs and memorabilia all around us, we would talk cricket and life long after the bright orange sun had dropped down into the rolling escarpments around Pretoria. They were life's treasured moments to be stored as indelible memories; the 1980s equivalent of Facebook.

League cricket in Pretoria was highly competitive. Not only were most players striving for a place in the Northern Transvaal Currie Cup team, but a nearby army base drew in top players from all around the country, doing their compulsory two-year army service. It was an eclectic mix: the visiting County Championship professionals, local club players, university and college cricketers, and shaven-headed transients serving their days in the South African Army.

Geoff Boycott and Bob Willis had both played for Northern Transvaal, as had former England bowlers Pat Pocock and Chris Old. Brian Lara was still to come, as were Richie Richardson and Ezra Moseley.

Former Springboks like Tiger Lance, Denis Lindsay, Jackie Botten and Ken Funston all played in Pretoria as, in later years, did Kepler Wessels, Pat Symcox, Fanie de Villiers and David Richardson; the current CEO of the ICC. I enjoyed the intense rivalry amongst the clubs, particularly with Afrikaner players who enjoyed nothing more than giving visiting 'Pommie' professionals a tough time. When the temperature in Pretoria climbed high into the 30s, it was one of my toughest challenges to keep cool – literally and metaphorically – whilst also dealing with the barrage of (mostly) good-natured sledging. It helped to learn a few words of Afrikaans, even if they were just an outburst of swear words, to dish back at the opposition. Those early months in Pretoria certainly enhanced my cricket education!

Pretoria Boys High alumni included Eddie Barlow, although he never played for Northern Transvaal. I also played a lot of cricket with and against one of the tallest left-arm spinners I had ever met – Willie Morris – whose son, Chris, is now a Test player with a million dollar contract in the Indian Premier League. Chris is probably the highest-earning of a list of Pretoria High's sportsmen which also includes 2007 Rugby World Cup-winning captain John Smit and US international footballer Roy Wegerle.

My modest progress with Northern Transvaal began with a Datsun Shield (55 overs) match against Border in Pretoria during October 1981, in which we overwhelmed our visitors. My 2-12 in seven overs helped the cause, but the real thrill was just playing representative cricket in South Africa. However, that feeling didn't last too long as 'Northerns' signed the Yorkshire and England fast bowler Chris Old and, from then on, were not going to need me.

He was the real deal as a cricketer and it was not even a contest between a player who had only just played the last of his 46 Tests with a vital role in 'Botham's Ashes', and a county player. However, Chris brought his well-known proneness to injury with him to Pretoria, so I became the constant travelling twelfth man; flying all over the country, as the chairman of selectors put it, "in case Chris has an injury". Months of net practices with the 'Northerns' squad were helpful from a bowling point of view, but ultimately dispiriting when your chances of playing depended on a medical bulletin on someone else.

My first-class debut for Northern Transvaal had to wait until March 1982. The visitors to Pretoria were Natal, a strong team skippered by my Gloucestershire teammate Mike Procter and including the great Barry Richards, and the giant fast bowler, Vincent van der Bijl, fresh from his sensational county season with Middlesex. My one and only Currie Cup match yielded one solitary wicket, that of my namesake Chris Wilkins, a hard-hitting opening batsman, who I managed to remove with a yorker for six. Vince van der Bijl was at his destructive best, rampaging through us like an elephant charging through the bush, taking 14 wickets for a paltry 111 runs, and yes, I was two of those 14 wickets. Big Vince was a genial giant of a man, an outstanding and whole-hearted cricketer, as popular in Pretoria as he was in Durban, although maybe not with us for those three days. While we lost by six wickets, the experience was a rewarding one.

It was a timely visit to Pretoria by Mike Procter, enabling us to talk about the forthcoming 1982 season, my third with Gloucestershire. Mike was a lot of things, but could never be described as garrulous. Everything in cricket came easily to him and he expected you to follow suit, or at least follow his lead. He wanted more from me for Gloucestershire but we were on different pages when he said, in effect, "You need to bowl quicker and you need to get some runs because we've got a tail that needs shortening." I guess it was his way of motivating me for the upcoming season, and I was looking forward to the challenge he had set for me.

It was around this time that the cricket world was rocked with the news that an English team was to play a series of matches against a full-strength South Africa team (then called the Springboks): the first of seven rebel tours to the politically isolated sports-mad republic. The South African Breweries English XI – captained by Graham Gooch – stayed for a month, playing three 'one-day internationals' and three unofficial 'Tests', but did not win a match. They had a decent line-up including Gooch, Boycott, Dennis Amiss, Peter Willey, Alan Knott, Chris Old, John Emburey, John Lever, Derek Underwood and Mike Hendrick. But the South Africans were too strong in virtually every department, fielding Jimmy Cook, Barry Richards, Peter Kirsten, Graeme Pollock, Clive Rice, Roy Pienaar, Mike Procter (captain), Alan Kourie, Ray Jennings (wk), Garth le Roux, Stephen Jeffries and Vince van der Bijl. Whilst every cricket ground was full to capacity, the rebels were much less popular in England and received three-year bans from international cricket. These were turbulent times for cricket, with South African Cricket defying the global sporting boycott and attempting to satiate audiences, and players, starved of international sport. Their clandestine measures would have long-term consequences.

At a personal level I was wholly unprepared for the excruciating pain in my left (bowling) shoulder in my next match for Pretoria High School Old Boys. It came in the middle of a spell of bowling, and lingered to the point that I could not continue. With only a few weeks before I was due back in Britain, this was worrying.

I was recommended to a blind physiotherapist called Dr. Peter Kelly, an Englishman who had emigrated to South Africa many years previously. A wonderful practitioner, he subjected me to an intensive course in physiotherapy, augmented by acupuncture, but warned that I had to give my shoulder complete rest before flying home, and should go easy on my return to the cold British climate before going full tilt in the new cricket season. The palliative warm sun and a daily swim had me feeling a lot better by the time I said farewell to my friends at Pretoria High School Old Boys. Little did I know of the awfulness that would engulf my life when I returned to England for the new season in April 1982.

# 11

# The Beginning of the End

*'My friend Wilko will always be remembered as a talented cricketer whose career was sadly cut short by injury, but the most prominent thought for me was a person immaculately dressed, with self-deprecating humour, who always played with a smile on his face – unless facing the might of the West Indian pace attack! His transition into broadcasting came as no surprise, his knowledge of many sports is outstanding and, like all quality commentators, he paints a wonderful picture for the viewer.'*

**David Graveney**

I arrived home just as the Falklands War with Argentina was breaking out. The British media was engulfed in nothing but news from those distant islands, and it made my own small world of professional cricket seem very small.

But it was a world that was about to come crashing down around me. Pre-season outdoor nets during an English April can seem the most inhospitable exercise on earth, especially after six months of warm sunshine in South Africa. The outdoor nets at Bristol were on the most exposed part of a ground so colossal that I always thought that Gloucestershire could make extra money by using it as a landing-strip for local businessmen's aeroplanes. In that first week of pre-season training I couldn't find the cricket landing area, let alone anything else.

Wrapped up in extra cricket sweaters on top of whatever warm undergarments you could muster, finding any kind of rhythm was nigh-on impossible. The wind was howling around the nets, blowing them from side to side, but something else was making me bowl like a complete novice. I watched in utter despair as one ball after another either flew straight over the batsman's head, landed five feet in front of me, or flew into the side netting. I'll never forget Andy Stovold shouting, "Wilkie, any danger you can get one to land near me so that I can have a chance at hitting it?"

There were a few giggles as this freak show was unfolding in the nets, but the pain that had returned with a vengeance in my shoulder was no laughing matter. I was in distress – mentally and physically – and at a loss to explain to the club's secretary-manager, Tony Brown, why I suddenly resembled an alien who was playing the game of cricket for the first time. Tony Brown – aka 'the Boss' – had been a high-class cricketer for many years, was a former captain and now very much in charge in his official capacity. He was easy to get on with – he'd offered me excellent signing-on terms for my three-year contract – and we had a good relationship. Conversely, I was never sure how well he got on with Mike Procter – by all accounts, it wasn't the most cordial of relationships – and he might have been unimpressed with players who spent winters away from home in sunny climes and appeared to have returned unprepared for the new season.

"What the hell is the matter with you, Wilko?", he inquired as I clutched my agonisingly painful shoulder while picking up a ball from the side netting. "My shoulder is hurting like hell, Tony, and I cannot let the ball go at without pain. I can't bowl!" What else could I say?

"Do you want to see the physiotherapist?", he asked. "I think it might be more than that. I might have to see a specialist," I replied. I explained that I'd felt pain in my shoulder a few weeks previously but had bowled at full pace without any pain in a Currie Cup match against Mike Procter's Natal.

I couldn't continue with the net practice; it was a complete waste of time for everyone and, with every ball I let go, the pain worsened. "Right," said Tony Brown, "you had better leave and make an appointment with the club's orthopaedic surgeon to get that shoulder looked at straightaway. Go and see Margaret in the office and she'll sort it out." When angry, he was not a man to exchange pleasantries with, and his face, by now, was thunder.

I felt a forlorn figure walking back to the clubhouse, not knowing how serious the injury was. I feared the worst, since the pain was much more acute than I'd experienced in Pretoria. Thankfully, with Dr. Keith Lucas, I was in good hands. Keith was consultant orthopaedic surgeon at Bristol Royal Infirmary, one of the top orthopaedic surgeons in the country, and had performed a few knee operations on Mike Procter. Our initial consultation confirmed my apprehensions. I was diagnosed with Adhesive Capsulitis, better known as Frozen Shoulder Syndrome. It occurs when the ligaments around the shoulder joint swell and stiffen to such an extent that normal healing doesn't take place. The surfaces of the shoulder joint are normal, but motion is limited because the tissues surrounding the joint have become tight, preventing proper movement of the arm and the shoulder. It can occur with any activity that involves rotating the arm, such as freestyle swimming, or throwing a ball or javelin, or bowling in cricket and is thought to be caused by severe inflammation in the joint due to overuse. Successful treatment of the condition depends on the fitness of the patient and the time allotted to regain fitness.

Tony Brown made it abundantly clear that I had to get fit as soon as possible and it was decided that I would undergo a shoulder manipulation operation. This happens under general anaesthetic, when the shoulder is moved, or sometimes dislocated, in order to stretch the sleeve (shoulder capsule) surrounding the shoulder joint. Corticosteroids and local anaesthetics can be injected to help reduce any pain or swelling, but this procedure is essentially a 'short-term fix' and does not cure the condition itself.

Dr. Lucas, who did the manipulation, said there was severe inflammation in my shoulder. His parting words were: "Take time with that shoulder. You will need to treat it gently for at least three weeks, and don't even think about bowling in that time. Don't even put a cricket ball in your hand. Just gently try and squeeze a tennis ball, or a squash ball, but do not exert that shoulder at all. Remember, no bowling. Don't even take your arm up above your shoulder. Given time, and the right rehabilitation, you will be playing again this season, but we won't know exactly when that will be. Much depends on how your shoulder reacts to the manipulation."

His prognosis was clearly at odds with that of the club's secretary-manager. I felt discomfort not just in my shoulder, but in the predicament I was now faced with. Despite my protestations, and against clear medical advice, within days I was bowling – off two or three paces – in the indoor nets. Even just starting with tennis balls, they left my hand with the power and direction of confetti at a wedding. It was a waste of time for everyone.

The problem was compounded by an instruction to only consult the club's regular physiotherapist, and these sessions would have far-reaching consequences. I was given a series of Corticosteroid injections directly into the shoulder, which relieve the pain but rarely cure the condition in the long-term. After a number of these incredibly painful injections, and with no tangible improvement in my shoulder movement, I was beginning to despair. The cricket season was well underway, and I was as much use to the club as a chocolate fireguard.

Imagine my horror to then be chosen to play in a 2nd XI match, against the RAF, at a ground I had never heard of: RAF Hullavington, near Chippenham in Wiltshire. I made my feelings known to the secretary-manager, but my protestations got me nowhere. It was one of those uninviting early season British summer days, bitterly cold and a howling wind, when the last thing you want to do is stand exposed to the elements and try and make out that you are enjoying playing cricket.

I had feelings of immense foreboding as I was given the new ball; I just knew it wasn't going to work. I clearly wasn't fit enough, only weeks after the shoulder operation. My anguish was complete when, after three or four deliveries of absolute dross, I came to a grinding halt; my arm did not want to go through the bowling action. The pain was excruciating. I was in a total mess.

The upshot was a return to hospital and another consultation with Dr. Lucas, who was singularly unimpressed with my so-called rehabilitation programme. On his diagnosis, I had to undergo a second manipulation operation, but this time the recovery process could – in his words – "take months". Medical specialists are not people to disobey. His business-like advice after the second operation left me in no doubt that this was a serious problem which might rule me out for most of the 1982 season.

I discharged myself from Bristol Royal Infirmary with my left-arm in a sling, carrying a small bag of overnight clothes in my right hand, and walked aimlessly away from the hospital; my world was upside down and I didn't know what was ahead of me. Buffeted in the turbulence of my cricket world, which appeared to be falling apart, I had turned to Dot in my moment of need. Of course, I knew that our marriage had completely broken down and I'd just spent six months away in South Africa, but I was still married to her. I contacted Dot and made the decision to confront her in the apartment that she was now sharing with her new partner. I had no idea that he would be there when I knocked on the door but I was now at my lowest ebb and I desperately needed to speak with her, even if it was just to say goodbye properly.

I still don't know what I had hoped to achieve by calling on their apartment but, with my arm in a sling and feeling like a bloke with no future, maybe I was looking for sympathy. I didn't receive it! To be fair to Dot and her partner, they had begun their new life together while I had been over 5,000 miles away in Pretoria. To say my head was in a mess was a huge understatement but I knew my life had to move on and accepted that Dot had started a new one with someone else. I left the apartment and headed to the home Dot and I had found together: the one she'd now left to find a new life. How could I blame her?

What could I do, except hope that my shoulder would recover at some time during the season? Back at the County Ground, the secretary-manager was also at a loss and not prepared to discuss anything with me in his office. When I left it, I knew that my future with the club was on the line. I was in my last season of a three-year contract and I had no idea when I would be able to play again.

The rehabilitation process was distressingly slow and it gradually became clear that I was going to miss most of the season. While India and Pakistan visited that summer, allowing great all-rounder confrontations when Ian Botham faced Kapil Dev and then Imran Khan, my season amounted to five 2nd XI matches in which I managed to deliver just over 100 overs of eminently forgettable left-arm pace bowling. I did not bowl one solitary ball in first-class, nor List A cricket that season. After taking more than 100 wickets in my first two seasons, this was hugely debilitating.

It came as no surprise when, at our end-of-season assessment meeting, the secretary-manager told me in no uncertain terms that my days with Gloucestershire were over unless I regained my full fitness and full pace. I would have to do something special to warrant another playing contract from the club. That meeting with Tony Brown was short and not terribly sweet. In his mind, I had cost Gloucestershire money because I had not played for the 1st XI the entire season. He was absolutely right, of course, but I also felt that my shoulder injury and its rehabilitation were not managed as well as they should have been.

We shook hands and exchanged parting pleasantries, but as I closed the door to his office at the County Ground and made my way to my car, a little voice in my head was saying that I was closing the door on my time in Bristol. That in itself was utterly distressing. I had rarely been happier than in the Gloucestershire team dressing room. I had made wonderful friends at Gloucestershire. David Graveney, in particular, was a tower of strength: not just for me, but for the team, taking over from the incapacitated Mike Procter in the latter part of 1981 before officially becoming captain in 1982.

A professional sportsman has to be on the park to earn his keep. It's tough enough being on the sidelines when you're fit and not making the playing XI, but being unable to play at all, as I was all season, is completely debilitating. My injury followed the loss of both Procter and Brian Brain, so Gloucestershire had to make signings, which they quickly did. The club signed two Barbadians: the wonderfully-talented Franklyn Stephenson, and the eminently steadfast and utterly affable John Shepherd, who was to follow 15 years of yeoman service to Kent with another seven for Gloucestershire.

The previous five months or so had been a cricketing write-off for me. Now I faced the challenge of regaining my fitness, my confidence and my entire self-belief. The 1982 cricket season – or its absence – had cost me dearly both professionally and personally. My shoulder, my cricket, and my personal life, had all fallen apart in Bristol. As I left the County Ground on my last day as a Gloucestershire player, I left behind a life of broken dreams, and maybe not just those of my own. I knew I had to get my act together and start afresh.

I left Bristol, my car loaded with all my personal possessions and headed west towards Wales. As I drove over the Severn Bridge, the symbolic link between England and Wales over the Bristol Channel, the sun was shining straight into the windscreen. Tears streamed down my face as I realised the enormity of the challenge that lay ahead of me. I had to get my life back on track, pick up the pieces and somehow put them back together so that I could play cricket again. But who would I play for? Who would accept me as a professional cricketer after missing the entire season with injury? Could I go back to Gloucestershire? Would they accept me back in Bristol? My life in the city was over, my marriage was history, and I felt I could not go back.

I had to get out of the country, and leave all the emotional baggage behind. I wanted to return to Pretoria, with the idea of regaining my fitness in the warmth. A shoulder specialist in Cardiff gave me the all-clear to resume my rehabilitation in South Africa. It would be up to me to prove my fitness in the ensuing months and, as I booked my flight from London to Johannesburg, I had no guarantee that I would ever get back to how I had been as a professional cricketer. Only time would tell, and that time would initially be spent on the Highveld of South Africa.

The return to Pretoria High School Old Boys and the wonderful Pretoria Boys High School would be my catharsis over the next six months. My first priority was to get fully fit, and try and regain whatever pace I had before the shoulder injury. I knew that the standard of cricket would test my mettle, so the rehabilitation process was down to me and how I managed it.

I was in a good place, literally and metaphorically, as two PHSOB members had also invited me to stay in their house. Six months at 192 Orion Avenue, Waterkloof, Pretoria would be my salvation. It was a beautiful, spacious home with a swimming pool – vital for my rehabilitation – located on one of the northern ridges overlooking Pretoria, with panoramic views to the south towards Johannesburg.

The house was perfect for viewing late afternoon Highveld storms; you could see them coming north as the blue skies over Pretoria were gradually blackened by the oncoming darkness, illuminated with savage flashes of lightning as the heavens sent their electric beams down to Mother Earth. It was the most exhilarating feeling to be in the eye of the storm on the Highveld, and then experience the calm after the event. Those early days in Pretoria were like looking into a mirror and watching a reflection of my life. The approaching storms, the turmoil of the tempest and the calm that followed. After the previous six months, I desperately needed to restore some equilibrium in many aspects of my life.

My two house-mates – Paul 'Beachball' Richards and Neal Parker – also turned out to be two of the most generous people I could have met as, when I was about to leave Pretoria the following March, I discovered they'd paid for my accommodation in their home out of their own pockets. I don't think I have ever been able to thank them properly for their benevolence. It was their kindness that enabled me to get my life back on track.

Using the facilities of the University of Pretoria, I worked hard to get fully fit, and it helped to be playing regular cricket on the weekends. I was confident of returning to the game, but which team was I going to be playing for? Too much had happened in Bristol, both personally and professionally, for me to consider returning there. I felt bad about leaving my Gloucestershire teammates, many of whom had become close friends, but also felt that I had to move on. Probably Gloucestershire saw it the same way too.

What eventually transpired was a conversation with the county of my birth; Glamorgan. Their new secretary, Phil Carling, made contact and raised the possibility of my return to the club. I discovered that they planned to sign a new captain for the 1983 season and were also interested in my services. I said that I needed time to think about it, but knew in my heart that a return to Glamorgan was the option I favoured most. As soon as I agreed to return to the club I'd left at the end of the 1979 season, the wheels started turning quickly.

A formal letter arrived by post (there was no email in those days) offering a three year contract. The new captain was to be Mike Selvey, a fast bowler who'd played for England against the West Indies in

1976 and won numerous trophies with Middlesex, the county he'd just left.

As a courtesy, I wrote to Tony Brown and David Graveney to tell them that despite two wonderful years with the club and the disappointment of the third year, I had enjoyed my cricket immensely but now felt it was time to move on. I doubt that I would ever have left Gloucestershire voluntarily but, after that dreadful six months in 1982 and the sheer upheaval in most aspects of my life, Gloucestershire appeared to have made their own plans in my enforced absence, and they too had moved on.

While rehabilitating in Pretoria, I signed a new three-year contract with Glamorgan. I was thrilled that they had not only offered me the chance to play, but had also shown the belief that I had a professional future which, in many ways, was more important. Phone calls with both Phil Carling and Mike Selvey gave me a new feeling of confidence about my game and my place with the county.

As my season in Pretoria neared its conclusion, I worked harder than ever on improving my fitness with regular gym sessions and a course of strengthening exercises. My life had moved on in so many ways, and I was looking forward to the challenge of returning to Glamorgan and proving myself as a professional cricketer.

My return to Cardiff also consigned to history my stint in Bristol and my playing days with Gloucestershire. The chapter had a feeling of finality about it when I received official notice in late April that Dot and I were now divorced. I knew that Dot was happy in her life in Bristol and that made me feel a lot better about a chapter in my life that had begun in our university days at Loughborough. It was time to move on and concentrate on my return to Glamorgan.

My intuition told me that this move was right. From a personal perspective, it was my best option. The new management at Glamorgan also augured well for the season ahead as Tom Cartwright had now moved on to be National Cricket Coach for Wales, doing outstanding work for young cricketers across the country.

After a year in the wilderness, the time was right for me to return to the first-class game. Nonetheless, there were still many questions buzzing around my head. Would I be good enough? Would my pace be the same? How would I fit in once again at the county I'd left three years ago? In hindsight, I knew that this really was a last shot at playing professional cricket, and that Glamorgan had provided that opportunity. My preparation had been sound, and I was ready for the challenge ahead.

A headline in a south Wales newspaper read, 'Prodigal Son Returns to Glamorgan'. My return was not exactly a ticker-tape reception, but I felt good to be back in the land of my birth and reunited with family and close friends. Now I had to justify their faith and produce the goods for Glamorgan. The landscape looked inviting, but this next chapter in my cricketing life would prove to be anything but a fairytale.

# 12

## No Shoulder No Cry

*'A popular player on the field and in the dressing room, Alan was always laughing and joking with a great sense of humour. As club captain, I can say with all sincerity that it was good to have Alan in the Glamorgan side.'*

**Alan Jones**

Glamorgan's pre-season brought the usual photo-call for the new squad, the dishing out of new kit and county sweaters, which not only had to be worn for these pre-season photographs but also because it was so cold at that time of year! I always felt that the county cricket season began too early. Early matches were rarely completed, and many did not even start.

Glamorgan's batting had been strengthened by signing of Pakistan's mercurial batsman, Javed Miandad, and it was clear that I would have to fight for my place in the pace bowling department. Competition for places came from the new captain Mike Selvey, Greg Thomas – who would go on to play for England – and veteran left-armer Malcolm Nash. The spinners included Barry Lloyd, Charles Rowe – a new signing from Kent – and Rodney Ontong, the South African-born all-rounder; all three were off-spinners.

My return to the Glamorgan team would, however, have to wait until early May in Cardiff, against Essex, who had a formidable team which included Graham Gooch, Keith Fletcher (captain), Ken McEwan (South Africa), Derek Pringle, Norbert Phillips (West Indies) and John Lever (England). Mike Selvey told me I would play in place of Nash and would share the new ball with Greg Thomas, while he bowled at first-change. I would have preferred to have bowled first-change, but was just happy to be in the side.

It was an uncharitably cold day in Cardiff, and Essex batted after winning the toss with Gooch opening, alongside the hard-hitting Scotsman, Brian Hardie. Greg Thomas opened the bowling for us and I have to admit that I was nervous. It was my first county match in 18 months and I'd waited for this moment for all that time, wondering if this day would ever come about.

Glamorgan's new captain was full of energy and encouragement, but I knew Mike Selvey's eye – and every other eye at Sophia Gardens – was now upon me as I delivered the first ball of my comeback from the Cathedral Road end to Brian Hardie, a destructive batsman who would go on to play 378 first-class matches for Essex, scoring 27 centuries. The ball left my hand reasonably well and it swung late, away from the expansive cover drive of Brian Hardie. It wasn't the swing I had intended. I always attempted an in-swinger with the new ball, and never ever tried to bowl an away-swinger with my first delivery. But Hardie got an edge to it, and John Hopkins took the catch at first slip. A wicket with the first ball of my career comeback for Glamorgan! There were mid-pitch celebrations and congratulations as Hardie walked off with his first-ball duck and I tried to take it all in.

That was it, though, from a wicket-taking perspective. Essex amassed 325-6 declared, with Keith Fletcher scoring 151 not out and Ken McEwan a stylish 107. My reward for 15 overs of fairly undistinguished left-arm medium pace – some quicker than others – was Hardie's wicket for 40 runs. But, more importantly, I felt I'd overcome a huge mental obstacle. I had finished the day without pain, and once again feeling part of the professional cricketing landscape.

Alas, those feelings of somewhat muted pleasure were not destined to last too long; instead they evaporated fairly early on in the season as I found myself in and out of the playing XI, and more out than in. Most of May was cold and wet and neither I nor Selvey enjoyed ourselves in Championship matches against the counties we had just left. Middlesex beat us at Lord's by an innings and 79 runs, then we lost to Gloucestershire by three wickets at Swansea. Zaheer scored a century, Javed failed with scores of 0 and 13 and I didn't take a solitary wicket.

My season seemed to go into freefall in June, just as the 1983 World Cup got going. I was left out of four Championship and five Sunday League matches and began to ask not only whether I had been right to return to Glamorgan, but if I was cut out to play professional cricket any more. The seeds of doubt were in my head; I was not playing, and it felt that I was allowing life to bypass me. I had a good degree from Loughborough University and I felt I wasn't using it, or my brain, in a proper vocation. This was not what either I or Glamorgan had envisaged, and I started to wonder what I might do outside cricket.

The historic day when India won the World Cup at Lord's – June 25th, 1983 – found me about 100 miles away on a windswept ground in the Leicestershire town of Hinckley. I got the wicket of David Gower, back in the Leicestershire side just three days after England had lost their World Cup semi-final to India in Manchester, but I was proving to be too expensive. I was clearly out of sorts, trying too hard, and it wasn't working.

Glamorgan had signed another paceman, the West Indian Winston Davis, who had hit the World Cup headlines just a couple of weeks earlier when he routed the Australians at Leeds, taking 7 for 51 in his ten overs, and bowling fast. He was a magnificent bowler, lithe and genuinely quick, even if he couldn't keep his place in the West Indies World Cup side. How could he against the Big Four: Michael Holding, Malcolm Marshall, Andy Roberts and Joel Garner?

Yet, somehow, I kept my place for the next match, against Kent, but was only the sixth bowler we used in a rain-affected match. I bowled nine overs, and had Bob Woolmer LBW for 97. Bob was furious, not because he thought it wasn't out – he was right in front to a ball that swung late into him – but because, as he told me afterwards in the bar, he was three runs short of scoring a century against all the counties, and I had spoilt his mission to accomplish the feat. Over a couple of glasses of wine, Bob just chuntered away in good humour, "Where the hell did you pop up from? You hadn't bowled all bloody day, and then you get one to bloody well swing after tea. You're not supposed to do that, you know!"

It was good banter. "Sorry, Bob, I'm not sure how I got the call from Selvey to bowl. In fact, I was having a good time chatting with your Kent fans in front of the hospitality marquees on the boundary edge!" The St Lawrence Ground was famous for its carnival atmosphere, the marquees forming a wonderful sight around this most picturesque of quintessential English cricket grounds. Just after tea, I had given up all hope of bowling and was enjoying the hospitality offered to me by some of the members.

"In fact, Bob, I don't want to make you feel any worse than you do, but I was actually into my second glass of champagne when I got the signal from the skipper to bowl!" "Bloody hell, are you kidding?" Bob queried. "No, I'm not, Bob. I was having a good time down there at third man, so please accept my apologies!" All he could do was shake his head and murmur, "Three bloody runs, that's all I needed, three measly runs!" We both saw the funny side to it, but I knew that I had yet again made a minimal contribution and was playing a part-time role.

I was surprised to play in the Championship and Sunday League matches which followed, against Sussex at Cardiff, but was dropped after conceding 38 runs in six overs, while taking the wickets of Imran Khan and Garth le Roux, on the Sunday.

I was left out for the next six County Championship and the next four Sunday League games, in effect a month out of the first team. The season is short enough anyway, given the amount of cricket lost to rain, and this one was going past me at such a rate of knots, that I was at a loss as what to do about it. When county cricketers are out of the side for any reason, the feeling of desperation is tangible. Injuries, of course, are part of playing a professional sport, but being left out for long periods of an already truncated season is difficult to assimilate. Those crucial mid-season weeks, from mid-July to mid-August, are the best time of the year but I was now seriously contemplating a career away from cricket. I simply wasn't cut out to be a part-time cricketer and I knew that this was the beginning of the end. I didn't tell anyone what was going on inside my head, mainly because I wasn't completely sure myself: a kaleidoscope of conflicting thoughts, and mental turmoil that was telling me that I had to make a profound adjustment to my mental compass. I was heading in the wrong direction playing professional cricket, and I knew that I wanted to change it.

My month's exile ended with selection to play against Kent at Sophia Gardens. It's a match I remember well, not for bagging a stack of wickets – I took one in the match – but for scoring a rather memorable – for me – 45 batting at ten, after being hit on the head and felled by a bouncer from the West Indian Antiguan-born Eldine Baptiste. We were trying to score enough runs to set Kent a fourth-innings target, and I thought Baptiste was no more than medium pace until this missile came out of nowhere, and I went down like a boxer after an unexpected hook! Fortunately, I was wearing a helmet, but I was seeing stars and snowflakes when I was helped back to my feet by the Kent captain, Chris Cowdrey, and other players. The next 30 minutes or so were as enjoyable as any I had experienced for a month. I managed to put bat to ball more often than not and was enjoying my stay in the middle – which didn't happen too often. On 45, Chris Cowdrey brought on Derek Underwood for a bowl and, having kept out Eldine Baptiste, I thought I would soon be notching a half-century. Alas, it didn't happen! 'Deadly' Derek produced a quicker ball that dipped in late under my bat and that was the end of the fun. Bowled Underwood for 45, and off to applause from my teammates on the dressing room balcony, and an ice pack on the lump on my head.

The Baptiste incident led to requests for interviews after the day's play. BBC Wales reported all of Glamorgan's matches and their reporter and commentator, Ron Jones, interviewed me. More important than the interview itself was the conversation we had after the match, which incidentally we lost. He knew that I had been struggling and I intimated that I would like to know more about the profession of broadcasting. Ron was a wonderful broadcaster, who went on to cover the Olympic Games, World Cup football and all major sporting events for the BBC's Radio Two and Radio FiveLive stations. Our conversation at Sophia Garden sowed the first seeds of interest in broadcasting as a possible alternative to playing cricket.

I had also learnt broadcasting from a playing colleague at Pretoria High School Old Boys. Trevor Quirk, a very decent wicket-keeper who played Currie Cup cricket for Northern Transvaal, was one of the most prolific talkers behind the stumps I had ever met and a well-known media personality. I visited him several times at the Johannesburg offices of the South African Broadcasting Corporation.

Trevor Quirk was the voice of many South African sports, but mainly cricket and rugby, and was quietly moving from radio into television. I was fascinated by broadcasting because it was so far removed from the life I had been leading. I was also impressed by the people I met in the offices at the SABC tower at Auckland Park in Johannesburg, with magnificent panoramic views all over the sprawling 'City of Gold'. With hindsight, while those months in Pretoria were intended to revive my cricket career, the really important element were those visits to the SABC offices, developing my fascination with broadcasting and laying a base for possibly developing a role within it.

My desire to learn grew by the day, especially when Ron Jones suggested that I might like to try some radio work. It was a turning point in my life. I wanted to throw everything into broadcasting, in order to embark upon a new career. I had told Ron about my visits to the SABC in Johannesburg, and that I was now serious about getting out of cricket. Ron was a source of great encouragement when he said, "Alan, why don't you think about it? Do you want to give it a go? Say some words for us, or maybe do a few minutes' commentary and we can record it for you?"

"Ron," I gasped, "that would be fantastic if we could do that. I have never commentated in my life, but if you think I could just try it then please could we do that?" "Absolutely no problem at all. Do you know if you're playing in the next match?" he asked. The following day I learnt that I'd be in the Glamorgan squad for the Championship match against Derbyshire at St. Helen's, Swansea, the second day of which happened to be my birthday.

My emotional wheels were now turning fast; I was both excited and nervous about doing commentary on BBC Radio Wales. A lot happened in the three days before the match. Firstly I met Tom Davies, the head of BBC Radio Wales sport, at their headquarters in Llandaff, Cardiff for a crash course in what was expected of me. I was to be used mostly as a guest adding expert comment to Ron's commentary, but what excited me further was that I would be able to 'try out some commentary' which would not go out on air, but would be recorded at the BBC in Cardiff. It wasn't exactly an audition, but it was a chance to hear what I sounded like on the air. Next came a series of telephone calls to Johannesburg, and conversations with Trevor Quirk and then Bob Law, head of English radio sport for the SABC. I had met Bob on my visits to the SABC; a Zimbabwean with a beautiful voice who still worked as a broadcaster as well as heading the department. I explained that I would be doing some radio work on a cricket match for BBC Radio Wales. Bob replied, with such enthusiasm, "That's great, Alan, make sure you record it and then send it over to us so that we can listen to the tape, and we can take things from there. Great talking to you and we look forward to hearing you on tape."

In my mind, this *was* an audition and I knew that if I did a reasonable job, it could start a new career. There were, as yet, no job offers but it was an opportunity for me to try something different. I was so excitedly nervous at the prospect that, frankly, I didn't really care whether or not I would be playing against Derbyshire.

Developments elsewhere would also have far-reaching consequences for me. During our match at Canterbury a few weeks earlier, I'd spent a few hours with the Kent and England fast bowler Graham Dilley. Conversations between county players often centred around playing and coaching opportunities for the coming winter, and Graham told me he would not be going back to The Wanderers Club in Johannesburg, where he had played the previous winter, while I was to be just an hour up the M1 motorway in Pretoria. He explained that they were looking for a bowler. "If you're interested," he said, "I'll put a word in, and you can sort it out with them. Have you got anything lined up for the winter?"

I answered that I had nothing lined up. Of course I knew all about The Wanderers Club, one of the greatest cricket clubs in South Africa, a historic sporting institution located in the north of the city with spectacular facilities for cricket, rugby, tennis, hockey, bowls, squash and many other activities.

"Wilko," Graham added, "The Wanderers is a fantastic club and they will look after you well. I will recommend you for the job and you'll get a phone call from a bloke called Tim Raaff. You'll have a great time there." "Cheers, Dill" I said, "and if it comes off for me at The Wanderers, I owe you big time!"

The call duly came. "Hi Alan, this is Tim Raaff, from The Wanderers Club in Johannesburg. Graham Dilley has recommended you for the playing and coaching job with us. Can you talk for a few minutes?" I was so excited, I could have talked for a few hours.

"Hi Tim, yes, I have spoken to Graham about the job, and I would be absolutely delighted to come over and play and coach for the club," I gushed. "Mind you, I've got bloody big shoes to fill, so please don't compare me with Graham Dilley, will you!" I said, half joking but ultimately seriously. "He is a Test bowler with serious pace, and you're not going to get that from me, but I think I can contribute in other areas as well." "Alan," came the reassuring voice down the telephone, "if Graham has recommended you, then we would be delighted to welcome you to The Wanderers Club in Johannesburg." "Tim, I cannot thank you enough for this," I replied, barely concealing my excitement. When will I hear from you next?" "You'll hear from me in a few days, Alan," said Tim, "but let's work on getting you here towards the end of September, would that be alright?"

"Sounds bloody perfect to me, Tim" I said. "I look forward to your next telephone call."

The pieces of my personal jigsaw were beginning to fall into place and with them a plan to go back to South Africa to look for a job outside cricket. Further calls confirmed that I would be going to play and coach for The Wanderers Club. Only my parents knew that I would be going back to South Africa, and I didn't tell anyone at Glamorgan.

The next piece of the jigsaw was the radio stint at St. Helen's. Mike Selvey told me I was playing on the morning of the match. We won the toss and batted and, given my place in the order, I knew that if we batted reasonably well I would have time in the early afternoon to join Ron Jones in the little radio box somewhere in the top of the grand clubhouse of St. Helen's.

Derbyshire had a decent attack – the mighty Michael Holding, very useful Danish fast bowler Ole Mortensen, the left-arm medium-fast Colin Tunnicliffe, and the England off-spinner Geoff Miller. We were four wickets down at lunch and I was afraid it was getting too tight for me to pop to the radio box but I'd made up my mind to go and was indebted to Rodney Ontong and Alan Lewis Jones for putting on a century stand for the fifth wicket. I started as a guest giving my comments alongside Ron Jones. That seemed to go well enough, but then Ron told me to prepare for a stint of commentary on my own.

This was it. It wasn't going out live on air, but it was a stint of radio commentary with Michael Holding, the great West Indian fast bowler, in full cry and the whole thing being recorded back in the studios of BBC Radio Wales in Cardiff. I did about a quarter of an hour on the microphone before heading rapidly to our changing rooms when we lost more wickets.

I felt absolutely exhilarated by the experience, and was shaking with a combination of nervous relief and excitement that I had completed the task on radio. Nerves took on a different complexion when we lost our seventh wicket, and I had to go in to bat, with Michael Holding bowling fast from the Mumbles Road End. I managed to stick around and somehow scramble 17 runs, before Holding sent my off stump flying for his third wicket.

Despite my excitement, I had to wait a while before I heard the tape at the BBC in Cardiff since, with the usual scheduling madness, we went straight from Swansea to Northampton for another County Championship match.

We drew at Northampton, where I scored a painstaking half-century which delighted me but put everyone else, including our dressing room, to sleep. Hotel telephone calls were expensive, but I had to make a couple to Johannesburg, informing both The Wanderers Club and SABC that I was intent on moving to South Africa not just for the winter months, but permanently.

The 50 at Northampton got me promoted to number eight for our next match at Taunton, where I scored a memorable 14 not out before joining Ron Jones in the radio commentary box. Ron took my interest in radio a step further by showing how to use the COOBE (said as COO-BEE), the suitcase-like Commentator Operated Outside

Broadcast Equipment which plugged reporters and commentators into the control centres in Cardiff and London.

I had one of my best days that summer on the following Sunday at Sophia Gardens, taking 3 for 13 including the wickets of Basil D'Oliveira and their captain Phil Neale, in an 83 run win over Worcestershire. Then it was back to Taunton on Monday to continue the county match. We bowled Somerset out for a first innings lead of four runs and reached 105 for 1 when we batted again. I decided to walk around the boundary, which was something which many county cricketers did during a match, to the other side of the ground where I could see Ron Jones – sitting with his COOBE – broadcasting for BBC Radio Wales. By now, I had struck up a real friendship with Ron, and he showed the patience of a saint in answering my endless questions about what a career in broadcasting entailed, how much training would I need, would I be able to change career and break into broadcasting and what prospects there were at the BBC.

From 105-1 Glamorgan lost a couple of quick wickets. Suddenly, Mike Selvey began waving frantically for me to get back to the changing room immediately. I said to Ron that I had better get back as quickly as possible, but for the life of me, I couldn't work out why 'Selve' wanted me back there. After a dash around the boundary I learnt what he wanted.

"For Christ sake, Wilks, what the hell are you thinking? Why weren't you watching the game from here?" Before I had time to answer, he followed up with, "Get your bloody pads on, you're going in as nightwatchman, if we lose another wicket." There was no time for debate, and I wanted extra padding because Joel 'Big Bird' Garner was working up a fearsome pace. Sure enough, we lost our fourth wicket and Mike Selvey turned to me and said, "Wilks, you're in, and make sure you stay there until close of play."

No pressure then! Just keep out a rampant Joel Garner for the next 25 minutes or so until stumps. One minute I had been talking about radio, and imagining myself in some commentary box somewhere, the next I was trying to fend off one of the world's great fast bowlers! Joel Garner hit me everywhere, from my throat to my toes, but I somehow managed to stay there until the umpires called time. I then had to face the wrath of the captain, who was clearly unimpressed with my no-show in the hour of need, much to the amusement of the changing room. The following morning, I didn't last very long and we were bowled out, leaving Somerset to get 241 to win the match, which they did fairly comfortably under the captaincy of Peter Roebuck.

As the season wound down, Wayne Larkins of Northamptonshire hit us for 252 at Cardiff, then Alvin Kallicharran smashed 243 for Warwickshire at Edgbaston. I was wicketless against Warwickshire and also in the final Championship and Sunday League games against Hampshire, so my final wicket for Glamorgan was David Steele, the former England batsman, who was playing for Northamptonshire. But I finished with something to say, and it was a word to the umpires.

The Hampshire game was bizarre. Glamorgan were in danger of a substantial fine for falling below the prescribed over-rate for the season, so Mike Selvey and Charles Rowe bowled 72 overs between them in quick time, with Selvey bowling off just three paces. It looked like a Charlie Chaplin film. My great friend, Chris Smith, elder brother of Robin, made a stylish 93 amongst the mayhem.

Mike Selvey had a mischievous sense of humour on that final day of the 1983 season, because he sent me in as nightwatchman with Glamorgan 76 for 2 and Malcolm Marshall in full cry. As I walked out to bat at number four, with Hampshire's players all very amused with this elevation in the batting order for me, a dark band of cloud came across the ground. The timing was perfect. The umpires, those two great stalwarts David Shepherd and David Constant, conferred, got out their light-meters, walked towards Rodney Ontong and me, and offered us the light.

"Rodney, Wilko, the light is not good enough. Would you like to stay on or go off?" said Shep, his rosy cheeks glowing in the gloom.

I looked at Rodney, then at Malcolm Marshall who was standing on the mark at the end of his run-up, and finally I looked at the empty crease, where I was due to take guard. I was in mid-pitch with Rodney Ontong and it didn't require a long discussion. This was no time to be a hero. It was cold, windy and not the place to be, with Malcolm Marshall about to run in with the wind behind him.

"We'll go off, Shep, no point in staying out here in this light!" I said in haste, and with great relief.

With a grin and a wink, Shep raised his voice to the Hampshire players: "Skipper, we've offered the batsmen the light, and they've decided to go off."

And that was it for me. While I still had two years on my contract, my professional career was over. The season had been a catalogue of uncertainty and lack of purpose. Neither Glamorgan nor I knew what my role was within the side, and the lack of consistency on either side led to my meagre return with the ball. I simply wasn't cutting it, and my mind was made up weeks before that final day. I'd had enough. In my mind, my cricket career was done and dusted right there on that day in Southampton.

The evening was a jovial affair, firstly in the clubhouse bar in the company of the Hampshire players, and then in the hotel where Glamorgan had organised an end-of-season dinner and drinks evening. Nobody had any idea of my plans as I looked around the room at the smiling faces of my Glamorgan teammates and listened to their banter. It was a memorable evening to end a not-so memorable season and, for me, that was it.

With the season over I finally got to visit BBC Radio Wales and listened to the taped recording of my commentary, a copy of which had already been sent to the SABC in Johannesburg. It was a weird feeling listening to my own voice, but it was a start of sorts and everyone has to start somewhere. I had no idea of what was in front of me, except that I was heading to Johannesburg to play and coach cricket for The Wanderers Club. That in itself was an incentive to move on to other things in life.

I still had the safeguard of another two years of contract with Glamorgan, but I knew deep down that my heart was no longer in the professional game.

At home, I started to separate the belongings needed for my trip from those to be stored in my parents' loft. I also put aside other possessions I might need in the longer term, such as a bundle of records and a hi-fi music centre for shipping to South Africa. It was time to say goodbye to my parents. I had no idea how long I would be in Johannesburg, but I wanted it to be a long stay. I yearned for a new career, and hoped that as well as playing cricket for The Wanderers Club, I could embark upon a career, possibly in radio broadcasting. That was my goal.

It was an emotional farewell, but I knew that this move had to be taken. I was wasting everyone's time, including my own, playing professional cricket. Mentally, I was ready for a change in my life.

# 13

# Familiar Places, Friendly Faces

*'Alan is a true gentlemen whose knowledge and passion for sport has served him well as a superb broadcaster. I spoke with Alan on many occasions whilst captain of the Springboks in 1994 and 1995 and I always looked forward to the interviews and discussions because he knew the nuances of rugby – he got it! Baie dankie Alan!'*

**Francois Pienaar**

I was heading back to a country I knew well, but this time to a new city and cricket club, and with the goal of breaking into a new career. The players and management of The Wanderers Club matched the magnificence of their setting, making the early weeks of settling in as straightforward a process as I could have wished for.

The chairman of The Wanderers Club was the great former Springbok wicketkeeper and batsman, Johnny Waite. He ran a cricket equipment business called L F Palmer Ltd, based in the centre of Johannesburg, with Sid O'Linn, a South African double football and cricket international who had played county cricket for Kent and league football for Charlton Athletic. These two wonderful gentlemen were very important in those early days in Johannesburg. I seemed to spend hours on end talking cricket in their famous store, then located on Commissioner Street, although it has since moved to the new Wanderers Stadium.

The Transvaal Premier League was some of the toughest and most competitive cricket I had ever played. This was hardly surprising given that the league was the supply chain for the hugely powerful

Transvaal team. On any given weekend the likes of Graeme Pollock, Clive Rice, Jimmy Cook, Henry Fotheringham, Alvin Kallicharran, Sylvester Clarke, Collis King, Kevin McKenzie, Vince van der Bijl, Rupert 'Spook' Hanley, Neil Radford, Hugh Page, Brian McMillan, Bruce Roberts and a host of leading provincial players, would all be playing Transvaal Premier League cricket.

I was not very amused when our wicketkeeper dropped the most straightforward of catches from my bowling, when Pollock had not yet got off the mark. The keeper's explanation was something along the lines of: "I am sorry. I was just looking at him, not his bat. I cannot believe that I am actually on the same cricket field as him. Oh God, what have I done?"

A very swift Pollock century followed, with the ball struck an alarming number of times onto different parts of The Wanderers Club real estate. Eventually he missed one, possibly through tiredness, more probably through boredom, and he was bowled. It was a moment to savour: Graeme Pollock bowled Alan Wilkins 109.

As much as I enjoyed playing high-level club cricket in Johannesburg, I was intent on getting a job outside the game. Bob Law listened to my taped commentary on the match at Swansea, and I poured my heart out to him, explaining that I was desperate to get into radio broadcasting; a move which would be the end of my cricket career. Bob said that the taped commentary was alright, but that I needed "a lot of work" and, in any event, there was no job vacancy at the time, but that there might be in a couple of months.

I clung to that "might be", knowing that I had to give Glamorgan three months notice should I decide not to return. Bob finally called during the Christmas holiday to say he now had a vacancy for a sports reporter/announcer, asking, "Would it be of interest to you, Alan?"

It was the call I had been dreaming of. I went in to the SABC offices, suitably attired with new shirt and tie, and barely able to control my unbridled excitement. A few hours of administrative formalities had me ready to start my new job the first week of January 1984.

My elation was indescribable, but there were important matters to attend to. First was the letter to Phil Carling, secretary of Glamorgan County Cricket Club, giving due notice that I would not be returning for the 1984 season and was retiring from the game. Then, now that I had a full-time job, I had to apply for permanent residence in South Africa.

My broadcasting career began in January 1984 when I was sent to cover the Transvaal Ladies Bowls Union Annual Championships at The Wanderers Club! What I knew about bowls, let alone the leading female players in the province, could have been written on a postage stamp. But it was an excellent entrance to my new career, a reminder that homework and preparation would be essential to covering anything other than rugby or cricket with authority. It was also an early salutary lesson in how to compile a report on a sport about which I knew absolutely nothing. I was required to phone in a two minute report on each of the three days of the event. By the end I was exhausted – three two-minute phone reports – and I was out on my feet, not helped by the ladies of the Transvaal Ladies Bowls Union insisting on my joining them for cocktails each evening. More lessons learned: don't mix the job with the social side of the sport, and maintain a healthy distance between broadcaster and participants.

The next couple of months were spent learning the procedures of every facet of radio broadcasting, from actual voicing of reports and live broadcasting to editing tapes, compiling programmes and interviewing techniques. The English Radio Service of the SABC had, in those days, some of the finest broadcasters I have ever known: Paddy O'Byrne, Christopher Bennett, Jeremy Dawes, Bea Read, Gail Adams, Peter Biles (who would go on to be a senior political broadcaster with the BBC in London), Mike London and John Bishop. Most were British expats who had lived in South Africa for years, and it was their personalities and excellence on the microphone which gave the English Radio Service such a wonderful reputation in the country. I learned my craft through on-hand training from this group of outstanding broadcasters, many of whom became personal friends.

I did not have to work on weekends, so was able to continue playing cricket for The Wanderers. The leading sports broadcasters in the land were well-established personalities, so as a newcomer I had to fight my way into the commentating profession: firstly by working at it and secondly by becoming an accepted voice in the business. That would take time. For now I was more than content in what I was doing. I was learning the ropes in a new profession. It would take time, a lot of dedication and no lack of effort to climb up the ladder.

Glamorgan did not respond favourably to my resignation. Phil Carling and Mike Selvey both rang to say that they were not prepared to accept my decision and that I ought to reconsider it. It was good of them to think that I could still make a contribution to Glamorgan's cricket, but I couldn't share their optimism on that score, and I had to politely stand my ground. I explained that I had begun a new profession and that I was going to stay in South Africa at least for the next few years. Given my very ordinary performance the previous season, I was surprised that I had received such support from both the secretary and the captain, but my mind was made up.

Also living in Johannesburg was Robin Jackman, who had now finished a wonderful career with Surrey and England and emigrated to South Africa. The Jackman-Wilkins Mankad story did the rounds in the golf clubhouses around Johannesburg; in fact, it went for a few years on the after-dinner speaking circuit! It was around mid-March, when a number of English cricketers who had wintered in South Africa were returning home for the new season, it hit me that I was not going back 'home' to play cricket. I was now embarking upon my first winter in South Africa, in itself a novel experience.

But my broadcasting career took a step upward around that time. I was assigned to cover the South African Formula One Grand Prix at the famous Kyalami circuit north of Johannesburg. To be there was extraordinary, never mind interviewing the likes of race winner Niki Lauda, that year's champion. Keke Rosberg, pipped to pole position by one hundredth of a second by Nelson Piquet, gave me an interview that haunted me for years! He had every right to, because I opened the interview with a daft question along the lines of: "How did your qualifying go?"

That interview never made it to air and not just because of the expletive he dropped in answer to my dull opening question. The finished product was almost impossible to edit, which was done in those days by splicing tape on a recording machine. You soon learn that well-constructed questions not only saved a lot of time and hard work, but it put the interviewee at ease. It was another salutary lesson in my early days of radio broadcasting, so thank you Keke Rosberg!

I had been looking forward to the start of the rugby season in April and, though not working, was fortunate enough to be offered a seat at Ellis Park for the second Test between the Springboks and England. It was an incredible experience, sitting amongst 70,000 rugby-mad South African fans with the winter sun blazing down on the burnt grass of Ellis Park. I had been used to the crowd noise at Cardiff Arms Park, but this was quite different. England succumbed to a rampant Springbok team 35-9, with the crowd seemingly baying for English blood. It was a good moment to remind some of the locals that I was a Welshman, not an Englishman; something that I would have to do on numerous occasions during my permanent residence in the country.

A typical week in those first months of radio broadcasting involved presenting the early morning sports bulletins, usually a five- to seven-minute slot during the morning *Radio Today* programme on the English Radio Service, a news and current affairs programme along the lines of BBC Radio Four's morning *Today* programme in the UK. The early shift involved a five o'clock start to collect overnight tapes from our reporters worldwide and the BBC World Service, then trawl through the wires of the Reuters news service to select items for the morning broadcast. Having selected the material, I had to script the sport bulletin, which would include taped excerpts. This was one of the most important early learning processes for me, since I was editing at the same time as producing and editing the radio sports bulletin. The bulletin had to be meticulously presented to the programme producer, and a copy of the script given to both the producer and the presenter. I would then enter the studio, usually during a taped item, sit opposite the presenter, settle down and mentally prepare to present the sports bulletin.

"Now, with the time at just past 7.25 here on *Radio Today*, with the first of the morning sports reports, here's Alan Wilkins." Those were the usual introductory words from Bea Read, or Gail Adams, two incomparable English Radio Service broadcasters. The next five to seven minutes belonged to the world of sport and the person presenting it.

Those moments were nerve-wracking at the best of times, and often chaotic. The bulletin might be running late, or an item might break just before you went on air. I learnt fast that it was 'sink or swim' on live radio. As my confidence grew, different personality traits could be used to personalise the presentation of the broadcast. I owe a huge debt of gratitude to my colleagues on SABC's English Radio Service in those early days. They not only showed great patience with me, but went out of their way to help: giving me advice and tips on voice delivery, breathing exercises, writing of scripts, and how to become a better broadcaster on radio. I devoured every ounce of information that came my way, and spent every hour I could in the offices and studios of the English Radio Service. Looking back I know that they laid the foundation for my career because the broadcasting was on a par with anything from the BBC. It was a privilege to be in their company.

Every sports bulletin seemed to morph into an international news bulletin when the South African 3,000 metre runner Zola Budd, competing for Great Britain, collided with Mary Decker, the American favourite for the race, at the 1984 Olympics in Los Angeles. The news element demanded a more serious editorial and delivery and I soon found myself being rostered on to the presentation of news bulletins, not just sport, This was yet another big step forward, because the presentation of news is essentially formal.

On October 31st, came the news that Indira Gandhi had been assassinated. This was a personal shock after being introduced to her at Eden Gardens three years earlier, and also had an impact on my broadcasting career. Because it was known that I had visited India and had met Indira Gandhi, I became the interviewee, not the interviewer, for a series of interviews on the impact the assassination would have not just in sport, but in a wider political perspective as well. I wasn't totally at ease on the political narrative, realising that sport was very much my comfort zone, but it was yet another step forward in broadcasting. Then, in the New Year, came my first cricket commentary on radio.

It was always my ambition to commentate, but I knew that as a newcomer I would have to wait behind a long queue of established cricket and rugby commentators.

In those days, cricket commentary on radio in South Africa (television arrived in South Africa only in 1976) was characterised by the incomparable Charles Fortune, an Englishman who emigrated to the country in 1935, taught science at St. Andrew's College, Grahamstown in the Eastern Cape, for many years, and began radio broadcasting in the late 1930s. He was the voice of cricket for generations of South African cricket enthusiasts and, as the South African journalist, Sue de Groot, remembers, "Charles Fortune spoke about the sky a lot, and the birds and the trees, and sometimes a little bit about the cricket, and he did it all beautifully!"

He was the doyen of radio broadcasting in the same way as his contemporaries, John Arlott in England and Alan McGilvray in Australia. I had met him when I was invited to The Wanderers Club radio box before Christmas. He was an imposing personality with the most distinguished voice, a stickler for the English language and one of the most respected broadcasters in the world. His right-hand man, his faithful scorer, was John Landau, a wonderful man who didn't just score with his pencil and scorebook, but embellished the commentary with all kinds of information on small notes deftly passed under Charles Fortune's nose whilst he was in full flow. Sometimes they made it into the commentary, other times they were left to rest on the desk next to the microphone. Charles Fortune was the first broadcaster to measure a batsman's progress by the number of balls faced, rather than the number of minutes spent at the crease; his and John Landau's innovation is now standard practice.

I made my live commentary bow on January 12th, 1985, with Transvaal 'B' v Boland at The Wanderers Club in the Castle Bowl; one tier below the Currie Cup, but still first-class. Live commentary would be broadcast throughout the Saturday afternoon sports programme.

Charles Fortune was in Port Elizabeth to commentate on the Currie Cup match between Eastern Province and Transvaal. I will never forget that moment in The Wanderers commentary box, waiting anxiously and nervously to begin my stint of commentary.

The audio engineer behind me gave me a thumbs-up signal and said "Good Luck, Alan, hope it goes well!"

The host in the studio crossed to Charles Fortune in Port Elizabeth and then, after about 15 minutes, he crossed to me at The Wanderers: "Now, it's time to go to Johannesburg, to a young man who is relatively new to South Africa, but we are lucky to have him with us at the SABC because he has not so long ago finished his county cricket career with Glamorgan and, before that, Gloucestershire." There was then a long pause. "Having studied his deeds with both bat and ball for both counties I would venture that Alan Haydn Wilkins, from Cardiff, enjoyed discernibly more enjoyment with leather than with the willow but, in any event, the numbers don't matter, it's his opinion that does. Welcome Alan, welcome to South Africa."

I was not prepared for that! I gulped with nervousness. How the hell could I follow that from Charles Fortune? Nico, the audio engineer, sensing my nerves, squeezed my arm, gave me a reassuring tap on the shoulder, another thumbs-up, and some words came out of my mouth. Some of them made sense. I was live on radio in South Africa, spouting away with butterflies the size of bats inside my stomach, but the sheer thrill of live radio broadcasting was just amazing. I was enjoying this moment like nothing else before and, just when I was feeling a sense of calmness after the early nerves, the studio host came through in my headphones, "OK, Alan, you can wind it up in the next thirty seconds, remember to give the score as your last words ... 20 seconds to go ... ten seconds ..."

I finished with: "So, Boland struggling here at The Wanderers at 114 for 6."

The studio host picked it up and I heard him saying, "Thank You Alan Wilkins at The Wanderers, and we'll hear more from Alan later in the programme."

I was a wreck! Hands soaked with perspiration, the back of my shirt sticking to my back with sweat, but I had done it: I had been live on air, and it felt exhilarating. I wanted to thank Charles Fortune for his wonderful introduction, using humour to let listeners know that batting hadn't been my strength as a professional cricketer, but in such an amiable way, while also informing our audience that I had actually played first-class cricket.

More commentary opportunities would come later in the season but my main role was studio-based hosting. One night I will never forget was May 29th, 1985: the European Cup final at the Heysel Stadium, Belgium, between Liverpool and Juventus. It turned out to be one of football's gravest nights. My role was to host the 15 minutes or so pre-match with preview items, and then hand over to the match commentators on site. The handover did not materialise for what seemed an eternity due to the clash between the rival sets of fans, resulting in the deaths of 39 spectators. The kick-off was delayed for at least an hour. I was completely unprepared, but somehow got through it alone, as there was no expert in the studio with me.

The domestic rugby season in South Africa was everything I had hoped it would be, even though the scheduled New Zealand All Blacks Tour was cancelled.

The leading rugby commentator was one of the most wonderful people I met in my early years of broadcasting. John Hamilton 'Chick' Henderson was born in Johannesburg, educated at Michaelhouse School in Natal, and went on to the University of the Witwatersrand and then Oxford University. He played in the back row for Transvaal and for Scotland – thanks to his Scottish mother – and was an internationally respected rugby commentator and protagonist for multi-racial sport, managing the South African Barbarians – the first multi-racial rugby team from the republic – on their tour to the UK in 1979. His was a respected voice of reason and he was a wonderful companion to me in those early years in South Africa.

Early rugby assignments – such as the few hours' drive to places such as Witbank, or Potchefstroom, to report, or commentate on rugby in those heartland Afrikaner towns – were part of my learning and discovery process, and a means of finding out more about this vast country and the people who inhabited it.

My first live radio rugby commentary was at the impressive Loftus Versfeld rugby stadium in Pretoria, home of the Northern Transvaal Blue Bulls, for the National Club Championship final between the Universities of Pretoria (the *Tukkies*) and Stellenbosch (the *Maties*). My co-commentator was former Ireland scrum-half, John Robbie, who had stayed on in South Africa after touring with the 1980

British Lions and playing in the fourth Test in Pretoria; the only one the Lions won. He has since become a leading radio and television personality but, on that sunny winter's afternoon in Pretoria, he was my commentator's crutch, helping me distinguish between the three Du Plessis brothers playing for the *Maties*, and the three Smits playing for the *Tukkies*. It was a bit like trying to sort out the Joneses from the Evanses in Welsh rugby! It was also John Robbie's first radio commentary, and the irony of the situation was not lost: an Irishman and a Welshman in Pretoria commentating on a rugby match between two predominantly Afrikaans-speaking teams. Despite the tongue-twisting challenges, we got there in the end!

The last sport I expected to be involved with was boxing, but the opportunity arose, and I found myself commentating live on some of the biggest fights in the country. Two of South Africa's most famous heavyweights, Gerry Coetzee and Pierre Coetzer, fought Americans in Johannesburg. Pierre Coetzer knocked out David Jaco in the sixth round with a punch that not only floored the American, but also detached half his nose as a gruesome bloody clump of gristle flew from his face onto my new beige jacket as I sat at ringside, making a personal note to myself for the next fight: don't wear a light coloured jacket to boxing.

Coetzee had become WBA World Heavyweight Champion in September 1983, knocking out the American Michael Dokes to take the title vacated by Muhammad Ali. He lost the title in December 1984 on one of the most spectacular evenings of entertainment I had ever witnessed. The flamboyant American Greg Page knocked him out in the eighth round at a packed Sun City stadium in Bophutswana. I was a spectator sitting four rows back from the ring, but was mesmerised by the brutality of these giant men smashing each other to pieces with ferocious punches. It was quite a gruesome sight, especially when Coetzee was hit so hard by an uppercut in the eighth round that both his feet left the ground before he fell in an unconscious heap on the canvas.

I was ringside again when Coetzee beat the American, James 'Quick' Tillis on points over ten rounds at Ellis Park Stadium. No light jacket on this occasion, and no real desire to do any more boxing commentary. I knew that no amount of research or dedication to the task would ever put me in a proper comfort zone, but it had been an enlightening experience, a lot of fun, and another building block in my burgeoning broadcasting career.

Sport in South Africa over the next couple of years was dominated by rebel cricket and rugby tours with Kim Hughes's Australian cricketers team, which played a total of 52 matches on two tours in 1985-86 and 1986-87, drawing capacity crowds for their 'international' matches, which were dominated by Clive Rice's South African XI.

It was a swansong series for the likes of Graeme Pollock who, even in his early 40s, silenced the battery of Australian fast bowlers spearheaded by Rodney Hogg, Carl Rackemann and Terry Alderman.

Following the footsteps of the Australian cricketers was the 'New Zealand Cavaliers' rugby team, which played four 'Test matches' against the Springboks in May 1986, losing the series 3-1. Of the 30 players who had been selected for the cancelled 1985 All Blacks tour of South Africa, only David Kirk and John Kirwan did not join the Cavaliers. Both would go on to feature prominently in the inaugural IRB Rugby World Cup the following year when David Kirk captained the All Blacks to victory in rugby's first global event.

Both rebel tours delivered full-on, high intensity unofficial international sport, giving South African fans the high-quality action they wanted but, at the same time, the rebel tag strengthened the cause of the anti-*apartheid* groups all over the world. Internationally, the forces against such sporting relations were growing stronger.

From a personal perspective my world was going in an upwards direction. I was promoted to the position of editor: radio sport at the English Radio Service, then fairly soon after that to manager: radio sport. It was a position of substantial responsibility, in charge of the entire output of radio sport across the country. This meant editorial decisions on which sporting events would be covered, which personnel would be used for reporting and commentating, the allocation of both human and technical resources and financial planning of a year's sporting calendar through a formalised budget. These were exciting times. I was liaising with sporting bodies across South Africa, meeting new people in different walks of life, getting to learn much more about the commercial aspects of running a national radio station and, all the while, maintaining my place as a commentator in both cricket and rugby. The rebel tours had given me the grandest opportunity to commentate at the highest level in both cricket and rugby and the domestic Currie Cup competitions, in both sports were of the highest standard.

Even so, I was flabbergasted to be the recipient of three national broadcasting awards in 1987: firstly, the Benson & Hedges Cricket Commentator of the Year, then the Nissan Media Man of the Year, and finally, the SAB Radio Sports Journalist of the Year for Commentary in cricket and rugby, the highest award given to national broadcasters in South Africa. I was honoured and humbled by such tangible accolades, and also happier then than at any time in my working life.

My personal life had also changed. I had met Mandi and tied the knot no more than three months from the moment I met her in Cape Town whilst working on the 'Test' match at Newlands between South Africa and Kim Hughes' Australians. I already knew her cousin, the South African batsman, Roy Pienaar, and the rest of her family. Ronnie and Heather Pienaar were Johannesburg-based cricket followers known all over the country, and I was staying in their Cape Town home when I received a phone call to say that Mandi would be calling over to collect some of Roy's personal possessions. It was a whirlwind romance where everything happened very quickly.

However, the landscape was to change dramatically. Firstly, my application for accreditation to work at the inaugural Rugby World Cup in New Zealand and Australia in May and June 1987 was rejected by the organising committee and so the working trip was summarily cancelled. Despite having a British passport, I was 'working for a broadcasting organisation that was not accepted' by RWC. I was in the same boat as virtually all sportspeople and media people in South Africa; we were outcasts in the international sporting fraternity. There was no way that sport could be separated from politics, and the rejection of my accreditation for the inaugural Rugby World Cup made me think about my position in South Africa.

I had been offered, but declined, the position of editor of the Western Cape for the English Radio Service of the SABC, based in wonderful Cape Town offices at Sea Point. I didn't consider it as a progression for me, and preferred to be in the central hub of Johannesburg, but I was now looking at the landscape from an international perspective. The reward for winning the Nissan Media Man of the Year was an air ticket to London, and it occurred to me that I could visit the UK for the first time since I'd left in September 1983.

I had discussed my future with the former Glamorgan and England captain Tony Lewis when he visited South Africa, and this prompted a decision that would surprise many of my friends and colleagues. I had decided that it was time to leave South Africa, and try and find a job with the BBC in London.

At roughly the same time, an incident occurred at our home that deeply affected both Mandi and me and stiffened my resolve to head back to Britain. It was a Sunday morning when I had been playing golf at The Wanderers Golf Club, just over the road from our apartment. Walking into the clubhouse, I was told that 'an incident had happened in our apartment' and that I should get home 'as soon as I could'. I sprinted the 100 yards or so at Olympic pace to find the door wide open and a sobbing Mandi in a distressed state. She had been out for the morning and had returned home to find two intruders ransacking our possessions. They had attempted to attack her, but she managed to open the front door and make a dash for safety out to the street. The police arrived and drove Mandi and me around the local neighbourhood to see if she could possibly identify the culprits, a futile exercise given her distress.

I cannot imagine what Mandi went through, but it changed her personality and with every justification. From that moment, Mandi found it difficult to lead a normal life. She could not stay on her own anywhere, and had to accompany me to work in the very early mornings when I was doing my radio programme. The position was untenable. I had to get Mandi out of South Africa, at least until she was able to return to some state of normality. Leaving Johannesburg to live in Britain was a chance to get Mandi back to proper health.

The wheels were set in motion, telephone calls made, letters written, telegrams sent over the wires and faxes sent; all pursuing an interview for a sports reporter's job with the BBC in London. Although I had by now begun TV work for SABC, presenting a series of regular sports programmes – and often in a bilingual setting alongside an Afrikaans presenter – I had to recognise that I was a rank novice when it came to the screen; my best way back to the United Kingdom would be in radio.

A meeting with Patrick Kohler, head of the English radio service, went a long way to helping me make up my mind. In an extraordinarily magnanimous gesture, he promised to keep my position as managing editor of English Radio Sport open for a year. He also knew that there were reasons for a change of direction in my personal life. He wished me well for my future, but said he hoped it would only be for the next 12 months.

An interview for the job of sports reporter with the BBC was arranged, and my flight booked for the first week of August 1987. The weeks leading up to my departure were as emotional as anyone might imagine. Feelings amongst my friends were mixed. Many wished me luck, but others felt that I was leaving South Africa when it needed support. Not everyone knew what had happened to Mandi, and it wasn't something that we wanted to broadcast. Saying goodbye was the worst feeling imaginable, but my gut feeling was that this was the right move. I was leaving alone. Mandi was due to follow me over, but we had not yet booked her flight. Of course, we should have flown back together, but we didn't.

Boarding the plane, I noticed the name on the nose of the British Airways Boeing 747: 'City of Cardiff'. Amid my tears, it made me smile. I was going back to Britain for the first time after four years in Johannesburg and, just like four years previously, there was no guarantee of a job. I was soon to discover that I was taking with me something that the BBC patently disliked.

# 14

# Back to the Future

*'Alan was an excellent county cricketer and is living proof that if you want to be a top sports broadcaster it is better that you have played one of the games to a high level. He may be Cardiff born and Cardiff bred but, in a broadcasting sense, Alan is "a citizen of the world".'*

**Tony Lewis**

My interview for the radio sports reporter's job with the BBC was set for Broadcasting House at Portland Place in London, but before that I visited the BBC Wales sport department in Cardiff. It was a matter of courtesy more than anything else, since I had told them that I was returning to Britain and hoping to secure a job with the BBC in London. I was completely taken aback when Onllwyn Brace, head of BBC Wales sport, and Dewi Griffiths, executive producer sport, made me a formal offer before I had even spoken to anyone in London.

"Alan," said Dewi Griffiths, "we know you're keen on working in London, but if it doesn't work out, then we would like to offer you a job here in Cardiff with BBC Wales television. We need a presenter for our *Rugby Special Wales* TV programme and we would like to offer you a one-year contract with the BBC here in Cardiff. Best of luck in your interview in London, but have a think about our offer here, if things don't quite work out up there in London."

I was stunned; it was the last thing I had expected, but it was just as well that BBC Wales saw something in me, because those in London clearly didn't. The formal interview, which entailed a practical task and an interview by a board of BBC network managers was not my finest hour.

"Mr. Wilkins," said Pat Ewing, head of BBC radio sport – smoking as she spoke – "we realise that you have a great deal of experience across a range of sports and we feel you have a possible future in broadcasting, but we have a problem with your accent."

"My accent?" I said. "Yes, your strong South African accent which you have brought back with you from your four years in the country. We cannot possibly countenance a South African accent on BBC network radio, certainly not in the current climate where there is virtually a global boycott against South African sport."

I was naturally disappointed, but I knew that I had picked up a South African accent. At the best of times I find it easy to imitate accents, but friends in Cardiff had pulled my leg that my newly-acquired clipped tones suggested I was more Witwatersrand than Wales.

Ewing, the first female head of radio sport continued, "I'm afraid that we cannot offer you a position here in London, but we suggest that you try and get something with BBC Wales in Cardiff, get to know a little bit more about how we operate within the BBC, and get rid of that South African accent! Maybe in a few years from now, you can look at whatever positions may come about in London, but it is not going to happen for you now. Best of luck."

There was no point in feeling sorry for myself. I knew that I had been offered a position in television with BBC Wales, and that was all I thought about on the two-hour train journey back from London to Cardiff. I duly signed a one-year contract with BBC Wales, with the initial assignment of presenting *Rugby Special Wales*, a Sunday compilation of the weekend's matches in Wales, plus rugby previews and features including the Five Nations Championship. The contract would start in early September, ahead of the 1987-88 rugby season.

I was introduced to the staff in the BBC Wales sports department as the new presenter of BBC Wales rugby and certainly felt like the new boy in town, especially as some people clearly did not like my connections with South Africa. I was nervous before my first programme; for one thing, it went out live so any slips of the tongue would be scrutinised by all and sundry. One thing you'll never achieve in broadcasting is to please all the people all of the time, but I was completely unprepared for the row that was about to break.

The Wales Anti-*Apartheid* Movement, based in Cardiff, instigated a fierce protest against my appearing on BBC Wales Television, and a sizeable group of demonstrators gathered outside the entrance to the BBC Wales studios in the Cardiff district of Llandaff. My name and photograph were on many of the placards, so I was relieved to see police in attendance as I walked through a gauntlet of chanting protesters to get into the building for the second week of my contract. It was unnerving and unsettling. Mentally, I was unprepared for it.

BBC Wales broadcast a statement whose line was that, "Alan Wilkins is a freelance broadcaster who has been contracted to work on sports programmes for BBC Wales. He is not employed by the BBC." There was debate in the press, where I was strongly supported by Wilf Wooller. It was an unsettling time, not the best start to a new broadcasting career with the BBC, and it didn't help that the head of HR at BBC Wales thought that I was actually South African! He asked, with all sincerity, "How are you settling in to Cardiff? I know this is a difficult time for you right now, but hopefully it will settle down soon. How is your family in South Africa? Are you speaking to them regularly?" I could only answer him as directly as I could: "Well, actually, I was born in Cardiff, I went to school in Cardiff and my parents are both Welsh. Furthermore, they live in Radyr, which is about ten minutes up the road from here, so yes, I do speak to my family quite regularly."

The President of the Wales Anti-*Apartheid* Movement in Cardiff was Hanif Bhamjee. I had met his brother, Abdul – a prominent figure in the governing body of professional football in South Africa – several times in my years in Johannesburg. I felt I had to approach Hanif Bhamjee personally and found out where he lived, taking it upon myself to call on him to discuss matters between us. It was a frank discussion in which I was able to get my point of view across, and the mood on his side was conciliatory. I don't know whether it was because I had met his brother in Johannesburg, but Hanif Bhamjee saw to it that the protests were scaled down. As so often, discussion had resolved issues between two parties with seemingly incompatible viewpoints. Matters improved from then on, but it was not all plain sailing. I still had to prove, to a new audience and a new set of colleagues, that I was 'of and from Wales'. It wasn't always the most straightforward process.

Neither was the process of assimilating Mandi into the Welsh way of life. She had arrived in a howling gale at London Heathrow and I think that the gods had planned on one of the worst winters imaginable to greet someone from the beautiful climate of Johannesburg. I swear I had never seen so much rain during the first winter that Mandi had chosen to spend in Wales. It was a tough initiation for her and I wasn't altogether certain that the idea of living full-time in Wales while I was attempting to establish myself with the BBC would work out.

This was the winter of the 'Great Storm' in mid-October, followed by 'Black Monday', the stock exchange crash on October 19th. Everything, it seemed, was crashing down around me. Not even the visit to Wales of the United States Eagles rugby team lifted the spirits in that dark and miserable first winter I spent back in my homeland. To say I missed the warmth of South Africa was an understatement, especially since I had been told that my job there would be kept open 'at least for the foreseeable future'. The easy option would have been to give up and return to Johannesburg, but I knew I had to stick it out for the long term. In cricketing parlance, I was up against a formidable batting line-up, and it was my mission to prove myself with the ball.

I had to give credit to Mandi for the way she persevered in her unfamiliar surroundings. We were living in a friend's apartment and his frequent absence gave us time together to discuss the future: but I knew that she was struggling. After battling the horrible Welsh winter in 1987, Mandi decided that she needed to get home to her family and to the warmth of Johannesburg. She left in early 1988 and hoped that I would follow and resume my job with the SABC. I was sorely tempted, but felt I had to stay and prove my mettle with the BBC. It was distressing for both of us, because we both knew that we would now go our separate ways. And that's the way it happened for the next few years, with Mandi leading her life in Johannesburg and me mine in Wales. We would eventually divorce in 1991 but would remain the best of friends.

I began, at last, to feel that I was making some inroads into my broadcasting career in Britain. The programming output from BBC Wales was as varied as it was challenging: rugby union was the cornerstone, but I became immersed in football as the Wales national team embarked upon its European Championship qualifying campaign with a match against Yugoslavia in the early spring of 1988. Football was new territory for me, but it was the start of a decade of my involvement as BBC Wales covered the fortunes of the Welsh team in its European and World Cup qualifying campaigns. Welsh football was served by some wonderful players in those years and it was astonishing that the team, featuring outstanding players such as: Ryan Giggs, Ian Rush, Mark Hughes, Neville Southall, Kevin Ratcliffe, Dean Saunders, Gary Speed, Barry Horne, and Chris Coleman, never qualified for a major tournament.

Learning about the nuances of football was straightforward compared with other challenges such as getting my head around the sport of bowls. I thought of it as the sport of gin-sipping ladies on sunny afternoons in Johannesburg, but this was serious stuff! The best bowlers from across Britain regularly competed at tournaments in Wales. My initiation was complete when I was assigned not only as a presenter but a commentator. It was the skill level – of the players, not of my commentary – which astounded me, with their extraordinary accuracy in both indoor and outdoor events. It was also a privilege to work alongside one of the greats of the sport – England's David Bryant CBE – a three-time World Singles Champion, both outdoors and indoors. My bowls education was completed by on-the-spot instruction from David Rhys-Jones, the legendary 'voice of bowls', a former professional who had been Bryant's partner in tournaments all over the world. I was never going to be an Oscar-winning bowls commentator, but it gave me an early opportunity to learn about a new sport, and how to commentate on it to a discerning British television audience. It was an invaluable lesson in broadcasting to have to learn about the nuances of a sport I had never played, its terminology, the tactics and strategies, and a range of vocabulary I had not used before. Sometimes, being thrown in the deep end is the best way to learn. It was largely down to me whether

I sank or swam, and it never entered my head that I would not at least keep afloat.

Being the new face of the BBC Wales sports department also meant a speedy induction into news reporting. The news department was a completely separate entity, but sports presenters and commentators were expected to report the news stories of the day. My weeks were soon filled with daily news shifts, which entailed going out to a venue, or to a training session, and getting interviews with sports stars who were newsworthy. If a Welsh rugby star was injured, then the Welsh public had to know about it and the news department wanted them to hear it first on BBC Wales.

The challenge of news reporting became all-consuming, but it was a priceless initiation into an important sphere of broadcasting. In those early days I was afforded the luxury of a cameraman and an audio engineer with the task of getting a good interview, getting the right shots, getting the right story and, most importantly, making the deadline for the news bulletin. This might entail a mad dash in two cars from BBC Wales HQ in Llandaff to some far-flung village in west Wales – it could easily have been a two-hour drive – to interview a rugby player who had been ruled out of the Wales team by an accident with machinery on his farm. The player had to be called to agree to the interview, then a time slot had to be agreed, then the location, then the race to get there. In some cases, a piece to camera would be required, so I had to mentally compose the story then think about how the item could be presented from the location. Some players – in all sports – are reluctant interviewees and the sight of the camera, and the audio engineer's sound equipment often led to camera nerves. What they didn't know was that I was nervous too! The nervousness on my side, however, was a form of nervous excitement; a mixture of pumping adrenalin and a desire to get a good interview, and a good story 'in the can'.

The BBC had some outstanding technical people who had gone through the best BBC training courses to learn their craft. I was indebted to people like David Jones, a cameraman of the highest calibre, and John Rees, an audio engineer who could hear a seagull fart from a mile away. Their expertise ensured that we always got sharp pictures and precise audio, and they also had a way of putting not only the sportsman or woman but the reporter himself at ease. Once the job was completed on location, they would make a speedy getaway back to BBC Wales HQ to get the tapes to the editors waiting in their video tape (VT) suites. Once back at HQ, it was my job to sit down and compose the news story with a written script, taking into account the interview now with the VT editor, and the shots filmed on location. On any given day, we could have two or three interview stories and the challenge of fitting each into a bulletin. Editing was a new skill that had to be learned quickly. Once again, it was sink or swim.

VT editors were worth their weight in gold. Much as I might want an extended piece, they would suggest taking a short clip based on what was important, and their expertise in reducing a seven-minute interview to thirty seconds – leaving the rest of it on the VT editing suite's floor – was essential to getting the bulletin prepared. These procedures take time, but you are always working to a deadline, and deadlines rarely change. Missing a deadline might mean losing your job. Once news stories were edited, compiled, voiced and packaged, it was my job to get the right graphics on the screen. This entailed a visit to the graphics department with a list of names, or maybe a table of scorers, matches or players, that had to be put on screen at a precise point. Everything took time but the better, experienced reporters of course took less time than the rookie.

With the sports bulletin packaged ready for broadcast 'live' during the main news bulletin, it was time to get ready to present the sports news. A quick change of clothing to a suit, collar and tie, and then to make-up to get a face put on to a face. The ten minutes in make-up were precious moments, and usually the time to take a few deep breaths, close your eyes and start thinking of your links to camera during the main national news programme. The entire five to seven minutes – seven if sport was lucky – was always a 'live' broadcast, always scripted and nearly always went smoothly, but there were inevitably moments which necessitated a fast change of plan. Maybe a VT package failed to run, so in place of a taped interview with the Wales football captain it was your job to pick it up and react, ad-libbing calmly until the next item was ready. As the presenter, you sat in a studio alongside the other presenter or presenters with three or four cameras pointed directly at you from a distance of five or six yards, sometimes even further away. The cameras often had the script on an autocue in front of them, so that every word you said to camera was written out on a glass slate in front of the camera lens. All you had to do, technically speaking, was just read it but, from early in my career, I was encouraged not to rely on autocue, rather to familiarise myself with the script so that in the event of a technical breakdown – such as the autocue grinding to a halt – I could easily pick up the thread of the story and continue as if nothing had happened. You had to think fast, coherently and without any sense of panic, and to keep your eyes fixed on the camera lens; look away, and you have 'lost' the attention of the viewer's attention watching at home.

The first year with the BBC in Wales was a fast-learning year; it had to be. I had a 12-month contract, at the end of which my performance would hopefully be assessed as favourable for a renewal. I knew I tested people's patience at the BBC, certainly in the news department, because I was always close to my deadlines, but that was the nature of the beast. With news, you lived on the edge, but it was exciting and an invaluable introduction to all facets of broadcasting.

I quickly learned that I was not going to make it as a story-breaking hard-nosed journalist. For one thing, I had not trained as a journalist *per se*, but I had had some voice training and other important areas of broadcasting expertise instilled in me by some outstanding broadcasters, initially in Johannesburg. I was also still thinking from a player's perspective, and not from a news point of view.

This led to a failure, on one particular occasion, to report an obvious story. The player concerned was Jonathan Davies, the Wales outside-half who before long would be off to forge an outstanding career in the professional ranks of rugby league for Widnes and Great Britain. I was watching the Welsh rugby squad training on the St. Helen's rugby ground in Swansea – it shares the land area with the cricket field – when 'Jiffy' pulled up clutching his calf muscle. He took no further part in the session and afterwards asked us not to mention the incident on the news, because he was hoping to be fit for the match the following weekend. I assured him I wouldn't. I headed back to Cardiff with interviews with some players, compiled the sports bulletin and presented it as part of the Wales Today news programme that evening on the news programme *Wales Today*. I didn't mention Jiffy's calf injury, but the following morning, the story was emblazoned all across the sports pages of the *Western Mail*. The head of news was furious the following morning, banging the table with a rolled-up copy of Wales' 'National Newspaper'. I had made my own decision, but I denied that I knew anything about the calf injury. I had made a promise to Jiffy that I wouldn't mention it, but as a sports journalist I had failed miserably.

Although I'd presented years of news bulletins – not just sport – but real, actual daily news, I knew that hard journalism i.e. unearthing and investigating stories, was not my forte. BBC Wales knew it as well. My ambition was to make it in pure sports broadcasting, presenting and commentating. I had a long way to go.

In May 1988, with my first rugby union season for the BBC drawing to a close, I was glad to see the warmer days of summer. It also meant a change of sport, hosting and commentating on many of Glamorgan's home matches. I was also playing league cricket on weekends for Cardiff Cricket Club, and was happier with my bowling form on my return to Wales than I was when I left over four years previously. I put it down to not having to perform for a living, but I felt I was also a better bowler for having played in South Africa.

Every day was a challenge in the first few years at the BBC, if only for the fact that it did nearly all of the sports broadcasting in the UK. London was the BBC network broadcasting hub, with BBC Wales, BBC Scotland and BBC Northern Ireland having their own personnel, presenters and commentators. They all also had their own programmes, and there was plenty of work with BBC Wales television and radio, based in Cardiff, but there was always the ambition of being selected for an assignment that would be broadcast across the BBC's UK network.

The BBC boasted some of the greatest presenters and commentators in the world of sports broadcasting, men who were legends in front of camera or with the commentary microphone. There were very few women sports broadcasters at that time. This would change in years to come, but back then it was the likes of the great Bill

McLaren, the Scottish schoolmaster who was the BBC's 'voice of rugby', who entertained British television audiences for decades with his rich Scottish brogue and his trademark turns of phrase. The BBC's coverage of cricket was centred around the unique talent of the wonderful Richie Benaud, whose calmness in front of camera and laid-back commentary became the stuff of folklore. Tony Lewis, the former Glamorgan and England cricket captain, was also very much part of the of the BBC's Network coverage cricket television commentary team, alongside such luminaries as Ray Illingworth, Jack Bannister and Tom Graveney.

Alongside Bill and Richie, every sport on the BBC had broadcasting giants on the microphone or in studio, either presenting – such as the incomparable Des Lynam – or describing the action, such as Harry Carpenter for boxing, David Coleman for athletics and football, Ron Pickering for athletics, Dan Maskell and John Barrett for tennis, Peter Alliss for golf, and Alan Weeks for swimming. In other words, in those glory years of the BBC's sports coverage, Wimbledon *was* Dan Maskell, cricket *was* Richie Benaud, rugby union *was* Bill McLaren. They were the voices of their sport, and an indelible part of British sporting consciousness.

The rival network was the commercial broadcaster, ITV. They also had regional stations, but could not rival the range of the BBC sports portfolio, while the proliferation of advertising during ITV programmes helped keep the majority of the audience tuning into the BBC for the big events. Not until the entry of the satellite broadcaster Sky Television in 1992 would this landscape change.

The BBC could claim to be the most respected sports broadcasting network in the world, largely because of its phenomenal expertise in all sports, drawing on a portfolio containing almost all the major sporting properties: Wimbledon, rugby's Five Nations Championship, international Test cricket and domestic cricket, Formula One motor-racing, domestic and international football, including World Cup and European Championship qualifying campaigns and tournaments, all the major athletics events and the Olympic Games. Government policy meant that some major events had to be shared, so that both BBC and ITV covered football World Cups and European

Championships. ITV's one jewel was exclusive rights, from 1991, to the Rugby World Cup.

BBC Wales took a significant step in 1989, in opting out of the later stages of the network's *Grandstand* programme, an institution in British broadcasting, to create its own Saturday afternoon sports programme called *Wales on Saturday*. It was a gamble, since no 'regional' station had previously opted out of the network, but it proved to be a success, and one of the most exciting programmes I ever worked on. I was assigned to present a 30 (sometimes 60) minute programme rounding up the day's sport in Wales. Soon every clubhouse television in Wales was tuned in from five o'clock for our package of results and highlights.

If ever a television programme epitomised the notion of team effort, it was this one. The logistics of getting everything on air, often less than an hour after the final whistle, was little short of a broadcasting miracle. The unsung heroes were the dozen or so reporters, all part-timers with jobs in teaching or other professions, who would attend a rugby or football match with one or two cameras, make notes during the game and then head at breakneck speed back to the BBC Wales HQ in Cardiff. This was winter in Wales, making roads hazardous. Some of our reporters opted to do the job on motor-bikes to ease negotiating busy Saturday afternoon traffic. It was this sort of boldness that made these hardy souls such valuable assets to the organisation.

Once back at BBC Wales HQ, their task was to edit an 80 or 90 minute match into a highlights package of about two minutes. The reporter then had to write a script and voice the highlights for live transmission. Often there wasn't time for the full operation. Handwritten scripts scribbled on a piece of paper would be thrust at me seconds before the highlights went out live, or the reporter himself would dash into the studio to sit alongside me, and read his own hastily-scribbled script to match the action that was going out on screen via a monitor in front of him. It was 'Mad Max TV' but the sheer thrill of getting this programme on air was a fantastic achievement for everyone involved; we broke all the rules, but nothing was going to stop this programme from being an unqualified success.

I have to mention the producer, Cerith Williams, and the director, Rob Finighan, who were both in my ear throughout the broadcast of the programme – the earpiece that presenters wear is not something there for show! It is the link to the director, producer and the rest of the production gallery, who are running the show from another part of the building. It was always a mad scramble, often with just seconds to go before we got on air, and it was almost always an ad-lib, seat-of-the-pants, make-it-up-as-you-go-along programme, but it was live sports broadcasting at its best. For everyone involved, it was a thrill knowing what could be achieved with so few resources and with such a small budget. It was a miracle we got on air, but we did. Looking back, I can say that programme by itself gave Wales a first-class television sports service.

My learning curve in broadcasting took an upward turn when BBC Network in London asked me to work on their flagship rugby union programme, *Rugby Special*, which was broadcast from London on Sunday afternoons. There was no regular Sunday sports programme in Wales, so I headed up to London by train on a Saturday evening, immediately after presenting *Wales on Saturday*. It was the start with London that I was hoping for; voicing English club highlights for a one-hour programme hosted by the former Scotland and British Lions centre, Chris Rea, was a stepping stone to what I hoped would be more work with BBC Network. It was a rewarding feeling to be called up, and the learning curve became steeper when the executive producer for rugby at BBC Network, Johnnie Watherston, told me that I had been selected to be the BBC Network match commentator for the 1989 English County Championship rugby final at Twickenham, between Durham and Cornwall.

It was a huge step forward, and one that I was nervously thrilled to be taking. It meant that a national TV audience, albeit one which had already heard me on highlights packages, would be hearing my rugby commentary. The great Bill McLaren was reserved for internationals, although I did wonder why the former England scrum-half Nigel Starmer-Smith, who'd commentated on other Five Nation games and presented *Rugby Special* for years, was not being used. It wasn't, though, the time to dwell upon selection policy within the BBC Network rugby department. My task was to do the job properly in front of a sell-out and eager crowd at Twickenham. The crowd was incredibly loud, especially the thousands of Cornish supporters who'd made their way to London in hundreds of buses, but their team went down 13-9 to Durham. I felt the commentary went well and the edited match was televised on *Rugby Special* the following day.

In due course, BBC Wales would have its own *Rugby Special Wales* programme, which later became known as *Scrum V.* The two architects for the high quality of this Sunday afternoon rugby programme were Gareth Mainwaring, the producer/director who also directed live rugby internationals for BBC Network, and Siôn Thomas, a creative genius whose talent for making features and programmes was unparalleled by anyone in the UK at that time. Rugby union coverage on BBC Wales television in those days was outstanding.

The early winter months were graced by the presence of Wayne Shelford's mighty New Zealand All Blacks, who won all 14 of their matches on tour, including a 34-9 trouncing of Wales at the beginning of November, but the rugby news in the world of television stole the headlines when it was announced that ITV had won the exclusive contract to broadcast the 1991 Rugby World Cup, to be jointly hosted by England, Scotland, Wales, Ireland and France. It was only the second Rugby World Cup, but BBC noses were put very much out of joint with the news that the grandest showpiece in rugby union would be shown exclusively on commercial television and not on the country's national public broadcaster. The landscape of major sports being broadcast on the BBC platform was changing and this was only the start of the erosion of the BBC's eminent stance in the world of sports broadcasting.

The New Year saw events in South Africa dominating the sporting and political headlines, with police in Johannesburg breaking up a demonstration protesting against the presence of Mike Gatting and his rebel English cricketers and, just a matter of weeks later on February 11th, 1990, after 27 years of in prison – mainly on South Africa's notorious Robben Island, off the shores of Cape Town – Nelson Mandela was released from prison. This historic decision, taken by South African President, F.W. de Klerk, would change the global sporting landscape, bringing to an end the country's sporting isolation and, subsequently, the *apartheid* laws which had so outraged the rest of the world.

A career of almost 12 years with the BBC provided me with just about every sporting assignment I could have hoped to be involved with, and accordingly, every sports broadcasting role. Each year seemed to become busier than the last and it was a wonderfully rewarding time to be involved with sports broadcasting. And there was always a new challenge just around the corner, as I found in 1990 when squash was revived in Wales due to the sponsorship of a south Wales businessman, Gerald Leeke, who ploughed over £2m into the sport by setting up the Leekes Welsh Classic squash tournament, held in Cardiff. It attracted the world's leading players, notably the Pakistanis Jahangir Khan and Jansher Khan. If ever there was a steep learning curve for a broadcaster, professional squash was it. It began with meeting my co-commentator, the great Jonah Barrington, the Cornish-born Irish player who won the British Open – then the *de facto* world championship – six times between 1967 and 1973, and known as 'Mr. Squash'. My squash had been limited to the occasional game with friends as a means of maintaining some level of fitness, rounded off by a few cold beers after the exercise; it was light years behind the level that Jonah had played all his life. But those years of smashing himself around the squash courts of the world had taken its toll and he was a sorry sight walking, or hobbling, with the most pronounced limp. His knees and hips had clearly seen better days. He knew I had been a professional cricketer, because his opening question was along the lines of: "So what does a cricketer know about professional squash?"

I could only reply with something like: "Not a fraction as much as your good self, Jonah, but I am here to host and do the lead commentary, whilst your expertise will be the key to the broadcast. The fact that you are Jonah Barrington gives us such credibility." Clearly, he wasn't overly convinced and I knew that I would have to work extra hard at developing this new relationship. I might have gone a step too far, however, when I popped up with the question: "Fancy a hit one day Jonah?" Despite his obvious discomfort in walking anywhere – he really did look to be in considerable pain –

Jonah Barrington would get onto the court every day and have a hit, with or without an opponent. I would regret asking him that question.

We arranged to play the following morning, hours ahead of the broadcast, so that we would have time to shower, have lunch and get ready for the day's commentary. I was clearly misguided on a couple of counts: firstly, I actually took pity on Jonah because I thought that this crippled former squash player would not last the pace in his obvious state of decrepitude. Secondly, I should not have told anyone that I was going onto the squash court with a former world champion, but I did.

I had made friends with the Australian professional, Chris Robertson, who was then ranked second in the world; 'Robbo' had made Wales his home while playing for the Welsh Wizards squash team in the British National Squash League, a thriving professional squash circuit packed with overseas stars.

When the following morning arrived, I was completely unprepared for two things: firstly, that the viewing balcony above the back wall of the squash court would be full of professional squash players. Secondly, that Jonah Barrington said he wanted 'a proper game'. I wasn't entirely certain what he meant by that remark, but after ten minutes on court at the Welsh Institute of Sport, I had a fair idea. The whole experience to this day is still a blur; all I know is that I was given the harshest possible lesson on how, in my case, *not* to play squash.

There he was, this hunched, crippled figure, barely able to move a yard or so left or right, but occupying the 'T' to such an extent he never moved from it. Meanwhile, I was sent careering around that court like a demented idiot chasing my own shadow. Resembling a well-cooked lobster, I came to a grinding halt and just said, "Enough!" Jonah had made his point, in front of a gallery of squash professionals. I had been marmalised into a quivering heap. It was the most extraordinary exhibition from someone who literally could not move, but whose nous for the sport was in his DNA. It broke the ice, if there had been any in the first place, and the handshake at the end of this physical thrashing signaled a commentary box friendship that made the event memorable.

The talk of the tournament, the world's richest professional squash event at that time, was the rivalry between the two great Pakistani players. Jahangir and Jansher Khan were unrelated, but between them dominated the sport for more than a decade. Jahangir is considered to be the greatest player in the history of squash. He won the World Open six times from 1981 to 1988, the British Open a record ten times in succession from 1982 to 1991 and from 1981 to 1986 was unbeaten in competitive play; during these years, he won 555 matches consecutively, the longest winning streak by any athlete in top-level professional sport.

Jansher began to challenge him in the latter part of 1986 and, after his victory in the semi-finals of the Hong Kong Open, went on to beat Jahangir in their next eight consecutive meetings and capture the 1987 World Open title. Jahangir ended Jansher's winning streak in March 1988, and won 11 of their next 15 meetings, including the 1988 World Open final in Amsterdam. They met a total of 37 times in tournament play, with Jansher just edging the head-to-head wins by 19 to 18. Jansher's record would boast a record eight World Open titles and six British Open titles. You had to feel for the Australian squash players at this time. Chris Dittmar, the supremely gifted left-hander from Queensland was on the receiving end no fewer than five time in the World Open finals, losing four of them to Jansher, and the fifth to Jahangir.

They played in contrasting styles. Jahangir moved with such stealth around the court, crouching like a cat, like a predator in search of his prey. Jansher was very different; standing tall and rarely looking troubled, it looked as if he was casually walking around, patrolling with such economy of energy and effort. The best players in the world were in awe of his ease of movement.

Chris Robertson's quest at the 1990 Leekes Welsh Classic was to achieve what no man had done before – beat both Khans in the same tournament. He beat Jansher, the world no 1, in an astonishing two-hour semi-final, covering every splinter on the court in an engrossing energy-sapping contest. Forty-eight hours later, he had to do it all again in the final against Jahangir. Alas, it didn't happen; the Australian was beaten 15-12, 15-6, 15-10. Jahangir had control for most of the match, but it was brilliant to watch and one of the most enjoyable sports I have been privileged to cover.

Events like that made the nineties some of the most rewarding years of my life. Rugby and cricket filled my diary each year, and I had the privilege of hosting the *BBC Wales Sports Personality of the Year* each year for a decade, awarding winners like 1991 Masters Golf champion Ian Woosnam. As well as bringing together the biggest names in Welsh sport, the event was a broadcasting challenge – staged in front of an audience of around 2,500 at the St David's Hall in Cardiff, a magnificent auditorium – being recorded for broadcasting to the BBC Wales audience an hour later. With a multi-camera operation, numerous sporting guests, interviews and sports demonstrations, it was a complicated show. There was also no autocue, so the entire script had to be learnt, word for word, off by heart. There was simply no room for any error, although the production could have been stopped at any time for a pick-up and a restart. It was a tribute to all who worked on it that not once in ten years did we have to stop for any error and pick it up on a restart. The live audience in the auditorium were treated to a splendid celebration of the sporting year and it was one of the most rewarding experiences of my life with the BBC.

The phone rang one day in early spring of 1994, and I heard a familiar voice from my days in Johannesburg. Mike Demaine was executive producer for cricket with SABC.

"Alan! Mike Demaine here in Johannesburg. Hope you're well. Can you talk now?"

"Mike, good to hear from you and sure, I can talk. What's up?"

"What are you doing this summer in the UK? Will you be home, or are you going to be away at all?"

"Mike, I have some BBC cricket to cover, but not much more than that."

"Great! That's good to hear...how would you like to be involved with us on the South African cricket tour to England and Wales this summer?"

"Involved? I'd give anything to be involved, Mike, what did you have in mind?"

"Well, the SABC is covering the entire tour live and we would like you to host it for us and be part of our commentary team. Would you be able to do it for us?"

I could hardly contain myself. "Mike, I am flabbergasted. I don't know what to say except that 'yes' is the answer. Please count me in!"

I was shaking with sheer anticipation and excitement. To be asked to host the return of the South African cricket team to England after an absence of 29 years was the biggest opportunity of my career to date. It was a three-match Test Series: Lord's, Headingley and The Oval, followed by two ODIs at Edgbaston and Old Trafford. My summer was planned.

The atmosphere inside Lord's for the return of the South African cricket team was incredibly emotional. The buzz of expectation inside the ground was the loudest I had ever heard. Every seat was sold and the television build-up was a truly emotional experience from my perspective. SABC Television was broadcasting from the roof of the pavilion – the modern media centre at the Nursery End had not been built yet – and when the two captains, Mike Atherton and Kepler Wessels, walked out to the middle for the toss, every person in the ground stood and applauded with such vigour that the noise was tangible on the roof of the pavilion. I'll never forget the noise inside Lord's at that moment.

South Africa were convincing winners of a match remembered for Atherton being fined for using dirt in his pocket to dry the ball, but it is the tea interval on the first day that I will never forget. I was told that the on-air guest would be Bishop Desmond Tutu, the first black Archbishop of Cape Town, a social and human rights activist who rose to worldwide fame during the 1980s as an opponent of *apartheid*. He received the Nobel Peace Prize in 1984; the Albert Schweitzer Prize for Humanitarianism in 1986 and the Pacem in Terris Award in 1987.

To this day, I will never forget the manner in which Bishop Tutu greeted me, with both his arms outstretched in front of him and his hands clasped around mine. His eyes looked straight into mine and, at that very moment, I felt the need to say something to him. I couldn't because we were due to go live on air. I thought it was going to be a tough interview, but it went well, due in no small part to the extraordinarily comforting presence of this wonderful man. With minutes to go before the players would walk back on to the field for the final session of play, I wrapped up the interview and he finished by clasping my hands once again, but this time in front of the camera. I felt my voice quivering at that very moment, and only just managed to get some words out with the tea-time score at the end of my 'pay-off' as I handed back to the commentators.

It was then that I had to say something to Bishop Tutu. I blabbered something along the lines that I had played cricket in South Africa during the time of the sporting isolation, and that I felt truly privileged to have met him, but I wanted to say more. I wanted to say sorry to him. But before I could say anything further, he simply put his hands up to my face, closing my eyelids as he did so. Tears were running down my face as Bishop Tutu simply said: "There's no need for you to explain anything, my son, there's no need for words. Bless you." And with that he left, leaving me on my own for a few minutes to compose myself. Whether he blessed me or not, I am not sure, but meeting Bishop Desmond Tutu was a deeply moving personal experience.

The second Test, at Headingley, was drawn following the only Test century of the prodigiously gifted 39-year-old Peter Kirsten's career, and England drew the series after pace bowler Devon Malcolm, fired up after being struck on the helmet by Fanie de Villiers, took 9 for 57, at the time the sixth best figures in Test history, at The Oval.

The South African sporting theme returned when I was sent to South Africa do to a preview documentary for BBC Wales Television ahead of that autumn's Springbok rugby tour. It was one of my most enjoyable assignments: our small team flew to beautiful cities like Cape Town and was able to gauge the largely supportive public response to the cricket tour.

When the Springboks came to Wales, BBC Wales kindly allowed me to assist them with social activities such as such as golf and sight-seeing. They were a delight to host, providing plenty of interviews for our television programmes and playing some wonderful rugby along the way.

They were playing Pontypridd, 12 miles north of Cardiff, when the news came through that Charles Fortune had died in Johannesburg, at the age of 88. Charles had been my mentor and, in spite of our difference in years, my friend. He had guided me in his inimitable way in my early years in radio, and to this day I still adhere to broadcasting advice that he gave me. He was one of the truly great radio sports broadcasters.

My ties with South Africa strengthened as a result of working with the SABC on the South Africa cricket tour to the UK, and I was invited to work for them at the 1995 Rugby World Cup, hosted by South Africa and with the Springboks competing for the first time. I had the pleasure of commentating for the SABC, the host broadcaster, throughout the tournament, but particularly on the quarter-final at Loftus Versfeld in Pretoria between Scotland and New Zealand. The All Blacks ran out comfortable winners, 48-30, with the massive wing Jonah Lomu scoring three tries. It was also the farewell appearance for the Scottish captain, Gavin Hastings. The Rugby World Cup that year gripped the country like no other sporting event had ever done. It gave rise to the term 'The Rainbow Nation' as people across the vast land came together in their support of the Springboks.

I was lead commentator for the semi-final at Kings Park, Durban, one of the most dramatic rugby matches in South Africa's history. Had it not been a World Cup semi-final, it's doubtful the match would have gone ahead. The rain that had been falling for days over KwaZulu-Natal in the lead-up to this historic occasion rendered the pitch virtually unplayable; conditions were atrocious on the waterlogged surface.

In the dying minutes of the match, the Welsh referee, Derek Bevan, disallowed what looked to be a legitimate try scored for France by their number 6, Abdelatif Benazzi, with the French forwards homing in on the Springbok goal line in pursuit of a chip ahead. Had the try been given, with barely two minutes remaining and with the conversion to come, France would have won. But the referee's decision not to award the try was made, and somehow the Springboks held on to win the semi-final 19-15. The Rainbow Nation breathed an enormous sigh of collective relief as the Springboks, led by Francois Pienaar, would play in their first Rugby World Cup final.

The other semi-final saw New Zealand overwhelm England 49-25, with Jonah Lomu scoring four tries, while the Springboks' victory in the final, against New Zealand, was one of the greatest days in South African sporting history, and produced the iconic image of President Nelson Mandela greeting Springbok captain Francois Pienaar, both wearing no 6 Springbok jerseys. The Rainbow Nation was united behind the Springboks, the new Rugby World Cup Champions.

I didn't get to work on that magnificent showpiece, nor did I see the Rugby World Cup final live in Johannesburg because I had to make a hasty departure back to Britain. My next assignment was Wimbledon, which was starting just over a week later. It would be my second Wimbledon Championships after my formal bow there for SABC in 1993. Working on such a variety of top class sport, I was living the dream. So were Pete Sampras, who took his third consecutive men's title, and Steffi Graf who took the ladies' championship for the sixth time.

I was now in my ninth year with the BBC, but clearly, as the last two years with the SABC had shown, there were increasing opportunities to work on international sporting events. The summer of 1996 would prove to be a consequential season for me. While I had worked on domestic cricket for the BBC, I was unlikely to break into their international commentary box since I had not myself played international cricket, and I felt it was time to consider where I stood on the broadcasting podium.

Under legislation demanding that a proportion of BBC outside broadcasts had to be produced by independent companies, BBC Wales' cricket was produced by Merlin Television, which was owned by two former BBC presenters: Peter Walker, the former Glamorgan and England cricketer, and David Parry-Jones, the former BBC Wales rugby presenter. Both were immensely kind to me in my early years, and they had also engaged an outstanding former BBC director called Simon Wheeler, who was now working for the television production company, Trans World International (TWI) – the production arm of International Management Group (IMG) – arguably the biggest television sports production company in the world.

Simon invited me to work on the Indian tour of 1996, led by

Muhammad Azharuddin. This opportunity proved to be the start of a new chapter in my life: India.

However, I was still determined to derive the maximum reward from working for the BBC. How could I not when I had the opportunity of sharing the commentary box with the great Richie Benaud? Just to sit alongside Richie was an education in cricket broadcasting. He was peerless, and so helpful towards me on BBC days when we worked on Nat West Trophy matches. It was not that Richie gave on-the-spot tutorials in the commentary box, but he showed a generosity of spirit towards someone who had never played the level of cricket that he had achieved in his illustrious career and would bring me into commentary with words that made me feel part of the team, and not just an addition to make up the numbers. His welcome in the morning was always the same, in that gentle Australian tone of his: "G'day Al ... how are you?"

He always called me 'Al', I never knew why, but his smile as he welcomed you was one that made you feel at ease immediately. Was I nervous the first time I worked with Richie Benaud? You bet I was. I was working with the greatest cricket commentator of them all, someone I had watched playing cricket, had once chased all over the city of Cardiff for his autograph and never once dreamt I would be working alongside for the BBC.

Whilst I felt my cricket assignments were gaining in credibility, 1997 gave another opportunity to travel when M-Net (now SuperSport) in South Africa asked me to commentate on that year's British and Irish Lions rugby tour, the first since *apartheid* ended and rugby union had gone professional. The Lions won 2-1, following the 1974 Lions, the 1996 All Blacks and the French in 1958 as series winners in South Africa.

Whilst opportunities grew in different parts of the world, the same could not be said at BBC Wales since we had lost the domestic rugby union contact to ITV. The effect on the BBC Wales TV sports department was tangible, and there was certainly a feeling of gloom about the place. To counter the loss of rugby, the head of sport, Arthur Emyr, a former Welsh rugby international winger, devised a new football competition called the FAW Invitation Cup, with prize-money in excess of a million pounds. It was certainly a good idea, but the teams competing were mostly those playing in the national League of Wales. I wasn't exactly enthralled by the prospect and neither, after the first match, was the head of sport.

My heart and my level of interest was not in football, certainly not at this level and I had not done enough homework for this opening match: Barry Town v Bangor City at Barry, a seaside resort about half an hour's drive from Cardiff. The game was a full outside broadcast with live commentary, and I was hosting it from a studio on site. When we arrived a couple of hours before the kick-off there were more security officials than fans, and that didn't change as we approached the kick-off. I had asked our football commentator, Ian Gwyn Hughes, for some information on the players, and any big talking points I should know, which I could put to my two studio guests. One was Bobby Gould, coach of the Wales national football team, the other was the chairman of Bangor City. Ian had told me to discuss the signing of the new striker in the Barry Town team and how poignant it was that the team he had left were the visitors, Bangor City. In other words, a big talking point and enough for there to be a keenly contested game in the very first match of this new tournament.

All was going well with the "Hello and welcome to the inaugural FAW Invitation Cup tournament here on BBC Wales, and tonight it's Barry Town against Bangor City, two famous Welsh clubs, and with me tonight two gentlemen steeped in professional football." I then mentioned the new striker to the chairman of Bangor City.

"He's a fine player, has scored important goals on big occasions, has the right temperament, is a quality player with a great reputation and tonight, he could make all the difference for you?"

"Alan," replied the Bangor City Chairman, "you've covered it perfectly, and everything you have just said is spot on, he's a wonderful player, has all the skills and experience and is the man to watch tonight, except for one big difference ... he's playing for them, not us!"

My smile disappeared into my crimson, blushing face. I hadn't done my homework, and I hadn't listened intently enough to our football commentator. It was a major gaffe, and I knew it. To be fair to my studio guests, they covered nicely for me, and we moved on to other topics of discussion, but when you're the presenter in the hot seat and you make such a glaring error, it sticks with you. The mistake is always with you. It is difficult to blank out of your head, but we got through the match and the post-match studio discussion without any further gaffes.

That was probably the beginning of the end of my association with BBC Wales but, in reality, this was a process that had already started two or three years earlier when I'd started to take on more freelance opportunities internationally. It's called ambition, but that ambition was not readily recognised or accepted by the management in late October. The voice on the telephone from Singapore was anything but Singaporean; it was, in fact, a rich brogue pertinent to a man from County Antrim, a proud Ulsterman:

"Alan, is that Alan Wilkins?" came the question, as if spoken by a policeman.

"Yes, it is," I said, rather hesitantly.

"Good, John Blair here, I am on the rugby committee of the Singapore Cricket Club International Rugby Sevens, and we're looking for a commentator. We've been given your name by a mate of mine from Northern Ireland, Ian Bremner."

Before I had a chance to reply that I knew Ian (he had coached Aberavon RFC) came the voice again.

"I'll be straight with you Alan ... we contacted Bill McLaren, but Bill said he's stopped flying long haul journeys and politely declined our offer. Second choice was John Inverdale, but John told us that although he presented rugby he didn't commentate on it. Third choice was Nigel Starmer-Smith, but we haven't been able to get hold of Starmers, so Alan, how would you like to be our commentator for the SCC International Rugby Club Sevens this year?"

There was a laugh at the end of his patter which made me laugh with him.

"John, how could I not consider your offer? Being fourth is better than not being asked at all, so count me in!"

At this stage of my career with BBC Wales. The football gaffe was symptomatic of what was going on inside my head; a myriad of thoughts but I was bursting with ambition to break into new broadcasting territory. My heart wasn't in this new football tournament and my ambitions lay further afield in distant climes: India.

The fact was, though, by seeking and accepting additional freelance roles I was not breaking any BBC rules; I had not been on contract with the BBC for the past two years and I was perfectly within my rights to work as a freelance broadcaster wherever I chose. Sure, there was the element of loyalty, but this is a process that works both ways and, around that time, I didn't believe that my loyalty was being matched by that of BBC Wales. I had even recommended another person at BBC Wales, a young broadcaster whose main sport was football, to host the new football tournament. Ollie Hides was a radio broadcaster, but I offered to train him in preparation for the development of his career in televised football. It did eventually happen, but not without disgruntled noises from the management.

One of the most memorable days of that summer of 1997 came on September 20th at Taunton, home of Somerset, when Glamorgan beat the home side to win the 1997 County Championship. BBC Wales was on site to cover the match as a live broadcast and, with Glamorgan inching nearer to only the third County Championship title in the club's 109-year history, BBC Network requested regular updates from us at the ground. There was an immense sense of pride in announcing my former county's triumph to a UK-wide audience. Glamorgan's overseas star, the mercurial Pakistani fast bowler, Waqar Younis, ripped through batting line-ups all season, but he was ably supported by home players like Steve Watkin and the off-spinner, Robert Croft. Leading batsmen included the captain Matthew Maynard and Steve James, who both averaged over 60 as well as former captain Hugh Morris.

Soon, another call from the other side of the world had me flying off again for work, this time to Singapore, to commentate on the Singapore Cricket Club International Rugby Club Sevens Tournament in late October. At this stage of my career with BBC Wales, I was not going to turn down any offer of work overseas. My first visit to Singapore would prove to be one of the most memorable and enjoyable experiences of my life, and I vowed to return as soon as possible.

The work at BBC Wales though was still going and next up was a trip to London in late November where the Wales rugby team was playing a 'home' match against the New Zealand All Blacks. The match was staged at Wembley Stadium, as the National Ground in Cardiff was being knocked down to make way for the Millennium Stadium to be built. The crowd of 76,000 saw Wales score a good try by Cardiff wing, Nigel Walker, but the All Blacks ran in five tries to overpower Wales for a comprehensive 42-7 victory, the 13th consecutive win for New Zealand over Wales.

For me, however, I felt I had a point to prove as I knew that certain people had their knives out for me, and that list of people included the then head of sport, Arthur Emyr. The working environment was anything but conducive to broadcasting with any sense of enjoyment, but on that occasion at Wembley, the small team on the *Wales on Saturday* programme pulled off a superb 'live' programme from the old stands of Wembley, which I hosted literally from the edge of my seat. At the end of that programme, I knew how well it had gone and, to be fair to Arthur Emyr, he was the first to say 'well done' but I also knew that he and I were at odds and that he wanted me out of BBC Wales. I couldn't put my finger on it, but you get an intuitive feeling when you know that someone wants you in their team, that they convey a sense of belonging and affiliation. With Arthur Emyr, at around this time, I felt we weren't on the same wavelength, and it almost felt like a power game with him. He always had a good sense of humour, and maybe it was his way of testing me for some reason. Maybe it was because I had been travelling away from Wales to overseas locations but whatever the reason, I knew that my face no longer fitted at BBC Wales in Cardiff. It was a question of when, not if, I would be finishing my broadcasting career with BBC Wales.

Yet at the same time I was working regularly for the BBC in London, on their national radio networks, Radio Five and Radio Two, working on sports bulletins throughout the week. This was a wonderful experience, working on some of the corporation's biggest radio programmes, and I was still working on BBC Network television sport. The problem appeared to be with the management in Cardiff and, as I tried to reason, wasn't it after all the same company? The management at BBC Wales in Cardiff clearly didn't see it that way.

Early 1998 saw me work on one more *BBC Wales Sports Personality of the Year* programme along with numerous meetings to discuss my future with BBC Wales. I had asked a good friend of mine, Alan Davies, the former Wales rugby coach, to represent me in negotiations with BBC Wales, but the negotiations got nowhere. This was nothing to do with Alan's skills as a negotiator, but was down, in my view, to the attitude of the head of sport and other senior managers.

As the rugby and football season was drawing to an end, I was offered the opportunity to travel to Mumbai for a cricket assignment, beginning just days after my last *Wales on Saturday* programme on May 9th. As a freelance broadcaster and, with no BBC Wales assignments scheduled, I accepted the offer and flew out to India, looking forward the challenge in front of me. Whilst walking along Mumbai's Marine Drive, I received a call from the BBC Wales sports department inquiring as to my whereabouts. It was no secret as far as I was concerned. "I'm in India. Mumbai to be precise. What's the problem?" I asked. The stern voice came down the line in reply: "You need to come and see us at the BBC the day you get back."

I had been summoned by the management to discuss my future at BBC Wales and that meeting took place on June 2nd, 1998, the same day I arrived back in Cardiff from India. I walked into Broadcasting House in Llandaff to be ushered into an office on the third floor of the building. There in front of me stood three solemn figures: Arthur Emyr, head of sport; Dai Smith, head of English-language content; and John Geraint, whose title was always a mystery to me, although he certainly had an opinion of me and my work. Not one of them could look me in the eye, which I found rather strange. It was a bizarre meeting because I was not under contract and I had not broken any rules, but this was the final whistle being blown on my period at BBC Wales.

"You have been working away in India, and you have been working in London," said John Geraint with his opening shot. "I actually saw you in Broadcasting House in London last week, so you must have been up there working for the BBC," he continued. I was flabbergasted with the words that came out of his mouth.

"Yes, I have," I replied, "and what is the problem working for the BBC in London? Aren't we all working for the same organisation here?" I put to him. "Yes, I was in London doing a few days of Radio Five and Radio Two, but how could that possibly be a problem?"

"The problem is that we need to know where you are because we have programmes here in Cardiff, and if you are not going to be here, then we need to find someone else," said Geraint with nods of approval from Dai Smith. But still no eye contact with any of them.

I know that I had not missed any programmes because the season had finished and May was always fairly quiet after the long winter season. Dai Smith was not my biggest fan, telling one monthly production meeting that my accent wasn't Welsh enough. I was handed a transcript of the meeting by a colleague, and was aghast to read such a critique of my accent, which had long lost its South African twang. I was Cardiff through and through and a proud Welshman but that wasn't enough according to the head of BBC Wales' English programming.

"Alan," said Dai Smith as he just about managed to catch my eye, "I'll cut straight to the point here. We realise that you have ambitions to work overseas and to broaden your horizons, and we also cannot match your financial expectations to stay permanently in Cardiff working for BBC Wales. Therefore, we feel that it is best that you go the way you have been going in the past couple of years and we will look for a replacement for you in Cardiff."

I agreed entirely with his rationale and, looking back, both sides had valid points. I wanted to spread my wings, but BBC Wales needed someone on a more full-time basis. I just felt that the ambience of the meeting was not right. I knew my days with BBC Wales were over, but then came one final request, which took me completely by surprise.

"But before we say goodbye officially," said Dai Smith, "we'd like to ask if you would help us on one final assignment – the Welsh rugby tour to South Africa – that would be taking place next month. With your connections and knowledge of the country, we would like you to be our host on site in South Africa. Would you do that for us, please?"

I was flabbergasted, but decided right there and then that it would have been churlish of me to refuse, so I agreed to do this final assignment for BBC Wales. The tour worked perfectly for me, since I was paid for visiting one of the great rugby countries of the world, but rather less well for Wales. The 96-13 annihilation by the Springboks in Pretoria remains the heaviest defeat ever suffered by one of the established rugby nations.

And that was it. There were handshakes as I left the room, and words of encouragement for my future in broadcasting, but I was finished with BBC Wales. I left the third floor and went to the sports department on the first floor to tell my friends and colleagues that I was no longer on the books of BBC Wales, but would still be going on a final assignment to South Africa in a few weeks' time. News in Wales travels fast though and, within a couple of hours, I was on the telephone with John Roberts, head of sport at ITV Wales, discussing their offer to join them as their rugby presenter and match commentator. ITV had won the rugby contract from the Welsh Rugby Union, and I would be joining them for the new season that would be starting in September 1998. A big chapter in my life was closing, but new opportunities would come my way.

The BBC years had been a huge part of my life: 11 years in which I was given the opportunity to develop as a broadcaster after my years as a sportsman, and after living in Johannesburg working for the SABC. A return to South Africa was next and after that, it was time to move on. I was nervously excited because almost a dozen years is a long time in broadcasting with one company. I would always cherish those years, and most of the people I met at BBC Wales. I could only feel privileged that BBC Wales had given me a chance to start a broadcasting career in Britain, and most of all, for their support at a very difficult time on my return from South Africa. But now, it was time to look at different landscapes and a new set of challenges ahead.

# 15

## Indian Hat-Trick

*'Almost 400 first-class wickets do not do justice to Alan's talent as a cricketer, but his ability to manage the disappointment of giving up his cricket career is remarkable. Congenial and friendly as he is with everyone, his evolution as a commentator is so impressive. His versatility as an analytical, knowledgeable and observant broadcaster is well known to audiences around the globe who enjoy his eloquent oratory.'*

**Sachin Tendulkar**

The 1996 Indian cricket tour to England would be my debut broadcasting international cricket to an Indian television audience. I had been invited to work on the 1996 Cricket World Cup by the British TV production company, Sunset & Vine, but this had clashed with the BBC's coverage of Five Nations rugby. I met up with the production crew for a couple of the tour warm-up games in mid-May. It was the first time I had met Harsha Bhogle, India's congenial television cricket anchor, and there began a friendship which has stood the test of time. The commentary team included the former Indian Test cricketers Abbas Ali Baig, Kirti Azad, and Atul Wassan, together with the former Somerset captain, Peter Roebuck, Simon Hughes from Middlesex, Harsha Bhogle and myself. The three Test series, won 1-0 by England, was to be remembered for the superb debuts at Lord's by two of the most important Indian players of the last two decades – Sourav Ganguly, who stroked a masterful 131, and Rahul Dravid who fell five runs short of a century – and the last Test umpired by the great 'Dickie' Bird. The Test series was broadcast by ESPN Star Sports and, although Pakistan were also touring England later that summer, because ESPN Star Sports did not have the broadcast rights so my presence in the commentary box was not required.

Learning to cope with the extra demands of commentating on Test cricket was a huge step up for me. Indian commentators delivered more commentary than their English counterparts – I think it was Harsha who explained that fans sitting at home in India would expect to hear more commentary, not less, as would be the case with someone like Richie Benaud. To be invited to work on a Test Series between England and India was one of the most thrilling assignments in my career. Watching (and describing) the greats of Indian cricket at the highest level – Sachin Tendulkar, Rahul Dravid, Sourav Ganguly, Mohammad Azharuddin, Anil Kumble, Javagal Srinath – was extraordinarily rewarding. But, having had a taste, I wanted more.

A telephone call from the offices of TWI in Mumbai during the first week of December 1997, with an invitation to work on the India v Sri Lanka ODI later that month, was the perfect Christmas gift. This was an opportunity I was not going to turn down – a return to India 17 years after playing on Eden Gardens and a chance to see some places I had never heard of. Coming straight out of the mid-winter cold of Britain was no preparation for the first ODI in Guwahati, the sights and sounds were an eye-opener for a pale-skinned Welshman in Assam, in the far north-east of India.

The match at Guwahati was reduced to 45 overs because of the thousands of fans who were trying to get into the ground. Another problem was my stomach, which decided it no longer wanted to be a part of my anatomy. To say that the middle overs were difficult was putting it mildly, but somehow I got through the day and my first international overseas commentary assignment. The commentary team for this three-match ODI series was Ravi Shastri, Sunny Gavaskar, Harsha Bhogle, Sri Lanka's Ranjit Fernando and myself; a very cordial commentary box, held together by the Australian producer, Michael O'Dwyer, better known around the world as 'Mod' and a talented broadcaster on both sides of the camera.

The day after Guwahati was an eye-opener and a first for me – a flight on one of the most enormous aeroplanes I had ever seen! TWI had booked the entire production crew on to a specially chartered Russian plane called an Ilyushin II-76, a massive aircraft that was designed to deliver heavy machinery to remote, poorly served areas, especially during times of war. Between 1979 and 1991, the Soviet Air Force Ilyushin II-76s made almost 15,000 flights into Afghanistan, transporting over 786,000 servicemen and 315,000 tons of freight into the war-torn country. Here, on the eve of Christmas 1997, it would transport a cricket commentary team, a full television production crew, and the trucks and machinery required for an outside broadcast. The destination was Indore for the second ODI that would take place on December 25th, Christmas Day for those of us who would be celebrating it.

I thought this aircraft would never take off! As passengers, we lined up like troops on benches along the side of the fuselage, staring straight into the wheels of the trucks that had been driven into the aircraft. The noise of the four engines powering up to a full crescendo was deafening; everything and everyone inside that monstrous aeroplane shook and rattled until we were airborne. It was no good trying to listen to what the captain was saying, not because of the thunderous noise but because the entire crew was Russian!

The flight from Guwahati to Indore took what seemed to be an eternity, and worse still, my deteriorating stomach developed into an excruciating fever. I was aching all over, and desperately needed to rest and see a doctor. It felt like the journey from hell. I spent the whole of the next day in bed and the doctor gave me medication, not the best preparation for the second ODI, which I was due to host.

Another full house greeted the players and the commentary team in Indore, but the match got off to a problematical start. After just three overs, the pitch was behaving so poorly that the two batsmen at the crease for Sri Lanka – Sanath Jayasuriya and Roshan Mahanama – appealed to the umpires, who then turned to the captains. Arjuna Ranatunga marched out to the middle to discuss the situation with India's captain, Sachin Tendulkar, and after a brief discussion, they agreed that the pitch was dangerous and that the match could not proceed. The ICC Match Referee, Justice Ahmed Ebrahim, from

Zimbabwe, ruled that the match had to be abandoned. That decision had to be conveyed to the thousands of Indian cricket fans packed into the Indore stadium.

By this stage, the fans were getting extremely agitated. I was asked by the executive producer to walk out to somewhere on the outfield to talk to a hand-held camera, and explain to viewers in India and on the world commentary feed that the match had been abandoned. It would have been better had the crowd been advised of this, their frustration and anger vented at me in the form of flying objects as I attempted to explain to a television audience that the match was abandoned. Nor was I feeling much better.

There might have been a real problem had no further cricket taken place that day. To their credit both teams agreed to play a 25 overs-a-side match, with no pace bowling on the dangerous pitch, so that at least the capacity crowd was placated. I hate to think what might have happened otherwise.

Back in the hotel for the evening, the TWI production crew managed to set up a wonderful Christmas dinner for those of us who wished to celebrate. I dragged myself out of bed to attend, and was glad I did so, because the camaraderie in the room was wonderful. Christmas dinner in Indore. A night to remember, after a day to forget.

The production crew and commentators left early the following morning – Boxing Day – for Bombay, and then to Goa for the third and final ODI to be played at the Nehru Stadium, Margao, on December 28th, where Sri Lanka levelled the series.

It would have been ideal to have celebrated the New Year in Goa, but return flights had been booked, and I felt rather sad at having to leave India after my first venture to the country as a broadcaster. On the plane heading back to London there was time to ponder the memories of my first Indian assignment; I knew both that I wanted more and that my BBC days would be coming to an end. But that's essentially the story of life isn't it, where one door closes and another opens? Except we can't predict when those doors come into our lives. For now, though, this felt like an Indian gateway to an adventure I had been craving.

This is the life! New Zealand v India in the first ODI ever played at Queenstown, South Island, on January 4th, 2003, with The Remarkables mountain range providing a breathtaking backdrop.

Pitch report at the Sydney Cricket Ground (SCG) for ESPN Star Sports in the fourth Test between Australia and India, January 2nd–6th, 2004. It was Steve Waugh's farewell Test (his 168th) in the baggy green cap.

The less glamorous side of broadcasting. On the roof of the Durban Hilton with producer, Jim Ribbans. It was as close as we could get to Kingsmead Cricket Ground, Durban, during the 2003 ICC Cricket World Cup. ESPN Star Sports did not have the TV broadcast rights for the event and, without official accreditation, ground access was prohibited so we used the hotel instead!

Cricket is like no other sport for forging friendships. With Graham Gooch and Martin Crowe in Cape Town, New Year, 2007. I never had the privilege of playing against Marty, but years after bowling against Goochie, I still felt the mental bruises.

Explaining a technical aspect about batting to a bemused Rohit Sharma before an IPL match in Mumbai. The handle on Rohit's bat in unusually thin, which is how Graeme Pollock liked his bats. That was the point I was making to Rohit, who clearly showed great patience by listening to me! (photo courtesy of Sportzpics)

I still have to pinch myself that I had the privilege of playing golf with two of my all-time cricketing idols: Sir Gary Sobers and Sir Vivian Richards, at the superb Apes Hill Golf Resort in Barbados, May 2010, in the good company of cricket journalist John Etheridge during the ICC World Twenty20.
Viv hit the golf ball out of sight and Gary was just 3 over for the round!

The 2007 Indian cricket tour to England:
Top Right: Enjoying a post-match chat with Sachin Tendulkar at The Oval.
Left: Thinking of my next questions
Bottom Right: A smiling Anil Kumble at The Oval after he had scored his maiden Test century, 110 not out. India won the three-Test series 1-0.

The morning newspapers were part of 'Wilko's World' each morning of the Test matches in England on the 2007 Indian cricket tour.
Left: Charlie Brougham – our reporter at Lord's – sees the funny side of things.

At The Wanderers, Johannesburg, with Ramiz Raja and Ian Chappell during the inaugural ICC World Twenty20 in September 2007. 'Chappelli' uses fewer words to make his point than Ramiz does, but they are both fantastic cricket pundits, and a joke is never far away from the conversation.

On top of the world on the Sky Tower in Auckland. An amazing feeling hanging on by a rope, but I would never subscribe to a bungee jump. Never!

My broadcasting career has given me the opportunity to catch up with old cricket adversaries and become good friends with stars from many different sports, such as (above) ex-England footballer and ESPN pundit Steve McMahon, Sir Ian Botham and Allan Lamb; (below left) Zaheer Abbas; and (below right) Sir Viv Richards.

Three former international cricketers-turned broadcasters: (L-R) Anjum Chopra (India), Lisa Sthalekar and Melanie Jones (both Australia) in Bristol during the 2017 ICC Women's World Cup.

With Isa Guha, former England cricketer, now television host and commentator. In 2015 Isa, Anjum, Lisa and Melanie became the first female commentators to work on the Indian Premier League (IPL) and they have become an essential part of the broadcasting landscape, all over the crickcting globe, at both men's and women's events.

MS Dhoni always has something to say out in the middle, and more often than not it was about his passion for motor-bikes, but he was briefly lost for words when India won the inaugural ICC World Twenty20 at The Wanderers, Johannesburg, in a dramatic final against Pakistan in 2007. (Top: photo courtesy of Sportzpics)

A history lesson from Ravi Shastri, pointing out the iconic landmarks of Mumbai – the Gateway to India and the Taj Mahal Palace hotel – with Ebony Rainford-Brent, the former England Women's cricketer, as we headed towards Ravi's beautiful home in Alibaug.

In good spirits on a day off from work during the 2013 ICC Women's Cricket World Cup at Ravi's Alibaug home, with (L-R) co-broadcasters, Alison Mitchell, Ebony Rainford-Brent and Melanie Jones.

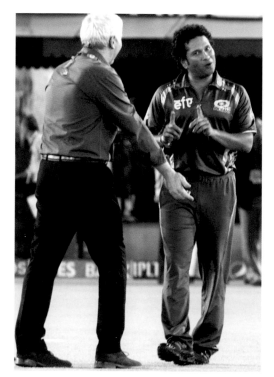

Left: Sachin – a man who always has time for people, I am constantly amazed by Sachin's self-effacing disposition and warm humility, given his constant place in the public eye not just in India, but all over the world. (photo courtesy of Sportzpics)

Right: Wasim – his sense of humour is infectious, he laughs like there's no tomorrow, and he can take the mickey unmercifully! The moment we met in Mumbai in 2000 was the start of a great friendship.

A serious Virat Kohli in a post-match interview in 2014. Virat is a superb thinker on the game, and he gives exceptional answers to questions, always well thought-out and considered, which makes the job so much more rewarding. (photo courtesy of Sportzpics)

In traditional Pakistani shalwar kameez for the final of the inaugural Pakistan Super League Twenty20 in Dubai, March 2016, with (L-R) Bazid Khan (son of Majid), my co-host Zainab Abbas, and commentators Pat Symcox (South Africa), Tom Moody (Australia) and Ramiz Raja (Pakistan).

In conversation with Roger Federer when the Swiss maestro stopped over in Singapore en route to the 2014 Australian Open in Melbourne. One of the most engaging sports personalities I have ever met, it's a privilege to spend time with the greatest tennis player I have ever seen.

Above, left: With Vijay at Flushing Meadows, New York. It was, in fact, the 2001 US Open, not the 2000 tournament, but the sign-writers hadn't been to the studio in time!

Above, right: The Wimbledon fortnight was like sitting in Vijay's front room with guests from the world of tennis popping in at any time of the day to say hello. Everyone knows Vijay!

Right: With Vijay Amritraj at the launch of his own wine label at the Taj London St James Hotel, June 2014.

Hosting the 2012 Australian Open with Vijay from the Star Sports studios in Singapore: Vijay looking clearly unimpressed by my service action.

Two stalwarts of television production at Wimbledon. On my left, TV director Deepak Gupta, and on my right, Phil Betts, the ever-smiling Australian television producer/director. These two gentlemen deserve a medal for their services to the industry, but more so, for putting up with all the nonsense they have had to deal with from Vijay and me. We certainly tested their patience over the years.

Hosting one of the early Vijay Amritraj Foundation (VAF) gala events in Los Angeles, in October 2007, with British film actress, Parminder Nagra: a fun co-host, and the event an unqualified success.

Left: The glamorous side of golf commentary! With Grant Dodd, a former European Tour winner, in our salubrious commentary booth at the Midea China Classic. We spent up to eight hours a day, four days running, doing live commentary from that rusting metal box.

Right: Pre-round practice at the magnificent Augusta National Golf Club the day after the 2012 Masters. A once-in-a-lifetime experience to play a full round on the hallowed turf at Augusta.

Sharing the stage and a joke with Tiger Woods in Delhi, February 2014. Tiger has a fantastic sense of humour. (photo courtesy of Paul Lakatos)

Some golf commentary boxes are better than others. On Sentosa Island for the 2009 Singapore Open with Dominique Boulet, a Hong Kong-born former Asian Tour professional, and Australian, Ian Baker-Finch, who won the 1991 Open Championship at Royal Birkdale.

Walking the fairways of Delhi Golf Club with Tiger Woods in February 2014. He shot a 63, never having seen the course before. (photo courtesy of Paul Lakatos)

On the 16th hole on the spectacular Augusta National Golf Course with Claude Harmon III, son of Butch Harmon, and grandson of Claude Harmon who won The Masters in 1948. I was fortunate to cover The Masters for seven consecutive years from 2007 to 2013, the year that Adam Scott became the first Australian to win the famous green jacket.

Left: Susie and I got married in Cardiff on August 22nd, 2014. It was also my birthday. What a day!

Right: I've done many different jobs in my life, but never thought I would be chauffeur to our wonderful dog Leo!

Left: My parents, Anne and Haydn, to whom I owe so much: a lovely photo taken in the Brecon Beacons, Wales.

Right: Doing a poor impression of Ian Chappell at the SCG before the fourth Test between Australia and India, January 2004.

A Welsh spring was no preparation for the incredible heat of Chandigarh, in the northern Indian state of Punjab: it was May 13th, and the mercury reading was 41 Celsius! An eclectic commentary team assembled for a rather odd-looking tri-series between India, Kenya and Bangladesh, once again having been invited by TWI to work in India: Harsha Bhogle, who was consolidating his place on Indian television as a cricket presenter and commentator, and Sanjay Manjrekar, who had played his final ODI and Test against the South Africans in November 1996. Sanjay was embarking upon a new career in cricket broadcasting and this was his first foray into the world where he is now, of course, a well-known, authoritative voice. The third member of the commentary team was the affable Trevor Quirk, from South Africa, whose puce-red facial complexion indicated that the Indian heat might prove a problem at this time of the year, and I wasn't far behind Quirky in the pink complexion stakes. We were warmly received by I.S. Bindra, president of the Punjab Cricket Association, at the cricket ground that is now named after him. A familiar face that evening was Gordon Greenidge, then coach to the Bangladesh cricket team. I was taken aback by Gordon's conviviality that evening – he talked more in a couple of hours than I had heard him for the best part of seven years in county cricket!

Our mode of transport for the series was, once more, the dreaded Ilyushin Il-76. Conditions at Gwalior for the match between India and Kenya were murderously hot! I had never in my life experienced heat and humidity like it. 48 degrees Celsius was insane, and a thermometer on the pitch gave a reading of 53 degrees! Conducting the toss, or doing the pitch report, was akin to wearing a suit into a sauna; there was no escape from the heat. Clearly, these conditions did not suit India because they lost to Kenya, despite having a batting line-up that featured Navjot Sidhu, Sachin Tendulkar, Mohammad Azharuddin, Rahul Dravid, Robin Singh, Jatin Paranjpe (who was making his debut) and Nayan Mongia. They had their revenge three days later, beating Kenya in the final at Eden Gardens.

It was a wonderful assignment, in spite of the intense heat. I was able to revisit The Oberoi Grand, the marvellous hotel I stayed in back in 1980-81 when I played at Eden Gardens, and I also had the privilege of visiting cities such as Bangalore, Hyderabad, Chandigarh, Chennai and Mumbai.

I will never forget my time in Gwalior, not just the cricket, but a solo adventure up to the very top of the Gwalior Fort in a tuk-tuk that I thought would never make it up the steep roads to the summit of that extraordinary eighth century landmark. Once there, the vista was breathtaking. An indelible experience if ever there was one, and just a pity that no-one in our commentary or production team wanted to come with me; the general consensus was that I was a bit mad to go out in the harsh mid-afternoon sun to do some sightseeing. I probably was but, during my playing days, I used to make a habit of visiting places I'd not seen before. I had no idea when I would be in Gwalior again, so best to make the most of it right there and then. All I knew was that the travel bug was very much in my system, and I would be seeking other assignments in India and other parts of the world. Right now, it was time for a move from the BBC to ITV and more challenges ahead.

# 16

# Wales Welcomes the Rugby World

*'I was fortunate to meet and get to know Alan when he was a sports broadcaster for ITV and I was the Wales rugby coach. Alan is an extremely talented broadcaster – knowledgeable, relaxed and with a good sense of humour – and having been a first-class rugby player himself definitely helped. We had many very enjoyable interviews. He was always great company and I have fond memories of the post-broadcast visits to the local for a friendly chat over a quality New Zealand wine.'*

**Sir Graham Henry**

The Welsh rugby tour of South Africa had come and gone in the summer of 1998, and I returned to Wales to cover more Glamorgan cricket which, ironically, was still being broadcast on BBC Wales. As the summer ended, I signed a two-year contract with ITV Wales to host rugby and commentate whenever that opportunity would arise. The ITV Wales rugby programme was called *The Front Row*, and the chief expert analyst was Nigel Walker, the former Olympic 110 metres hurdler who competed for Great Britain in the 1984 Olympics in Los Angeles. Nigel made the successful transition to a rugby union career after his athletics days and he was probably the fastest winger in the world at the height of his rugby career. He was articulate, a natural broadcaster, and had a sound knowledge of rugby. What helped make our television programmes so enjoyable was the genuine rapport and friendship we struck on and off the screen. What was refreshing about Nigel was the wider perspective he brought to analysis, a product of his years as one of Great Britain's foremost athletes, and it made for good television on ITV. It was the start of a new life away from the BBC but it was tremendously rewarding.

It was around this time that I met Susie, a teacher of textile technology in a leading Welsh school and we began dating on a regular basis; we attended the same health club in Cardiff, which was a decent social club as well. Susie was not a mad sports lover, which suited me in one sense, since for years I had been submerged with virtually every sport that had been thrown at me. Our relationship was easy-going and we got on well. Susie had her job and I had mine, but the landscape would change for both of us. These were happy and settled times even though we were soon to uproot from Wales on an adventure that would take us 7,000 miles to the other side of the world, but with Susie, it felt completely the right move.

A gap in the rugby schedule in early November allowed me to return to Singapore for a second consecutive Singapore Cricket Club International Rugby Sevens. This reinforced my desire to see more of the world and I knew that I would one day want to live in the Far East but, for now, I had a fresh challenge with my new colleagues and paymasters at ITV.

Rugby union was very much my focus, and I enjoyed commentating on a thriller of a game between Wales and Argentina at Llanelli's home ground, Stradey Park, with Wales running out winners 43-30, in what was the first match for Graham Henry as Wales' new head coach. The match had more significance for me because ITV in London had also asked me to commentate on the international at Twickenham between England and Australia.

The support I received from John Roberts, head of sport at ITV Wales, and Bob Symonds, rugby editor and commentator, was so encouraging in those early days with ITV. It felt like a new family, and I couldn't have wished for a warmer welcome; it certainly banished to a distant memory the back-stabbing and derisory comments by a minority in my last years with BBC Wales. I had always believed then, and I still do now, that in life what goes around comes around. Be kind to people whenever you can, even if that sounds a bit altruistic, but in the business of broadcasting, it is not a bad practice. Be kind to people when you know you're going up in the world, because one day, the journey will change direction, and you'll possibly find yourself seeing the same people on your way down.

The next week all the focus was on the England rugby team and their November international against the Wallabies at Twickenham: from my point of view, my biggest day so far with ITV. The evening before the match was spent at the Petersham Hotel in Richmond, where the former England scrum-half, Steve Smith, was in fine form regaling stories of bygone years. He was the expert commentator alongside me and we had one thing in common; we'd both attended Loughborough, albeit at different times. Clive Woodward, the England rugby coach and another former Loughborough student, was also in the dinner party and, all in all, I felt I was in good company.

The following day, England disappointed a full Twickenham by losing 12-11 to Australia with a lacklustre performance; I didn't think I hit too many heady heights either with my commentary, but a couple of days later was asked to do the commentary on the Rugby World Cup qualifier between Scotland and Spain at Murrayfield, in Edinburgh. From a commentary perspective it was a more entertaining match because Scotland, as expected, overwhelmed Spain 85-3 with many tries and flowing movements. It was also good fun working with Scott Hastings, the former Scotland centre and younger brother of Gavin.

Most of all, 1999 was a year of World Cups, first cricket then rugby. I was delighted when the invitation came from the BBC in London to work on the ICC Cricket World Cup in May and June.

My schedule took me all over England, up to Edinburgh for Scotland against Bangladesh, over to Amstelveen in the Netherlands for South Africa against Kenya, back to Chelmsford for one of the great matches of the tournament, when Zimbabwe beat the much-fancied South Africa team, and finally to Northampton, where Bangladesh pulled off the most unlikely victory against Pakistan. In the BBC television commentary team that day were two of cricket's greatest players: Sir Viv Richards and Pakistan's former World Cup winning captain, Imran Khan. Imran was never the most loquacious person at the best of times. Here, as Pakistan began losing both the plot and the match to lowly Bangladesh, his silence was deafening.

His face turned to thunder when yet another Pakistan wicket fell. He decided something had to be done, and when we needed him to be at the front of the commentary box for his next stint of commentary, he was nowhere to be seen. We just caught a glimpse of him clambering over the temporary scaffold where our BBC commentary box had been erected, moving like a cricketing Zorro over the pipes and railings onto the balcony of the Pakistan dressing room. In a flash, he had opened the glass sliding door behind which the Pakistan team was watching the match, and all we heard was a "What the hell...?" in a big booming voice as the door slid shut with a crashing thud behind him.

The commentary box didn't see Imran for at least an hour and a half, by which time Pakistan had all but lost the match. When he did return to the box, it somehow didn't seem appropriate to ask him what on earth was going on. His face said it all. Their loss that day did not affect Pakistan's progress in the tournament because they went on to face Australia in the final at Lord's three weeks later, but none of us in that BBC television commentary box that day will ever forget either the outcome of the match, or Imran's response to the events unfolding in front of us.

While I was not involved in the knockout stages of the ICC Cricket World Cup, compensation came with calls from Singapore to host Wimbledon, and ITV to be part of their 1999 Rugby World Cup commentary team.

With the Cricket World Cup group matches finished, my next assignment was an 11-day trip for ITV Wales, doing a feature on rugby in the Pacific, which involved Samoa and Japan initially, and then flying over to Auckland across the International Dateline to watch the New Zealand All Blacks in training. More than 5,000 fans watched them at the superb North Harbour stadium in Albany, North Shore, Auckland. After an intensive training session, it was amazing to watch the entire All Blacks squad form an orderly queue in order to sign autographs for every fan in the ground. The All Blacks took professional rugby to another level, and watching a training session, followed by an autograph session with fans, illustrated that perfectly.

Next up was hosting Wimbledon for the Singapore-based network ESPN Star Sports. I had met their CEO Rik Dovey some years earlier when I had talks about joining Sky Sports in London. That move never materialised. It is always a subjective issue in the business of broadcasting: management and executive producers either like your face and/or your voice, or they don't. Rarely is there any grey in between. Clearly my face didn't fit with Sky, but I did keep in touch with Rik, and now he had moved on to head the ESPN Star Sports network in Singapore. My life was about to change further by meeting one of India's favourite sons: tennis legend, Vijay Amritraj. It would be my third Wimbledon Championships but the 1999 tournament was my first of 16 with Vijay.

Links with Singapore were strengthening all the time, and I was invited to work there for a month 'to test the water' ahead of a possible permanent appointment.

The month in Singapore started July 29th. A business class flight is a good way to start when a company is trying to entice someone into moving to the other side of the world to work. An outstanding five-star hotel overlooking the Singapore Marina was another way of sweetening the deal. But the most important aspect was the work environment. That would be pivotal in my thinking, and my eventual decision to move to Singapore to live and work. In the five weeks spent 'testing the water' the schedule was a busy one: hosting Tri-nations rugby – Australia, New Zealand, South Africa – a range of programmes featuring cricket from all around the globe, Premier League football from England, and regular bouts of tennis. Singapore's timezone meant I got used to work extending into the early hours and catching a taxi back to the hotel at 4 am after hosting Liverpool v Manchester United. It was all an extraordinarily surreal experience, altogether rewarding in a host of ways and I had seen enough to know that this would have to be a career move. Singapore would happen but before that, though, there was a Rugby World Cup.

A commercial company like ITV does things differently to the BBC. The World Cup welcome weekend in London, for presenters and commentators, took place at a reception in Planet Hollywood, the outfitting in New Bond Street with American clothing company Gant, an evening hosted by ITV executives at the Marriott County Hall followed by lunch the following day. It was difficult not to feel bowled over by the entire experience and this was just the welcome weekend!

The following week I met Rik Dovey in London to agree to my move to Singapore. Although Rik wanted me to start working in Singapore within weeks I made it clear that it could not be before the New Year, given that I was under contract with ITV Wales for another year.

A fortnight later I knocked on the office door of John Roberts, head of sport at ITV Wales. "John, I need to talk to you about something important" was probably not my most convincing opening line, but he came back with a stunner: "You're going to bloody Singapore aren't you?", he said with a smile, both in his tone and on his face.

"Well, I haven't made any specific plans – how can I when I am still under contract with ITV Wales – but that's why I have come to see you today. I want you to consider my request to be released from my contract so that I can start in Singapore in the New Year."

John Roberts was one of the most decent men in television sport and I felt dreadful sitting in his office asking to be released from my two-year contract but, for a host of reasons, from personal to professional, I felt I had to leave Wales and make a fresh start in another part of the world.

"Well, there's no point in me trying to stop you, if you really want to go and live on the other side of the world, but if you can give us a few weeks to sort things out as far as our schedules are concerned, that would be much appreciated." It was a generous attitude on John's part, and one that I will always be grateful for, although he still had to go through the human resources and contracts department to get my request agreed.

"Don't worry, I'll sort this with HR," he said, "but I want you to know that it has been great having you here at ITV working on our rugby and I wish you every bit of luck in Singapore. We've got a Rugby World Cup ahead of us, so let's concentrate on that and we can finalise matters towards the end of the year. How's that? In the meantime, enjoy the World Cup!"

Frankly, I don't know what I would have done had John Roberts not agreed to let me go, but I felt relieved that I'd managed to have the conversation with him. It had been on my mind for weeks. My priority right now was the Rugby World Cup which would be starting in two days' time. I had been given the task by ITV of hosting the opening ceremony from the Millennium Stadium in Cardiff. The full rehearsal was scheduled the following day, with the script due that afternoon so that I'd have time at home to read it, practise my delivery and basically familiarise myself with the theme of the opening ceremony.

The following day at the Millennium Stadium, everyone at ITV Sport working on the 1999 Rugby World Cup was there for the rehearsal: studio presenters, studio pundits (such luminaries as Francois Pienaar, Michael Lynagh, Gareth Edwards, Sean Fitzpatrick, Gavin Hastings) match commentators, reporters, producers, directors, floor managers, heads of audio and camera facilities, executive producer (Rick Waumsley) and the ITV head of sport, Brian Barwick, who had only recently moved over from the same position at the BBC.

The rehearsal for the opening ceremony went off without too many problems. I was positioned in the ITV commentary box in the stadium's second tier on the halfway line, one of the best vantage points in the world for watching international rugby. The rehearsal was a lengthy affair that continued under the floodlights, and we eventually finished at around 8.30pm. Everything felt good and that's what rehearsals are for, of course, to ensure that every person on the job knows his or her role off by heart. There was an air of tangible excitement before the biggest rugby show on earth got underway the following day. What could possibly go wrong?

October 1st, the start of the 1999 Rugby World Cup. The weather was good, the roof of the newly-completed Millennium Stadium was open and the entire stage looked magnificent. A capacity crowd of 74,000 inside the stadium was making an incredibly loud noise with the opening ceremony about to start. I was in position in the commentary box an hour before the scheduled start, and the adrenalin was pumping hard; it was not difficult to get psyched up about this special day welcoming the world to my home city

Cardiff, capital of Wales, and being a small part of a huge television operation.

Over 1,000 Welsh male and female singers had combined in massed choirs on the protected, hallowed turf, as the build-up to the opening ceremony gathered momentum. First on stage, the Welsh rock band, Catatonia, who sang their world hit single *International Velvet*, a raucous song that got the crowds going wildly. Next, the walk-on by two of Wales' greatest singers – Dame Shirley Bassey and Bryn Terfel, the world-famous bass-baritone opera and concert singer. Together they sang the Rugby World Cup anthem *World in Union* in perfect harmony, in a rendition that stirred every emotion in every person in the stadium, including me. It was all very emotionally charged.

Next was the performance by hundreds of young Welsh schoolchildren in a pageant called 'The Birth of the Red Dragon', supported by 20 Royal Marine commandos who abseiled from the stadium's east and west stands. The commandos hoisted the wings of a giant, skeletal red dragon – the icon of Wales – in a ceremony rich in symbolism and drama.

It was during this dramatic part of the opening ceremony that I realised that the words of the stadium announcer were exactly – word for word – the same as the ones assigned to me on my script. Approximately seven seconds after the stadium announcer's words, I was repeating them, *ad nauseum*, to a worldwide television audience in over 200 countries. The audio microphones in the stadium were so sensitive and the tannoy system so loud that every word from the announcer, who happened to be Gerald Davies, one of Welsh rugby's greatest players, and every word from me – the exact same words – was heard crystal clear on every television set around the world.

After so many years with the non-commercial BBC, I was so relieved that we'd now be heading for a commercial break. As we broke away for advertisements, I removed my headphones and said to Brian Barwick, head of ITV Sport, who was sitting next to me: "Can you hear what is happening here? I am repeating every bloody word that Gerald Davies is uttering! We have the same damn script!" Brian responded by patting me on the shoulder with the

216

reassuring words, "Don't worry about it, you're doing a great job, you're sounding great!" But the next bit came as a surprise: "If you feel like ad-libbing, just do what you think is best, you'll be fine!"

To this day, I am not sure what I managed to cobble together for the rest of the opening ceremony. I did try to ad-lib some of it but that, in my opinion, made it worse and I was hearing the words of the announcer so clearly in my headphones. It's at moments like that, when the programme is live and you have little control over what goes out on air, that you either sink or swim. I think I probably sank to a depth I wasn't prepared for, but possibly managed to get my head above water by the end of the ceremony.

It wasn't the finest hour in sports broadcasting, but the tournament was now underway. With the opening ceremony over, I made my way out of the commentary box, the head of ITV Sport congratulated me but, inside, I knew that it had not been a memorable hour on the microphone. Fortunately, the opening match of the tournament was about to start – the hosts, Wales, against Argentina, in what turned out to be a scrappy game, and certainly not a spectacle of rugby. I watched from the comfort of the stand, but couldn't get out of my head what I felt was a botched performance for the opening ceremony.

The following morning I was on a plane for the short flight from Bristol to Dublin to commentate on the second match of the tournament, Ireland against the United States, from the famous Lansdowne Road stadium in Dublin, one of the great cities of the world, and absolutely magical for rugby. The match commentary went well, which made me feel a whole lot better about the day before, but there was no time to dwell on anything. Next day, it was another flight, this time at 7am from Dublin to Manchester for the match between Samoa and Japan at Wrexham Football Club's Racecourse Ground, which was to kick off at 1pm. There was little time for working on team lists with such a schedule, but it was exhilarating to be working on the tournament, and with such a fast turnaround in matches that required live commentary. A couple of football grounds were used for this fourth edition of the Rugby World Cup, and proved a great success because their smaller capacities made for an intimate atmosphere. The Samoa v Japan game was a super advertisement for rugby union, with Samoa running out clear winners by 43 points to 9.

The Pool C matches were all played in France and I was delighted to be given a number of them for commentary, working alongside Scott Hastings – the former Scotland centre – brother of Gavin, and Brendan Mullin, the former Ireland centre. After two matches in Bordeaux, France v Namibia and Fiji against Canada, I had to rush back to Leicester for the Pool B match between Italy and Tonga, a thrilling game which the Tongans won 28-25.

After such a hectic start to the tournament I was glad of a couple of days at home in Cardiff, to catch my breath and prepare for two more matches in France. Fiji had proved to be a real force in this group and it would boil down to the final group match, between France and Fiji, to decide which would go thorough to the quarter-finals. In anticipation I had done a stack of preparation, knowing that I would have Canada v Namibia, followed by the crunch match in Toulouse.

Then, on the Tuesday, came the telephone call from Rick Waumsley, ITV's executive producer. The conversation began in a friendly enough fashion: "Hi Alan, hope you're enjoying the tournament. You've had some really good games and we're enjoying your commentary. Well done!"

"Thanks Rick, that's kind of you to say," was the simplest reply, "I'm so looking forward to doing the big match next Saturday between France and Fiji. I've watched both teams and have covered them training in my time in France, so it should be a hell of a game."

The other attraction about this match between France and Fiji was that it was going to be broadcast live on ITV 1, the flagship channel of the network, not on one of their minor channels (ITV 4) and every sports commentator in the world wants his work to be seen or heard on the main broadcasting network. This was due to be a huge step upwards for me in my career, until the next line from Rick Waumsley: "Well, Alan, there's been a change. You won't now be doing commentary on France against Fiji in Toulouse next Saturday. We've made a late change in the roster." I was stunned.

"What do you mean, Rick, what late change?"

"I'm telling you that you and Scott Hastings will not be doing commentary on France against Fiji next Saturday in Toulouse, but you'll now be making your way back on Friday – after the Canada v Namibia match on Thursday – for Friday evening's match in Dublin between Ireland and Romania. You'll receive travel instructions shortly from our production department."

I couldn't let it go at that. "Well, Rick, what kind of a decision is that? Scott and I have done virtually every match in France in Pool C, and now you're taking the big one away from us, plus the fact that we have prepared for it like no other game, because we've been in France more than anyone else. So, who is going to do the France v Fiji match?"

"We're sending down John Taylor and Steve Smith after they have finished England against Tonga at Twickenham on Friday afternoon. You'll be on your way back to Dublin that day."

John Taylor (former Wales and British Lion) was ITV's number one commentator and Steve Smith (former England and British Lion) was the number one summariser but, in my view, this decision made no sense. Neither man would have seen France or Fiji in the pool matches, and Scott Hastings and I had covered all the games in France.

"Rick, with respect, that is a crazy decision and it doesn't make any kind of logical sense. For what it's worth, I think the decision sucks."

"Well, Alan, you're not paid to make executive decisions and I am," came the terse reply down the telephone, "and it's nothing for you to fall on your sword for so just accept the change in roster and get on with it."

"Don't worry, Rick, I am not going to fall on any sword. I just don't agree with it, but as you say, you make the decisions." The conversation came to an abrupt end, but that was that. It was the decision of the executive producer and Rick Waumsley was correct – he was paid to make the call on the commentary team for whichever match he chose, but it made no sense at all. Scott Hastings felt the same as me.

We did what we had to do. A flight from Bristol to Brussels the following day and from Brussels to Toulouse in the south-west of France for the dead rubber match between Canada and Namibia the day after. What should have been a day relaxing and doing last minute preparations for the big match on Saturday October 16th turned out to be a needless, arduous day of travel. This started badly with ticket problems at Toulouse airport, continued with a delay from Toulouse to Birmingham and then onto Dublin, capped by arriving in Dublin just 90 minutes before the kick-off between Ireland and Romania, and finding that there was no room booked for me at the hotel. I'd had this feeling before in another career! There was no time to do anything but dump my luggage with the hotel concierge, change in the men's toilet, and head to Lansdowne Road to do live commentary on a match which Ireland won comfortably 44-14 against a plucky Romanian team.

The following week I was on the Eurostar to Lille in northern France for the quarter-final play-off between Argentina and Ireland in the Stade Felix Bollaert in the nearby town of Lens, another football stadium. It proved to be one of the most dramatic matches in the World Cup so far, and I was delighted to work alongside two former great Irish players in Brendan Mullin and Hugo MacNeill, but not so delighted for Ireland, who lost the match 28-24.

A couple of days later it was a flight back to Dublin for the quarter-final. The whole of Ireland had expected their team to be there, but the result in Lens meant that France played Argentina, beating them 47-26 in a pulsating encounter which banished some of the demons from my difference of opinion with Rick Waumsley. One score by wing Philippe Bernat-Salles was voted the try of the tournament, not for the accompanying commentary, but because of the classical French flair in running the ball out of their own 22 with beautiful athleticism and individual panache.

France went on to produce one of the greatest shocks in the history of the game when they beat New Zealand 43-31 in the most extraordinary display of uninhibited running rugby ever seen at Twickenham. The All Blacks were stunned. The rugby world was stunned. There would be no Jonah Lomu in the Rugby World Cup final.

In the other semi-final, Australia beat South Africa 27-21, after extra time, to make the 1999 Rugby World Cup final in Cardiff, a showdown between the Wallabies and *Les Bleus*. That was a match – won by Australia 35-12 – I was delighted to commentate on, not for ITV but for the SABC English Radio Service, with my good friend, Gerald de Kock.

It had been the most extraordinarily rewarding year with three momentous sporting events: the Cricket World Cup, Wimbledon and the Rugby World Cup, all within the space of six months. The rest of the year had a rather surreal feel about it as the weeks ticked away not just towards the end of the year, but the end of the century and the millennium. My world was about to change as well. I would be saying goodbye to Britain and embarking on a new life and career on the other side of the world. Asia beckoned and a new position with one of the world's great broadcasting networks, ESPN Star Sports, based in Singapore.

Furthermore, the future was not going to be just about me and my ambitions, but it would now include the aspirations of Susie as well, since we had decided to start a new life together in south-east Asia; something that excited us both immensely.

As the New Year celebrations began all over Wales, Susie and I spent that final evening of 1999 in the company of Lynn Davies, the great Welsh Olympic long jumper, who'd won Olympic Gold in the 1964 Olympic Games in Tokyo. A close friend and a person who always sees the positive, not the negative, Lynn and his wife Meriel were wonderful company and they shared our excitement about leaving Wales for Singapore in early 2000. Never shy about talking about his athletic achievements, Lynn – known in Wales as 'Lynn the Leap' – reckoned that although his leap in Tokyo was special, the one I was about to make to Singapore had just as much significance.

"You may not win a gold medal," Lynn said sagely, "but the experience you're about to have in the Far East is something you can't put a value on. Go and give it your best shot."

With those words ringing in our heads, we said goodbye to 1999 and welcomed the year 2000 into our lives, which were to change in so many ways.

Singapore was next and it was everything I'd hoped it would be, and much more. It was the start of an adventure far removed from our accustomed British way of life, but it helped that Singapore was such an easy place to start a new life. For one thing, virtually everyone speaks English and all the street and road signs are in English, a legacy of Lee Kuan Yew (often referred to as LKW) the country's first Prime Minister, who governed for three decades. He was recognised as the nation's founding father, a visionary leader who oversaw the transformation of Singapore from a stagnant British crown colony with a natural deep harbour, to an Asian Tiger economy as the sovereign city-state transitioned from the third world to first world in a single generation.

It was with palpable sadness when I was in New Zealand for the ICC Cricket World Cup in March 2015, when news came through that Lee Kuan Yew had died of pneumonia at the age of 91. LKY's years in office had touched the lives of everyone in Singapore, locals and expatriates alike, and his funeral was the most extraordinarily emotional day, felt by all of us who had been privileged to live in Singapore.

Although I had only signed a two-year contract with ESPN Star Sports, from February 2000, I knew that Susie and I would be staying in Singapore an indefinite time. Susie soon began work as a lecturer in fashion design and textile technology at LASALLE College of the Arts, and later also at the Nanyang Academy of Fine Arts (NAFA) two of Singapore's leading arts institutions.

In our early years in Singapore our way of life was markedly different from that we were used to in Britain. One example was how our daily travel routine completely changed. Because cars were so outrageously expensive, we used public transport and taxis to get around. For Susie, that meant getting a series of early morning and late evening buses as she went about her business lecturing some of Asia's most aspiring students of fashion. In the constant heat and humidity of Singapore that wasn't always the easiest task, neither were my efforts to flag down a taxi on a rainy day, which was nigh on impossible. Eventually I gave in and bought a car – a classic 25-year-old Mercedes 200E – which looked great but cost me a fortune in repair bills and general upkeep, but even in the confined spaces of

Singapore's road system we did find that having our own transport wasn't just a luxury but an extremely welcome convenience.

The Singapore Cricket Club was central to our social activities in the early years but, even as a former professional cricketer, that wasn't the most straightforward process. The cricket convenor at the time of my arrival was a delightful man called Abu Omar but he was a stickler for procedure and, despite my cricketing CV, he wanted to see me bowl in the nets before he would decide on whether I could join the club.

At one of the first net sessions I was thankful that David Jones, a 1st XI cricketer who hailed from Hong Kong, and his Malaysian wife, Tracy, did their best to persuade Abu that I was a decently experienced cricketer in my time. David also had the incredible knack of being able to name any player in the world with his full set of initials – your ideal man in a pub quiz on cricket!

"Abu," said David, "A. H. Wilkins (with emphasis on the A. H.) is a former county cricketer who opened the bowling for Glamorgan and Gloucestershire. We really don't need to be running the rule over him here on a Wednesday evening at our club nets with youngsters and the lads in attendance."

"No!" replied Abu, "I want to see him bowl before I decide if he can join the club as a full-time member." At this point I thought I should have some input into the conversation. I turned to David and said: "It's alright, thank you for your support, but clearly Abu wants his way as cricket convenor, so I have an idea." I then turned to Abu, who was wearing his cricket kit: "Abu, why don't you put your pads on and go in the net and I'll bowl at you, so you can have a closer look at my bowling and then you can make up your mind quicker?"

Clearly, that wasn't in the convenor's thinking but in fairness he did go into the net – padded up – even if it wasn't for long, as I bowled in such a fashion that his mind was made up fairly hastily. "Right," said Abu, "I'll see you in the bar after practice!" The funny side of my 'trial' wasn't lost on anyone at the nets, certainly not on David and Tracy Jones whose warm hospitality in those early months ensured that Susie and I made friends quickly at the SCC and we became close friends from that moment.

Another friendship kindled at the SCC was with the late Grant Stanley, who coached at the club for many years until his untimely death in October 2017. A giant of a man, in his heyday Grant bowled left-arm pace in many parts of the world including 20 years as a professional in Scotland. In Singapore he bowled left-arm spin and, with hands the size of buckets, he turned the ball miles. I would reminisce for hours with Grant on the veranda of the club, talking cricket and life in general; he was a gentle giant of a man and is sorely missed.

Soon after my arrival, Jim Bovill, the ex-Hampshire cricketer – and a fine frontline bowler in his day – also arrived in Singapore. Younger and quicker than me, Abu made the correct decision to welcome Jim into the club without a 'trial' and it was a pleasure watching him bowl on some of Singapore's flat pitches. Wednesday evening cricket practice sessions were generally well attended; most of the guys had full-time jobs in the city and they popped over to the club straight after work. Susie and Jim's wife, Claire, also teamed-up to run around the Central Business District and the Padang – one of the most famous playing fields in the world – the land shared by the Singapore Cricket Club and the Singapore Recreation Club but ultimately owned by the Singapore Government.

Being an active playing member of the Singapore Cricket Club meant there were always sports tours to famous clubs all over the region but, in October 2002, the SCC embarked upon its first ever cricket tour to India and it proved to be a memorable visit. Memorable initially for the wrong reason, in that when we all met for breakfast on the morning of Sunday, October 13th, at the wonderful Cricket Club of India (CCI) at the Brabourne Stadium in Mumbai, we were all devastated by the news that we had lost eight friends from the rugby section of the SCC, victims of the Bali Bombing the previous evening. The sense of loss was acute, and the feeling of helplessness palpable as we had only just landed in Mumbai the day before for a cricket tour, whilst our friends in Bali had flown to the Indonesian island for the Bali Tens rugby tournament.

The solemnity of that day engulfed us all and it was difficult to think of playing cricket, but our hosts at the CCI and then at the Mumbai Gymkhana where we were due to play our first match went

224

out of their way to help soothe our spirits with their sporting balm. For some reason – and I'm still not sure why they were there – the CCI were also hosting three of the finest cricketers of all time in Sir Viv Richards, Michael Holding and Mike Procter, who were soon involved with our evening entertainment on a swelteringly humid evening in Mumbai.

The match against the CCI at the beautiful Brabourne Stadium was a keenly contested affair with the CCI captained by former Indian Test batsman and 1983 World Cup winner, Sandeep Patil. I relished the challenge of bowling to Sandeep and was deliriously happy when the ball swung late and crashed into Sandeep's front pad, bang in front. We all went up in unison, claiming the LBW, but it was to no avail. The umpire was never going to give Sandeep Patil out in his home city of Mumbai, but he rather placated us when he said quietly and politely: "Not out ... not today!"

I was the envy of our entire touring party when it was discovered which room I had been allocated at the CCI. Initially I had been given a small bedroom across the road from the famous club, but a quick conversation with an official did the trick and I was moved into the outstanding Vinoo Mankad Suite in the CCI main building itself; it was a truly spectacular suite, so palatial that I reckon the whole team could have stayed in it quite comfortably. They didn't but most of them visited during the evening and ensured that the drinks were put on my room bill!

From Mumbai we flew to Delhi for a match at the National Stadium Grounds against the Aviva Insurance XI – the company hosting our tour to India. The company had also ensured that they wouldn't be coming second in this game by including Ajay Jadeja, Sameer Dighe and Venkatesh Prasad, three Indian Test cricketers, in addition to Michael Holding, in their team, but mercifully, the great West Indian fast bowler was there only as a guest. The evening function in Delhi saw us enthralled by the litany of stories from Bishan Singh Bedi who I reckon could easily venture into comedy if he chose.

A five o'clock wake-up call the following morning for our departure to Agra meant that there wasn't too much humour on the team coach for our visit to the Taj Mahal, especially when the bus broke down halfway into the journey, but it was worth it once we got there. The Taj Mahal is a truly magnificent monument. The return journey to Delhi – all six and a half hours of it – was equally monumental.

Our final match was against the Punjab Cricket Association in Mohali and what a joy it was to take the train from Delhi to Chandigarh, another memorable experience in the first-class seats we had booked for the journey. Word must have gone along the wires from Delhi to Mohali after our defeat against the Aviva XI because the team we faced on the beautiful playing surface in the Punjab Cricket Association Ground was decidedly short of talent, and youth. We won the first game in such quick time that we agreed to play them again and duly won that match as well. The feeling amongst the team that evening at the official function was one of contentment after two wins in the day and a good way of signing off the Singapore Cricket Club's inaugural tour to India. The biggest laugh of the evening was provided by an official of the PCA when, during his lengthy official speech, he decided to make specific reference to me.

"We are delighted to have here in the Punjab someone who is well-known in cricket circles across the whole of India as he is on our television doing a fine job with his hosting and his cricket commentary. We are proud and privileged to have this famous man amongst us tonight, someone who played such a high standard of cricket in England, who has played against some of the biggest names in our sport, and to have him here tonight is a very special feeling for all of us, a familiar face on ESPN Star Sports. Ladies and gentlemen, please welcome Alan Wilson!"

The entire group of Singapore Cricket Club players fell to the floor in hysterics. They laughed and cackled and generally had the biggest laugh on me in what was a salutary moment. I was 'Wilson' from thereon for the rest of the night and at the airport check-in the following day in Delhi when the SCC bade farewell to India.

Established in 1852, the Singapore Cricket Club is today a premier sports and social club in Asia, yet it is the second oldest sports club in Singapore, junior by ten years to the Singapore Sporting Club, now the Singapore Turf Club. It stands at the centre of the city's colonial heart, a public space that has witnessed many of Singapore's triumphs and defeats, upheavals, independence and the annual National Day Parades on August 9th.

Nearby historic buildings include Raffles Hotel; St. Andrew's Cathedral; City Hall, on the steps of which the Japanese surrendered to the British in 1945; the Old Supreme Court, now the National Gallery of Singapore; Old Parliament House, now the Arts House; Victoria Theatre and Memorial Hall, and Empress Place Building, formerly government offices and now the Asian Civilisations Museum.

Cricket was played on the Padang as early as 1837, only 18 years after Sir Stamford Raffles founded the settlement of Singapore in 1819, but it was not until 1852 that the first meetings were called to discuss the formal establishment of a cricket club. The roll call of visitors to one of the world's most famous cricket clubs is extraordinary – from Bradman to Border – and during my time at the club it was a pleasure to welcome Waqar Younis, Wasim Akram, Sunny Gavaskar, Sachin Tendulkar, Ravi Shastri, Ian and Greg Chappell, Jeff Thomson, Graham Gooch, Danny Morrison, Dean Jones and Pat Symcox as some of the more regular visitors to Singapore.

As the years went by, though, it became increasingly difficult to maintain any kind of regular playing regime and there were two main factors that led to my decision to hang up my cricket boots for good and hand my bat to a good friend, Ash Raivadera, who I knew would use it better than me. The first was the increase in workload with ESPN Star Sports, and my simultaneous expansion into golf commentary on the Asian Tour for World Sport Group. The second was an increasingly fragile body that was taking longer to recover from playing a day's cricket in the humidity of Singapore, coupled to the after-match replenishment of fluids, the combination of which made the decision to bow out of cricket a straightforward process. The body won over the mind!

There were pros and cons of living in Singapore but how could we not enjoy living in a major metropolis of the world where the streets are sparkling clean and its architectural treasures have been beautifully restored. Where its four main ethnicities – Chinese, Malay, Indian and Eurasian – co-exist in tropical tolerance with a large

227

community of foreigners who live without fear of crime. The feeling of safety in Singapore is tangible, more than any other country I have ever visited.

Singapore's parks – especially the spectacularly luxuriant Botanic Gardens – its museums, art spaces and architectural icons are world class, with many of them breathtaking in their majesty. It was a privilege to be a part of the fabric of Singapore for so many years, being able to live and work in one of the world's most dynamic cities, conveniently located as a superb location from which to cover the Asia-Pacific region with Australia and New Zealand very much on the radar.

In my case, Singapore was the south-east Asian hub for nearly every familiar name in the broadcasting world – BBC, ESPN, Star Sports, Discovery Channel – and at the time of my joining the company, ESPN Star Sports was comfortably the biggest sports broadcasting network in the world.

If there was a downside to our utopian world in Singapore it would have to be the ever-rising cost of living, especially in contrast to the neighbouring countries of Malaysia and Indonesia, and Singapore now ranks as one of the world's most expensive places to live. Housing, alcohol, cars – anything foreign – are all expensive and there's never getting away from the oppressive heat and humidity which, with Singapore's location just two degrees off the Equator, is constant for 365 days of the year. One way of combating the humidity is to visit any of the city's growing number of shopping malls and bask in the ice-cold air conditioning whilst at the same time ponder the endless tide of consumerism which can engulf you if you're not prepared for it – but even that gets tiring after a while. There's only so much shopping you can do but try telling Singaporeans that! All in all, though, it was the most extraordinary experience to live in one of the world's most exciting cities and it was sports broadcasting that took me there.

# 17

# Singapore Fling

*'I have known Alan throughout my broadcasting career. Over the years our friendship has flourished, not only for cricketing reasons but due to his friendly and warm personality. Having the ability to commentate on any sport is a tremendous God-given gift and Alan has become easily one of the most respected voices in international sport. He has the rare gift of making his analysis very exciting yet extremely dignified. Very few have achieved the status and credibility he has and, if you're lucky enough to get to hang out with Alan after a game, he can make you laugh so hard that you cry. Alan has always been in my corner, so if I was given a choice to pick my top 11, he would always be in my team.'*

**Wasim Akram**

Within an hour of touchdown at Changi Airport I was in and out of my hotel and relaxing at what would become my home from home for the next 15 and a half years – the Singapore Cricket Club. Having been a temporary visiting member for three years I made a number of friends and would, in time, become a full paying member but for this first evening – on February 3rd, 2000 – it was time to let people know that I would be staying in Singapore for at least two years, the duration of my initial contract with ESPN Star Sports.

ESPN Star Sports (ESS) was a joint venture formed in 1997 between ESPN Inc (partly owned by the Walt Disney Company, and through ESPN International, which Disney itself directly owned) and News Corporation, two of the world's leading cable and satellite broadcasters. The Pan-Asia ESS network would build up its portfolio to showcase an unparalleled variety of live sports from around the globe 24 hours a day, to a cumulative reach of more than 350 million viewers in Asia. ESPN Star Sports had 19 networks covering 24 countries, each of them designated with local native languages to deliver an outstanding product across Asia-Pacific. Its great advantage was being based in Singapore and able, at a flick of a switch, to broadcast any sports event to its Asian territories and the subcontinent.

ESS's Indian headquarters were in Delhi, and would later move to Gurgaon, but Indian government restriction on satellite uplinking meant that virtually all programming was produced in Singapore. Even when licenses were granted for events like cricket's Champions League, the live transmissions were channeled through Singapore and then back to India.

The working environment in Singapore was extremely friendly, and I had made friends at ESS on my month's visit the previous year. I already knew that Singaporeans worked especially hard and were not afraid of long broadcasting hours that stretched well into the early hours of the following day. In my first year my feet did not touch the ground and that was exactly how I wanted it: to be totally immersed in all manner of sports.

I relished hosting coverage of Six Nations and Tri Nations rugby union and international cricket from all over the world, and compiling the accompanying non-live programmes, but also soon learned to adopt the speak of a 'petrol-head' when assigned to host Formula One Grand Prix, World Super Bikes and Moto GP. My body's metabolic system was then fully challenged by English Premiership and Champions League football, which often started late one night and went through to at least 8am the following morning.

John Dykes and I were the main hosts at ESS in my first year in Singapore and, when the years ended, we were asked to decide which sports we wish to focus on. 'Dykesy' was essentially a football man and I was happy to give up the long, overnight football broadcasting to immerse myself in rugby, cricket, tennis and golf, as well as keeping tabs on the likes of Valentino Rossi, Kenny Roberts and Max

Biaggi on Moto GP, and Michael Schumacher, Mikka Hakkinen, David Coulthard and their fellow racers in Formula One.

The big bonus – mid-year – was the July trip back to Britain to host Wimbledon in the company of the peerless Vijay Amritraj. As well as enjoying every minute working with this extraordinary human being, the trip back to the UK provided me with the opportunity to return home to see family and friends although, within a few months of arriving, Singapore already felt like home. Singapore was an easy place to live and friends encouraged me to take up cricket again so that I could join the Singapore Cricket Club as a playing member.

Those days were tough on the body. On the televised rugby weekends I would get home after Six Nations rugby and have only a couple of hours' sleep before getting up to play a full day's cricket on the Sunday for the SCC. At times the heat and humidity in Singapore were overpowering. I must have been mad to have come out of retirement to play club cricket in Singapore, but I relished the challenge and loved the camaraderie of the Cricket Club.

Rugby union was also very much on my agenda but, towards the end of my years living in Singapore, a number of the rugby broadcasting rights on the network fell away. This was disappointing, particularly for expat rugby fans, but executives had to weigh up the income generated against the cost of the broadcast rights so rugby union fell casualty to rising costs in a part of the world where it would be considered a minority sport.

Cricket strengthened my ties with India, since ESPN Star Sports broadcast the national team's matches outside the country. My involvement became as much a way of life as a professional commitment, bringing me into touch with some remarkable personalities.

My first tour with India was to South Africa in October and November of 2001. Sourav Ganguly's team played a Tri-Series involving Kenya and the home nation, followed by a three-match Test series against Shaun Pollock's South African team. Our commentary team for the tour comprised Sunny Gavaskar, Ravi Shastri, Navjot Singh Sidhu, Geoffrey Boycott, Harsha Bhogle and myself, an eclectic mix of people entrusted with delivering the stories through commentary back to India and other parts of the world.

231

The small print in my contract meant that the company could ask you to do just about anything. I had not realised this would have me working as a part-time chauffeur for the commentary team, driving a big VW Kombi mini-bus with some particularly expensive company assets around various parts of the country. We should have had microphones in the mini-bus, because the stories kept us in raptures for hours on end. Ravi Shastri always sat in the front seat. No-one else (except the driver) had any chance of occupying the front seat, and the other three took their places in this luxury mini-bus as we drove from Bloemfontein to Kimberley, a journey of almost three hours, and from Port Elizabeth to East London, a trip in excess of five hours.

Only one member of our team refused to travel in the mini-bus. You know him: he scored over 8,000 Test runs for England. Geoffrey missed out on some memorable hours as we motored across the vast plains of South Africa and along the eastern seaboard. I learned more about Indian cricket in that mini-bus – in the company of Ravi, Sunny, Harsha and Sidhu – than any book I had read. The stories were gold. Sidhu came into his own telling outrageous yarns, and he was always the first to laugh at his own stories.

The Tri-Series was an altogether strange set of matches. Sourav Ganguly and Sachin Tendulkar twice put on huge first-wicket stands, each scoring a century both times, but India also lost once to Kenya and were undone by South Africa's pace attack in the final at Kingsmead, Durban.

The Test series is remembered for Virender Sehwag announcing himself in Test cricket with a century in the first Test in Bloemfontein, but still more for the furore surrounding match referee, Mike Denness, at the second Test in Port Elizabeth which developed into a row that threatened to rip world cricket apart on racial lines.

Denness, Scottish-born but captain of England in 12 Tests between 1973 and 1975, perceived two serious incidents during the match. The first was what he thought was excessive appealing, orchestrated by Harbhajan Singh, bolstered by several Indian teammates and not dissuaded by Ganguly the captain. The second centred on allegations that Sachin Tendulkar had been found tampering with the seam of the ball, and it was the suggestion that India's favourite son had cheated that caused the furore.

Tendulkar had bowled on the third day of the Test, just four overs of gentle seam-up, but he made the ball swing more than anyone else had managed. Close-up camera shots showed Tendulkar using his thumb and forefinger on the seam of the ball which, in Denness' opinion, was ball tampering. What got lost amid the commotion was that Tendulkar was accused of not informing the umpires that he was cleaning the ball, rather than tampering with it.

On the fourth day, Denness informed the Indian camp that he would be banning Tendulkar for one match, suspended for a year, for his actions and that Ganguly was to be given a similar suspended punishment for not controlling his team and the excessive appealing.

It got worse. Virender Sehwag was to be banned from the third and final Test for claiming a catch off Jacques Kallis that had clearly bounced, and for attempting to intimidate the umpire by charging at him as well as using 'abusive language'. Shiv Sunder Das, wicketkeeper Deep Dasgupta and Harbhajan Singh were also to be handed one-Test bans for excessive appealing. All six were then fined 75 per cent of their match fees. The on-field umpires had cited four players whilst the action against Tendulkar and Ganguly had been instigated by Mike Denness.

Players leaked the news to the travelling Indian media, who immediately accused Denness of racism, and that's when it all spiralled into a nasty row. Ravi Shastri, a mentor to Sachin Tendulkar, was furious with Denness for not answering questions at the post-match press conference.

"If Mike Denness cannot answer any questions, why is he here?" asked Ravi. "We know what he looks like." In Denness' defence, ICC regulations prevented him from discussing the matter, but when the escalating row hit home in India, the BCCI President Jagmohan Dalmiya demanded that Denness be removed from the final Test, where he was once again the nominated ICC match referee.

The threat was that the Test might not take place at all. India pulling its team out would have had significant financial repercussions for the South African Cricket Board (UCBSA). The ICC had to back their own match referee but the two cricket boards were being directed by their respective governments and, on the eve of the match, replaced Mike Denness with the former South African wicketkeeper, Denis Lindsay. Their action was declared unlawful by the ICC chief executive, Malcolm Speed.

The third 'Test' went ahead at Centurion, but was declared 'unofficial' by the ICC and so does not count towards records. This was tough on South Africa's captain, Shaun Pollock, who scored an undefeated century, but admitted that he felt it lacked the feel of a proper international match.

The pity is that it was all so unnecessary. The Indian players were aggrieved that no action was taken against any of the South Africans, but Denness' hands were tied since none had been reported by the umpires.

He would serve as match referee in only two more Tests and three ODIs, and was not reappointed by the ICC the following year. An unfortunate affair all-round.

I drew the short straw for the 2002 Indian tour of the Caribbean, assigned to anchor the entire tour from the ESPN Star Sports studios in Singapore in the company of Navjot Singh Sidhu. The time difference meant a start time of around 8pm with the live cricket broadcast going through the night to the following morning. With a full highlights programme to record after the day's play, Sidhu and I would be leaving the studios at around 9am most days. It was the dreaded night shift which, over seven and a half weeks with someone who told his stories and jokes repeatedly, became a penance. Don't get me wrong, those famous Sidhuisms were very funny the first few times, but most of them had reached their tell-by date not even halfway through the tour.

The Indian cricket tour to England in 2002 is remembered for a tough Test series drawn 1-1, with Rahul Dravid scoring three centuries, including 217 at The Oval. A monumental Indian batting display at Headingley, built on a first-day 68 by opener Sanjay Bangar under fearsomely difficult seaming conditions, India reached 628-8 declared with Tendulkar scoring 193, Dravid 148 and captain Ganguly 128, equalising England's opening win at Lord's.

The next one-day series culminated at Lord's with the match that saw England captain Nasser Hussain gesturing towards critics in the media box after making 115, and his Indian counterpart Sourav Ganguly wildly waving his shirt above his head from the pavilion balcony after India, at one time 146 for 5, chased down 326 to win.

My chauffeuring duties continued that long summer as I had the pleasure of driving the expensive cargo of members of the commentary box around the motorways of England that had become so well known to me as a professional cricketer. The ESPN Star Sports cricket commentary team was one of the most cohesive groups of men you could have wished to work with, hence the outstanding work conducted by the award-winning British film director, Jonathan Finnigan. He filmed a promotional campaign at Trent Bridge called *A Few Good Men* in which Sunny, Ravi, Boycs, Harsha, Wilko and Sherry were the protagonists. The team leader was Huw Bevan, a Welshman, the head of production based in Singapore and an acquaintance from my early BBC days. For some inexplicable reason, Sidhu always called him 'Marshall', and I believe that he was the one person in life for whom Sidhu had utter reverence. Believe it or not, in Huw's presence, Sidhu was almost sheepish. They were happy times.

ESPN Star Sports broke new ground in November and December 2002, broadcasting from Bangladesh for the first time as the host nation played the West Indies. There was no Shastri, Gavaskar, Sidhu or Bhogle for this assignment, but the commentary box comprised the inimitable Tony Cozier, alongside the former West Indies fast bowler, Ian Bishop, former Bangladesh top order batsman, Athar Ali Khan, former Indian opening batsman and good friend, Arun Lal, and myself.

Over the course of three ODIs and two Test matches in Dhaka and Chittagong I had the immense privilege of working with the incomparable Tony Cozier. That voice! It was also my first meeting with John Gloster, the physiotherapist with the Bangladesh team, who went on to work with India. John and his medical bag kept me on my feet for the most part of that tour on my inaugural visit to Bangladesh, as I struggled to cope with the heat and the spicy food. The team physio is one of the most important people in any international team set-up and John Gloster's work with the players of Bangladesh and later, India, deserved medals for service beyond the call of duty. He worked all the hours under the sun, and then those hours long after it had gone down. On a long tour, the physio becomes the man who players visit on a regular basis, for comfort as much as anything else, believing that in his bag of medical supplies there is a tablet or a gel that can cure anything. More pertinently, the personality of John Gloster, and before him – with India – Andrew Leipus, earned not only the utmost respect of the dressing room, but also its support. Unashamedly, I have to add that the commentary box was also a beneficiary of the work performed by these hardy souls.

As the Bangladesh tour ended, India went to New Zealand for a two-match Test series and seven ODIs. It was my first visit to New Zealand, and it is not difficult to see why New Zealanders regard their country with so much pride. It is breathtakingly beautiful. One such place was the venue for the fourth ODI – Queenstown, Central Otago, in the South Island – one of the most stunning landscapes on mother earth. The backdrop to the cricket ground is the Remarkables mountain range, with peaks reaching almost 8,000 feet. India, however, didn't reach any great heights, losing the first ever ODI match held at Queenstown.

It was also my chance to meet and get to know Martin Crowe, New Zealand's greatest ever batsman, and one of the finest thinkers the game has ever had. A conversation with Martin Crowe about anything to do with cricket was pure gold. I valued Martin's company and our friendship, and it was with utmost sadness that he tragically lost his battle to cancer at the tender age of 53 in 2016. He was a truly remarkable man. RIP Martin Crowe.

ESPN Star Sports were outbid by Sony for the television broadcast rights to the 2003 Cricket World Cup in South Africa, but went with plans to broadcast programmes pre-match and post-match from a studio in Cape Town, the idea being to harness the popularity of *A Few Good Men* and keep the momentum going on the ESS networks.

The studio was strategically located on Bloubergstrand Beach, along the shores of Table Bay, 15 Kilometres north of the city of Cape Town. It had a classic view of Table Mountain as the backdrop, which immediately told viewers where we were. The lucky host was usually Harsha Bhogle, although he was suddenly more subdued than usual though when a real-life cheetah was brought into the studio to sit alongside him!

Since we were not TV rights holders we were not accredited for the grounds so my role was to introduce viewers to different parts of South Africa from unconventional locations, such as the roof of the Hilton Hotel in Durban, with Kingsmead Cricket Ground in the background, or from my hotel room in The Wanderers Hotel with The Wanderers cricket ground behind me, or from the slopes of Table Mountain, from where any view is truly spectacular.

The pieces to camera were no problem and for the most part worked according to plan, but there was plenty of trouble with the confounded video satellite phone that we had to use to do live updates. The technology was far from perfect and, in most cases, my live updates on the video satellite phone made me sound like a Dalek: a fictional extraterrestrial race of evil mutants portrayed in the British science fiction television programme *Doctor Who*. During the Cricket World Cup of 2003, it looked like I was auditioning for a role in the series.

April 2003 brought a tri-series whose final, between India and South Africa, was not played due to the monsoon rains that engulfed the Bangabandhu Stadium in Dhaka. It was during the third match of the tournament, between Bangladesh and South Africa, that Sidhu and I got involved in an incident on air.

A graphic appeared on the monitor in front of us, with a list of former Indian cricket captains and I stumbled over the one name – it might have been Maharajkumar of Vizianagram – and after I made another attempt at saying it, stumbled again. I might have got it right third time.

Sitting alongside me, Sidhu interjected and said, on air: "You have never been able to pronounce Indian names properly have you?" Whether Navjot expected me to answer his question, I don't know. I had always prided myself on pronouncing Indian names correctly, but this one did trip me up. It happens. I tried to make light of it, by saying something along the lines of: "Well, Sherry, try this one for size" – as I spelt out the English place name 'B-I-C-E-S-T-E-R' at which point Sherry got a little flustered. The commercial break came at an opportune moment because there was no point in labouring the situation but, as soon as we went to the break, I held my finger on the 'mute' button on the console in front of me and just said quietly to Sherry: "You shouldn't ever do that live on air, Sherry. It's not right to try and trip up a fellow commentator, especially when it is as sensitive as pronouncing Indian players' names."

On hearing that, Sidhu lost it: "F**k off! Don't you talk to me like that." Or words to that effect, but he had forgotten to hold the mute button down on his microphone, so the profanity went out live on air, even though we were in a commercial break. Viewers in India might not have heard it, but viewers in South Africa did because their television network had not gone to a commercial break.

The incident was blown out of all proportion because someone from the Indian media was sitting in the back of our commentary box. Once he'd heard the commotion at the front of the box, he was immediately on the phone making sure that the incident was carried in his Mumbai tabloid newspaper the following day.

I have said it before, and will always say this, about Navjot Singh Sidhu: he is a highly emotional person who immerses himself into his work, whether it is television or politics, with a fierce passion. There is nothing insipid about Sidhu, he is pure emotion. Unfortunately, this was one moment when he forgot to abide by the rules. We patched it up in a couple of days.

My first visit to Australia could hardly have been better; a hard-fought four-match Test series for the Border-Gavaskar Trophy between India and Australia. The series was drawn 1-1 and saw the end of Steve Waugh's 168-Test career, with double hundreds from Ricky Ponting (twice), Sachin Tendulkar and, most significantly, Rahul Dravid's 233 and 72 not out in India's historic four-wicket win in Adelaide.

In the commentary box another career was starting, and Wasim Akram soon became a permanent fixture with ESS cricket. Wasim volunteered to work at ESPN Star Sports HQ in Singapore for three months to learn about the business of sports broadcasting, and impressed everyone in the production team with his appetite to learn about television. Very few former players – let alone, one of the game's all-time greats – would have volunteered to learn about broadcasting the way that Wasim Akram did. He didn't need to, but he wanted to.

Every tour in these years had significance, such as India's first full tour to Bangladesh in 2004 where Sachin Tendulkar equalled Sunny Gavaskar's record of 34 Test centuries, which had stood for years. Describing that moment in live commentary, as Sunny congratulated Sachin on the field of play, was a treasured moment.

The 2007 World Cup prompted my debut in film-making in Bollywood. Harsha and I were invited to Mumbai to shoot for a cricket-themed film called *Hat-Trick*. The success of the film depended on the success of India in the tournament, so when India bowed out after losing group matches to Sri Lanka and Bangladesh it was the end not only of their World Cup, but of a promising future in Bollywood for me. Or possibly not!

For once, I was grateful that ESS did not have the broadcast rights when Pakistan's coach, the former England all-rounder, Bob Woolmer, died during the tournament. Even though I was thousands of miles away from the Caribbean, safe in the sanctuary of Singapore, I sensed a pall of sadness and sorrow over that edition of the Cricket World Cup

That year's tour of England brought Rahul Dravid's team a series victory and me a first opportunity to meet and work with former Australia captain, Ian Chappell, somebody else I had respected as a player who now became a colleague and friend.

A masterful raconteur whose recall of incidents in the game from years gone by is unprecedented, Chappell's presence in the commentary box made the stay in England a more memorable experience, and the motorway trips pure entertainment. Mind you, the swear box was in danger of bursting open within the first few weeks, only to be rescued when Chappell accepted the challenge of using no more swear words at any point in the day or evening. He accepted – and mastered – the challenge. Imagine Ian Chappell as innocence personified. Harsha Bhogle was one of the judges.

The world's cricket landscape changed dramatically with the inaugural ICC World Twenty20 in South Africa in September 2007.

It was also the start of the reign of MS Dhoni as India's captain, which began with a dramatic five-run win over Pakistan in the final in Johannesburg. Twenty20 cricket delivered a prestigious product on the world stage, a forerunner to the Indian Premier League which would begin its multi-million dollar extravaganza the following year.

In March 2009, ESPN Star Sports broadcast the ICC Women's World Cup for the first time. The tournament was held in North Sydney and went a long way in promoting women's cricket globally. In a tournament full of surprises India beat Australia in the third place play-off and, in the final, England, captained by Charlotte Edwards, pulled off a win against Suzie Bates' New Zealand team that saw England crowned World Cup Champions.

The commentary team for the event comprised Wasim Akram, Danny Morrison and myself. We also had the benefit of being accompanied by three of the leading players in the women's game: Belinda Clark, the former Australia captain who was the first female player inducted into the Australian Cricket Hall of Fame in 2014; Mel Jones, former Australia top order batter, and Debbie Hockley, the former New Zealand captain.

In November 2016 Debbie Hockley became the first woman to be elected President of New Zealand Cricket. Melanie – or 'MJ' – has become the leading female voice in the game in both men's and women's cricket and her journey will surely serve as a source of inspiration for more female cricketers to move seamlessly into cricket broadcasting.

Mel Jones, Lisa Sthalekar, Isa Guha (who played for England in that 2009 Women's World Cup final) and India's Anjum Chopra are the first female voices to work on the Indian Premier League. There's no doubt in my mind that their presence has instigated a morale-boosting injection of interest in women's cricket worldwide, certainly in India.

The success of that 2009 World Cup broadcast ensured that interest in women's cricket was given a timely boost, so much so that the viewing figures for the 2013 ICC Women's World Cup held in India – where Australia beat West Indies in the final held at the Brabourne Stadium in Mumbai, confirming Australia as winners of the ICC Women's World Cup for a record sixth time – were appreciably higher.

The 2017 British summer featured two major ICC tournaments: for the men, eight countries competed for the ICC Champions Trophy, culminating in an overwhelming victory for Pakistan over India at The Oval on June 18th. Six days after that stunning win for Pakistan's men, the ICC Women's World Cup got underway at Derby, when India's women announced themselves in the eight-nation tournament with a resounding win over England. Over the next 30 days – using the county grounds at Derby, Bristol, Leicester and Taunton with the final held at Lord's – the 11th edition of the Women's World Cup showcased women's cricket like never before, with all 31 matches televised on the traditional television format and across all digital platforms to a global audience that reached record numbers.

The ICC Women's World Cup final at Lord's between England and India was a sell-out, bursting at the seams with a new profile audience, but it was disappointing to see so many empty seats in the members' pavilion. Those who stayed away missed out on witnessing one of the most thrilling and dramatic Lord's finals in memory. England won the World Cup in the 49th over by just nine runs against a relatively young and inexperienced India side. It was the fourth time that England had won the World Cup, going back to the inaugural tournament in 1973, which was staged two years before the inaugural men's World Cup.

Not just the final, but the entire tournament confirmed the enormous progress that women's cricket has made. It was my third Women's World Cup tournament, and I would be hard-pressed to name a tournament that has given a commentary box so much pleasure. The talented broadcasters: Melanie Jones and Lisa Sthalekar (Australia); Anjum Chopra (India); Charlotte Edwards, Alison Mitchell and Isa Guha (England); and Natalie Germanos (South Africa) combined perfectly. Their unbridled enthusiasm, deep cricket knowledge and impeccable broadcasting was simply outstanding, and it was a real privilege for the three male commentators – Ian Bishop (West Indies), Sanjay Manjrekar (India) and myself – to be able to share the duties with such a respected team during the flagship event in Women's Cricket.

England's Anya Shrubsole won the Player of the Match award in the final for taking 6 for 46, and opening bat, Tammy Beaumont earned the Player of the Tournament award, but without trying to sound too altruistic here, each and every player who appeared in this edition of the Women's World Cup, was worthy of an award.

India's irrepressible bat, Harmanpreet Kaur, smashed the World Cup defending champions, Australia, for the most astonishing score of 171 not out from just 115 deliveries, with 24 fours and seven sixes, in the semi-final defeat of Australia in Derby: an innings which led former England captain, Charlotte Edwards, to proclaim: "That was the best innings I have ever seen. Ever."

The tournament gave a global exposure to superb cricketers and over the next few years we will hear much more about the achievements of England's World Cup stars – Heather Knight (captain), Tammy Beaumont, Sarah Taylor, Natalie Sciver, Anya Shrubsole and Alex Hartley and India's Poonam Raut, Harmanpreet Kaur and 19-year-old Deepti Sharma.

It may well have been the last World Cup for two of India's greatest female ambassadors, their captain, Mithali Raj, the first woman to score the milestone of 6,000 ODI runs, and the evergreen fast-medium bowler, Jhulan Goswami, for whom bowling is a way of life.

South Africa's Lizelle Lee, Laura Wolvaardt, Mignon du Preez, Marizanne Kapp and their captain, Dane van Niekerk were outstanding, as were Sri Lanka's Chamari Athapaththu, who scored the tournament's highest innings of 178 not out against Australia; New Zealand's Suzie Bates, Sophie Devine, Lea Tahuhu and their 16-year-old leggie, Amelia Kerr; The West Indies' Stafanie Taylor, Deandra Dottin, Afy Fletcher and Hayley Matthews.

Australia have the outstanding world number one bat, their captain Meg Lanning, while Ellyse Perry will continue to enhance her all-rounder's reputation. Pakistan will look to their captain, Sana Mir, along with Kainat Imtiaz and Diana Baig to fly the flag proudly for years to come.

The 2017 Women's World Cup broke all manner of records, further confirmation of the impressive strides the game has made and justification of the investment the ICC has made in transforming women's cricket into a much more professionally structured sport. Women's cricket has had an extraordinary journey in recent years, and how apt it was that before the start of play in the final, there was a round of applause for the incomparable Rachael Heyhoe-Flint – who had died six months earlier – the true pioneer of women's cricket whose indefatigable work ensured that women's cricket established itself on cricket's landscape in the first place. Baroness Heyhoe-Flint's portrait hangs in the Long Room at Lord's, where she belongs, and how the great lady of cricket would smile if she knew that the custodians of the game have now acceded that women cricketers will take their place on the honours boards in the Lord's Pavilion alongside the men. No-one worked harder for parity in the women's game than Rachael Heyhoe-Flint. You only had to be at Lord's for the 2017 final to know that women's cricket has truly arrived.

The 2009 ICC World Twenty20 saw Dutch cricket have its greatest day when they beat the home nation, England, at Lord's in the opening match of a tournament eventually won by Pakistan, while England took the women's title.

It was during this tournament that I discerned a change of attitude or policy towards me from ESS, finding myself left off the commentary roster for a number of the 'bigger' games as the tournament built up to the knockout matches. Not shy in asking questions, and knowing that I had been 'here' in my cricketing days, I sought clarity from Huw Bevan, head of production, as to why – in my opinion – I wasn't getting a fair deal on commentary.

Why, I asked, were there large gaps in the roster where I was not included on any decent matches ? It was glaringly obvious that I had been sidelined. We were having a frank discussion at the back of the Lord's commentary box, and I needed some plain-talking on the matter. The answer couldn't have been terser: "Because you're not Indian and you didn't play Test cricket!"

It was a conversation stopper. It wasn't as if I could argue against either point because it was factually correct. I asked him to expand upon the statement he had just made.

"Viewers in India want to hear commentary from former Test cricketers and the big stars. That's the reality of the situation and the position you are in Wilks, I am sorry." Huw Bevan has always been totally straight in giving his views, but right there at the back of the Lord's media box in the middle of the 2009 ICC World Twenty20, it didn't sit so comfortably to know that I was basically regarded as a B-Grade actor in a big film. What had happened to *A Few Good Men*?

Feeling a little aggrieved with my new-found status as a second division cricket commentator, I just tried to take a positive spin on it and vowed to get on with the job. After all, it was only a week before I would be at the All England Club for Wimbledon.

As it happened, I worked on a fantastic game at The Oval where England beat Australia in the women's semi-final, courtesy of a scintillating 76 not out from 53 balls from England's Claire Taylor. It was such an entertaining a game that Mike Selvey, the former England fast bowler, Glamorgan captain, and now cricket correspondent for *The Guardian*, rated it the best of the tournament. England's victory in the Lord's final over New Zealand was one-sided, but the big plus for the women's game was that the semi-finals and the final had been televised and that women's cricket received a significant boost in the process.

England's men may have been humiliated as World T20 hosts but they were winners of the title only 10 months later in the West Indies in a competition played in place of the originally scheduled Champions Trophy. Australia won the women's tournament, but my abiding memory of the trip comes from the golf course and a round with two of my idols – Sir Gary Sobers and Sir Viv Richards – on the magnificent Apes Hill golf course in Barbados. It was the kind of day that boyhood dreams are made of and the golfing day of a lifetime. Sir Viv hit the ball miles – he won the longest drive – would you expect anything less? Sir Gary was near flawless as he dropped no fewer than three or four shots all day. The other player in this sponsors' day four-ball was John Etheridge, cricket correspondent for *The Sun*, who reckoned he had never been so nervous on the golf course. I concurred.

An unexpected second brush with Bollywood came in June when an Indian film company asked ESPN Star Sports to hire a couple of cricket commentators for a film located at Trent Bridge. The film, *Patiala House*, starred Indian actors Akshay Kumar, Anushka Sharma and Rishi Kapoor, and was directed by Nikhil Advani. Sanjay Manjrekar and I were the ESS commentators, and it was a great experience working on set to see someone like Akshay Kumar in action. I have no idea how much the film grossed in India or anywhere else, but can share with you the figure I was paid for my part in the film: nothing. Absolutely nothing. It was a *quid pro quo* arrangement: the film company had the services of Sanjay and myself, and ESPN Star Sports had its logo plastered all over the commentary box walls for those clips. I could see clearly how Bollywood was not going to make me rich, or famous.

Apart from the opening ceremony at the Bangabandhu Stadium Dhaka, and the first match of the tournament, played at Mirpur in Dhaka between Bangladesh and India, I spent the rest of the tournament in Sri Lanka, mainly Colombo, but also at the superb Victoria Golf & Country Club near Pallekele. The down time between cricket days provided perfect opportunities to savour the company of Ian Chappell, Tony Greig, Wasim Akram and Ramiz Raja. Many an evening was spent at the stunning Albatross Lodge, high on the hills overlooking Lake Victoria, with our host Nirmal Ranasinghe and his family warmly welcoming all of us into their home for dinner and drinks. One of the privileges of my work has been to meet some of the greats of the game. I felt I got to know Tony Greig much more in our time spent in Sri Lanka; he was like a walking encyclopedia on cricket, so much so that a three-hour journey with Tony driving from Pallekele to Colombo in the early hours passed so quickly.

Tony Greig was regarded like a god in Sri Lanka: he knew everyone, he had friends in high places, and one day organised for a small group of us to be looked after by the Sri Lankan Air Force. This began with a welcome in the Officers Mess in Colombo by Air Vice Marshall, KVP Jayampathy, followed by a one-hour – very noisy – flight in a SLAF plane to Trincomalee and from there, a bird's eye view in an open SLAF Bell helicopter of the north-east coast of Sri Lanka that had been devastated by the 2004 Tsunami. It was a solemn, but totally meaningful, experience.

It was India's sporting triumph, of course, but my last match was the semi-final in which Sri Lanka edged past New Zealand. I did not see the final, and did not know who had won until the day after because I was *en route* to Augusta for the Masters golf tournament.

The next ICC World Twenty20 enabled me to become more familiar with the beautiful country of Sri Lanka but, more than that, it was the last time I saw Tony Greig. The big man always loved his round of golf on days off followed by a large glass of red wine and a cigar; and so it was at the Victoria Golf & Country Resort, where a handful of former players-turned commentators played golf on September 26th.

Simon Doull, David 'Bumble' Lloyd, Tony Greig and I were joined by Sir Richie Richardson, who was officiating as an ICC match referee. The cricket stories were coming thick and fast, fuelled by good wine and banter and a selection of Tony Greig impressions – virtually everyone in the commentary boxes across the world did impressions of Tony Greig – and then, suddenly, Tony coughed and clutched his ribs, and kept coughing amid calls from the group to throw his cigar away and give himself a chance.

"No, it's not the cigars," said Tony, "I think it's more than that. To be honest, I think I've got the Big 'C'." In that moment we all went quiet, just for a moment, but it was a moment that all of us around that table, sitting under the stars at Victoria Golf Resort, will never forget.

We implored him to go and see a doctor, to get out of Sri Lanka, get home to Sydney, forget the cricket and go and get checked up. "No, mate, I'll see this tournament through," he said, "and then I'll go and see about it again when I get home." He wasn't going to leave a cricket tournament in the middle, no matter how badly he felt.

We would have one more evening to remember, on September 28th, when the Ranasinghe family invited us – Tony Greig, Bumble, Simon Doull, Russel Arnold and our TV director, Gavin Scovell – to their beautiful Albatross Lodge to sample the delights of *al fresco* dining under the stars. None of us knew it at the time but, for some, it would be the last time we would see Tony Greig with a glass of red wine in his hands and the accompanying cigar.

The final match in Pallekele, which saw Lasith Malinga tear through England to take 5-31 to ensure that Sri Lanka would take their place in the semi-finals, was my last commentary gig with Tony Greig.

I was out of Sri Lanka even before the semi-finals and within four days after the final, in which the West Indies beat Sri Lanka, was in Johannesburg for the fourth edition of the ill-fated Champions League Twenty20 (CLT20), a tournament that promised so much, but ultimately failed because of poor TV ratings. ESPN Star Sports had paid the exorbitant sum of US$900 million for the TV rights to broadcast the CLT20 around the world in a ten-year deal that lasted only six years. The 2015 CLT20 was scrapped, and financial settlements agreed. A champions league, with winning teams from around the globe competing to decide the champion T20 team of the world, was a good idea. But, it never caught the imagination of TV audiences and one of the most expensive projects in the history of cricket ended up on the scrapheap.

Ian Chappell phoned me from his home in Sydney on October 20th, while I was working at The Wanderers in Johannesburg on a CLT20 double-header. Chappelli's mood was sombre: "Wilko, the news of Greigy is not good mate. He's got lung cancer and the doctors have given him three months."

It was the news we had all feared, the news that Tony himself had confided in us on that balmy evening in Pallekele just a few weeks earlier. Initially diagnosed with bronchitis in May, the condition lingered and worsened during the ICC World Twenty20 in Sri Lanka. On his return to Sydney, tests showed that he had lung cancer. Typically, he said he would fight it as hard as he could, but tragically, it was one battle he wouldn't win.

Tony Greig died of a heart attack at his home in Sydney on December 29th, at the age of 66.

It would take another book to describe the contribution that Tony Greig made to the game of cricket: first and foremost as a player, then as someone whose involvement with Kerry Packer bettered the game, and the lives of everyone involved in it before his second innings, as a broadcaster who entertained television audiences all around the world. He was a larger-than-life personality and he gave everything to life itself, through the game of cricket or with his family. That I was fortunate to have played against him in my early years as a professional cricketer and, to have spent time in his company in the commentary box, on car journeys, and helicopter flights around Sri Lanka, left my life enriched with a wealth of experiences and comradeship only he could have provided.

The New Year could hardly have begun worse, with the news that Christopher Martin-Jenkins, or 'CMJ' as he was widely known, one of the world's most respected cricket writers and broadcasters had died peacefully at home at the age of 67, another victim of cancer. In Tony Greig and Christopher Martin-Jenkins, the game of cricket had lost two of its most authoritative voices.

On the field, I was invited to work on the four-Test series between Australia and India, but was only available for the last two Tests. I was due to fly to Delhi on March 12th, but Huw Bevan called me into the ESPN Star Sports offices in Singapore with news that took me completely by surprise.

"Wilks" said Huw, "things are changing in this company. I can't disclose everything to you right now, but I am giving you six months' notice on your new contract, and we'll have to renegotiate it once you have returned from India."

Another conversation stopper from my Welsh colleague! I couldn't stay too long because I had a plane to catch, but it was strange given that I had only just signed a new three-year contract. As it transpired, ESS was being disbanded following Rupert Murdoch's News Corp's buyout of ESPN in November 2012. ESS would disappear from Singapore – and the rest of the world – and be rebranded Fox Sports in Singapore. In India, Star Sports and Star Cricket would stay the same but my new contract, which still had to be negotiated, would be with Star India Private Limited, based out of Mumbai. None of us involved at presenter-commentator level in the organisation was privy to the business machinations but it gradually became clear that one of the world's foremost television sports broadcasting networks – and one which had given me some of my best years in broadcasting – would cease to exist. Those years would be difficult to emulate: nigh on impossible, in fact.

The third Test at the Punjab Cricket Association Ground in Mohali was my debut in Test match commentary in India, with the hosts winning again and Shikhar Dhawan's 187 made his debut a good deal more memorable than mine. It was a thoroughly enjoyable experience with a wealth of personalities in the commentary box: Sunny Gavaskar, Ravi Shastri, Laxman Sivaramakrishnan, V.V.S. Laxman and Sanjay Manjrekar providing an Indian point of view; Allan Border and Matthew Hayden ensured that we knew a bit more about the visitors. I guess I would consider myself the neutral voice in that commentary box.

I won't forget March 19th, 2013, a day off in between the third and fourth Tests. It was spent in good company on the fairways of the enchanting Delhi Golf Club, where I hit my first ever hole-in-one, at its 17th hole. It is an extraordinary feeling. It happens, you pick the ball out of the hole, shake hands with your playing partners and move on to the next hole. The feeling of satisfaction doesn't linger long enough, unless, of course, you happen to be playing with three very thirsty Australians: Rodney Marsh – then chairman of selectors for Cricket Australia – Allan Border and Dean Jones. Those three gentlemen ensured that my 'ace' would be celebrated in true Australian style. Put another way, Lodi Gardens restaurant ran out of beer very early that evening.

I had previously been refused permission, in spite of an invitation from the Board of Control for Cricket in India (BCCI), to work on the Indian Premier League, but the hiatus between the disbanding of ESPN Star Sports and any new agreement with Star India allowed me to work on the 2013 tournament. I was captivated by the combination of cricket skills and sheer entertainment on display. It was an eye opener. But the real highlight of that year was to be on commentary when Sachin Tendulkar's innings ended in both his 199th and his 200th – and last – Test matches.

In the first of the two Tests against the West Indies at Eden Gardens, Tendulkar was adjudged LBW by the English umpire, Nigel Llong, but television replays clearly indicated that the ball was going over the top of the stumps. In the second Test at the Wankhede

Stadium, Mumbai, Tendulkar was caught at slip in acrobatic fashion by West Indies captain, Darren Sammy, off the off-spinner, Narsingh Deonarine, for 74. He had batted flawlessly, and a century was looking inevitable.

As a commentator you want to deliver the right words for the moment: once you've said the words live on air, they are in the television archives for all time. I wasn't altogether happy with my description of the final innings of his unparalleled career because it happened almost in slow-motion. Darren Sammy caught the ball behind his back, Tendulkar stood there for a moment, then he turned away from the pitch and began his walk back to the dressing room. He paused, the crowd paused, I paused. The moment had gone. Tendulkar's final visit to the crease, even though none of us in the commentary box knew it: it was only the first innings. The West Indies team wasn't the strongest, and the likelihood was that Tendulkar would not bat again, but in that moment of commentary, those few precious seconds, your mind had to think of the pertinent words instantaneously.

It was as the Indian team was doing a lap of honour after the match had finished that my colleague, Harsha Bhogle, hit the perfect note with his description of all that was unfolding in front of us. Ian Bishop was sitting alongside, but 'Bish' knew exactly what was needed in that 30 minutes or so – he said very little. It was one of Harsha's finest hours; the way he found the right words to use in that highly emotional atmosphere was outstanding. Few could have done it better. It was Sachin Tendulkar's moment, beautifully portrayed by Harsha with a fine piece of commentary that perfectly matched the occasion. That is a skill that cannot be taught. It is something innate.

I spent the 2015 ICC Cricket World Cup in New Zealand, and had no complaints about that. The 'land of the long white cloud' appeals in so many ways and there were many memorable moments to cherish: Ireland's superb win over the West Indies in Nelson, Afghanistan's first ever World Cup win when they beat Scotland in the most dramatic finish in Dunedin, Martin Guptill's onslaught for 237 not out against the West Indies in the quarter-final in Wellington when the Kiwi smashed 237 not out, and the semi-final at Eden Park, Auckland, which proved one of the best matches in the tournament.

It was an extraordinarily tense finish and those of us in the commentary box thought that Ian Smith was going to pass out with a combination of sheer emotion and unbridled passion for the home country. New Zealand just got over the line to take their place in the final. It was a full house at Eden Park which, because it is also one of the great rugby stadiums in the world, makes for an intimate atmosphere for a game of international cricket. It was also a full house in the commentary box, since Star Sports had rostered 11 commentators to work on that semi-final: Ian Smith, Simon Doull, Graeme Smith, Shaun Pollock, Rahul Dravid, Sourav Ganguly, Michael Hussey, Shane Warne, Brendon Julian, Michael Atherton and myself. It was just as well we weren't paid by the word.

It would be the last time that I would see Marty Crowe, who had been inducted into the ICC Hall of Fame during the New Zealand v Australia match at Eden Park on the last day of February. The following day I took a taxi from my Auckland hotel out to Kohimarama Beach to meet Marty and we chatted about anything and everything. He always had the most discerning views on the game and on broadcasting; a finer intellect you would find difficult to match in the cricket fraternity. After a couple of hours, Marty said he was feeling a little tired and felt like having a sleep. We said our goodbyes and it was with a sense of foreboding that I left Marty and his lovely wife, Lorraine, on the lawn outside their home. I decided to walk back to the city centre of Auckland, a journey which took about two hours along the beautiful coastline around Auckland, alone with my thoughts.

November found me commentating on the Cricket All Stars. This was a three-match series played on baseball stadiums in New York, Houston and Los Angeles between teams of greats organised by Sachin Tendulkar and Shane Warne, and was well attended by the significant Indian and Pakistani expat community in the States who flocked to the stadiums to see these icons of the game in the flesh.

The players had an absolute ball in the three matches even if there were some aching bodies at the end. It was a truly exhilarating sight to witness Pakistan's Shoaib Akhtar bowling fast to Australia's

Matthew Hayden, who was wearing a microphone and talking to us in the commentary box as Shoaib was running in. It was grand entertainment even if the likes of Courtney Walsh and Curtly Ambrose were a way off their best and, all in all, it was a great concept and one that I believe will happen again in the future.

Yet another T20 league had been born in February 2016 as the inaugural Pakistan Super League got underway in the UAE. It, and the second edition in 2017, attracted record television audiences in Pakistan, and the decision was made to hold the 2017 PSL final not in Dubai, but Lahore.

The days leading up to the final were full of emotion for everybody in the commentary box. Naturally, Ramiz Raja and Bazid Khan (son of Majid Khan) were thrilled that the PSL final was going to be held in Lahore. So too was my co-host, Zainab Abbas, but the three foreign commentators: Danny Morrison, Melanie Jones and myself, were desperately torn. There had been bomb blasts, including one in one of the city's most secure districts in Lahore in the days leading up to the final. The foreign offices of both Great Britain and Australia advised strongly against travelling to Lahore.

I know that we all endured sleepless nights over making the right decision especially after the British television production company to whom we were contracted pulled out of going to Lahore. Each of us sought advice from as many reliable sources as we could and, in the end, all decided that our families and our personal security took priority. The decision not to travel to Lahore was one of the most difficult I have had to make in my broadcasting career.

I wanted to see Lahore (even though we wouldn't have seen much of the city) and to complete the job professionally. It was the most bizarre feeling, sitting in a hotel in Dubai watching Peshawar Zalmi win the second edition of the PSL at the Gaddafi Stadium in Lahore, knowing that I could have been there. It was a great comfort, however, when thousands of Pakistani cricket fans – who largely understood and were sympathetic to our predicament – engaged me on Twitter. Thank God the PSL final went ahead without any incident. Without wishing to delve further on this incredibly emotive issue, our thoughts were also with the people of Lahore that night.

Twelve months later, in March 2018, I took the decision to travel to Pakistan for the play-offs and tournament final, and to, at last, experience a country I'd heard so much about. The decision also ensured that I finally completed my global cricketing odyssey to every major cricket-playing nation.

In India, 2016 was the year of Virat Kohli. He batted as if his life depended upon it, whether in the IPL or in Tests, subjugating opposition bowlers with masterclasses in the most clinical and effective fashion. With him as captain and leading from the front, life for visiting teams to India proved an almost impossible existence, with the twin spin combination of Ravichandran Ashwin and Ravindra Jadeja compounding the agony. New Zealand and England were swept away in three and four match series respectively. Ashwin broke records with virtually every spell of bowling in 2016, and it was no surprise when he was awarded the Sir Garfield Sobers Trophy for ICC Cricketer of the Year, as well as being voted the ICC Test Cricketer of the Year for his unprecedented achievements.

With MS Dhoni stepping down from captaincy, Team India is now very much under the tutelage of Virat Kohli. The qualities we see now in his guardianship of Team India are similar to those we saw in 2008 when he led India to their ICC Under-19 World Cup triumph in Malaysia. Kohli was born to lead. His brand of cricket and his approach to how the game should be played is a style that is rewriting the game in India.

In the blink of an eye the baton has been carefully passed on from the most wonderful hands to ever hold a cricket bat, in Sachin Tendulkar, through to one of the safest pair of hands in MS Dhoni, and into the most exciting pair of hands in the modern game in Virat Kohli.

What a privilege it has been to be witness the line of transition through Indian cricket, and to be able to describe it through commentary on television and radio. It has been the best seat in the house, and I count myself blessed to have been given the opportunity to occupy one of those seats in the commentary box.

# 18

# Vijay

*'In an age when some like to sensationalise just to attract attention, Alan is someone who does not seek controversy or the limelight. He says what he sees and that is what endears him to the players. I do not recall him trying to be cheeky or intrusive and his knowledge of sport and commitment to his chosen profession is so profound that he simply does not need to indulge in short-cuts. He has been a sportsperson himself, and he allies his familiarity with the pressures and pulls of sport with his professionalism. His love for sport is reflected in his commentary and that in turn has made him very popular with the sports-loving masses, who see themselves in him.'*

**Virat Kohli**

I will never forget walking into the All England Club on the morning of July 21st, 1999, for my first day of tennis with ESPN Star Sports. I had been told about my co-host, the legendary Indian tennis player, Vijay Amritraj, but I wasn't quite prepared for our first meeting. For a start, he is a giant of a man and his voice filled the room. I had been told that Vijay was in the media restaurant underneath the broadcast centre at the All England Club, and so I made my way down there; it was 8am, and the broadcast centre was humming with people.

The producer, George Greene, took me down to meet Vijay and there he was, sitting with a group of tennis luminaries – I can't remember them all but I do recall seeing John McEnroe, Peter Fleming, Darren Cahill, John Lloyd, Virginia Wade and a hundred other faces, all of whom had tennis coursing through their veins.

When Vijay stood up from his coffee and his breakfast raspberry muffin for us to be formally introduced, I suddenly felt slightly out of my depth and a little awkward in the presence of such tennis aficionados. But Vijay was so warm and welcoming, introducing me to the people around him at the coffee table.

I had swotted up on as much tennis as I could, at least familiarising myself with current players, but when I was given the task of scripting a formal introduction to open the Wimbledon Championships live on air, my mind suddenly went as blank as the sheet of paper in front of me. The programme opener had to be a formally-scripted collection of sentences, with the words matching the pictures on the screen. Then, as it was the first day of the 1999 Championships, there were the seeded players to talk about, and who were favourites for the men's and the women's events.

I had hoped that Vijay would help me through this process, but it became abundantly clear at the very start of our wonderful working and personal relationship that he had more important matters to attend to. No sooner had he said: "Alan, lovely to meet you, welcome to Wimbledon and let's have some fun," he was off talking to another group of people in another part of the restaurant. The laughter and hugs with other former players-turned commentators carried on as if it was a college reunion. I could see and hear how immensely popular Vijay was. He had time for everyone, his welcome was warm with everyone, his smile genuine, his presence – even in the company of friends he had played with and against for decades – was simply awe-inspiring.

But right there and then, I needed help with the scripting on the opening segment to the first ever programme I would be hosting for ESPN Star Sports. I was a bag of nerves. Vijay had left me at the coffee table to get on with the day's first task, and I needed guidance. It came from the former British number one Andrew Castle, one of Vijay's group of friends that I had just been introduced to. He was also working on his notes for the day.

"Are you okay," Andrew quietly asked from across the table, "can I help you with anything?" He must have noticed the beads of nervous perspiration running down my forehead, but if ever there was a friend ready to help it was Andrew Castle right there and then.

255

"Andrew, I need a line or two on the seeds in the men's and women's events, so if you have a couple of minutes, I'd be eternally grateful."

"Sure," he said, "let's have a look." They were like words from heaven as he guided me through the seeding in the men's event – top seed, Pete Sampras – from Pat Rafter, Yevgeny Kafelnikov, Andre Agassi, Richard Krajicek, Tim Henman down to the number 16 seed; and in the women's event, the top seed – Martina Hingis – from Steffi Graf, Lindsay Davenport, Monica Seles, Jana Novotna, Venus Williams at six, down to Anna Kournikova who had entered the seedings when Serena Williams (seeded ten) withdrew due to flu and a high fever. I am forever in Andrew Castle's debt for that breakfast session.

Although I was only hosting (commentary would come in later years), I found the first couple of days bewildering, but thoroughly enjoyed the adrenalin-filled hours of introducing tennis matches from the manicured courts of the All England Club during those, my first championships when Lindsay Davenport won the ladies' title, and Pete Sampras won the sixth of his seven men's titles.

Some things must have gone right during that Wimbledon fortnight because it was after this tournament that Rik Dovey, CEO of ESPN Star Sports changed my life with the blunt question "Do you want to come to Singapore to work?"

As we know, I said "Yes", but at that the moment I was savouring the fortnight I'd just spent in the company of Vijay Amritraj, with whom I had struck an immediate friendship that has transcended normal working relationships. He is an extraordinary human being, in whose presence you feel privileged. In life, you meet people from different backgrounds, from different parts of the world and, metaphorically, from another world, yet I have not met anyone in my life like Vijay Amritraj and for that reason alone, I feel blessed. I know that other people feel the same way: he is universally loved by his peers in the world of tennis, and it is no surprise to me that to a company like Rolex, for whom Vijay is an ambassador, he is held in the highest regard. Very few former and current sports stars stand above Vijay Amritraj in the world of Rolex, whose *'His stature in India – think Himalayas'* promotional tagline for the former Indian number one is so apt. It's been a pure joy to work, and share memories, with him.

My first ever visit to the city of New York, for the 2001 US Open Tennis at Flushing Meadows, was a fateful assignment and one I'll never forget. Venus Williams had beaten her sister Serena in the women's final, and Australia's Lleyton Hewitt had taken down Pete Sampras, in the men's final on September 10th. The following day we were checking out of our hotel – on East 48th Street, Lexington Avenue, midtown Manhattan – when the second of two airline passenger jets hit the Twin Towers of the World Trade Center. The hotel manager had already told us that: "there appears to be a problem at the Twin Towers...we understand that a light aircraft has hit them...but we are waiting for clarification," but already there was a commotion in the lobby. Television screens were now showing the Twin Towers with plumes of smoke billowing into the blue sky.

Suddenly, the true horror was unfolding in front of our eyes and it was only just past nine o'clock in the morning. Within minutes, the hotel informed us that JFK Airport had been closed down and that no flights were being allowed to leave the city of New York in the foreseeable future. We were advised to hold on to our rooms which we did for the next five days as America was put on a full security lockdown. Our hotel managed to stay open as East 48th was the last street not evacuated for security purposes. The next five days were the most surreal experience, with a total blockage of all mobile phone communications in and out of the city of New York, except that it *was* so real.

Our small, mostly Singaporean, group eventually got permission to travel to JFK Airport where we boarded an ANA jet to Tokyo, for a connecting flight back to Singapore. The events of that week will remain with me always.

The return to New York in late August 2002 proved to be one of the most emotional sports events I have ever attended. The men's final on the last Sunday will forever be etched into my mind. How on earth the two great Americans, Pete Sampras (seeded 17) and Andre Agassi (seeded six) managed to even hit a ball in that emotionally-drenched Arthur Ashe Tennis Stadium, I'll never know. The giant United States flag that had once adorned the World Trade Center was somehow salvaged and brought to the stadium, to be walked onto the court by a brigade of New York firefighters who had survived 9-11. A flock of white doves was then released into the darkness above the stadium and the American national anthem was played. Tears flowed. Words were impossible. Neither Vijay, nor I, could speak. Neither of us wanted to. The picture on the television screen said it all. The most poignant picture of all.

On to 2003, and the beginning of the era of Roger Federer's dominance of the sport he has commanded with elegance, style and panache. How do you begin to describe an era in men's tennis that has been graced by Roger Federer, Novak Djokovic, Rafael Nadal and Andy Murray all at the same time? How do you begin to describe an era in women's tennis that has been dominated by two sisters, Venus and Serena Williams, who have arguably given sport *the* most compelling story of all time?

Vijay Amritraj argues that no other sport comes close to providing the drama that we see on Wimbledon's Centre Court, in Flushing Meadows' Arthur Ashe Stadium, on the Philippe Chatrier Court at Roland Garros and on the Rod Laver Arena in Melbourne. When you watch a final between two of the finest tennis athletes of all time, it is difficult to disagree with him.

The building of a retractable roof to cover the entire centre court at Wimbledon not only ensured that tennis would always be played whatever the weather in London, but it has changed the way that we broadcast the event.

Before the roof, when there were rain breaks – and in London there are many of those – there was always time to indulge in some studio discussion, banter and viewers' questions. Many of these sessions were sponsored, such as 'Rolex Vijay on the Spot' and they were some of the most enjoyable sessions of the day, because we both felt that it was a way of interacting with our viewers. Vijay has the most fantastic sense of humour (he once had his own comedy show on American television) and at times it was almost impossible to keep a line of conversation going with his witty one-liners.

On other wet days, Vijay, because he knows everyone in the tennis world, and they know him, would be able to bring a special guest into our All England Club studio – it could be Boris Becker, Jimmy

Connors, Martina Navratilova, or even Roger Federer himself – and it was a treat for all of us to welcome such luminaries into our studio. Our Wimbledon television director, Phil Betts, had the unenviable task of trying to keep to timings on these sessions, a job easier said than done when Vijay is on a roll.

It was a tremendous disappointment when Star Sports India decided not to have the tennis studio on site at the All England Club for the 2015 Wimbledon Championships. Vijay and I hosted the 2015 Championships from the studios in Mumbai and trying to recreate the atmosphere with a studio set came nowhere near the real thing. Although we had Vijay's son, Prakash, on site reporting for us at the All England Club, and he did an outstanding job, not actually being there ourselves took away the real feel of the Wimbledon Championships. I would like to think that, as with the retractable roof, the door could be opened again after it's been closed, and it would be a welcome return for the studio to be returned to the All England Club.

I would consider myself extremely fortunate to have had one of the best seats in the house at Wimbledon and at the US Open in New York, and to have worked alongside one of the greatest personalities in tennis in Vijay Amritraj. Of course, we didn't please everyone with our programmes or with our commentaries, but in this business, you have to have a thick skin and adhere to the old adage that 'you can't please all of the people all of the time.'

In recent times, new tennis broadcast opportunities have appeared on the sporting landscape, especially in India: There's the International Premier Tennis League (IPTL), owned and run by Mahesh Bhupathi, who has done well to bring the world's greatest tennis players to India, Singapore, Dubai, Manila and Tokyo.

Players such as Roger Federer, Rafael Nadal, Novak Djokovic, Andy Murray and Serena Williams have to work out how much tennis they can accommodate in their full calendars, but this is one event where the fun factor is a part of the deal.

Similarly, the Champions Tennis League (CTL) – owned and operated by Vijay Amritraj – is a pan-India team tennis tournament held across at least six Indian cities: Mumbai, Hyderabad, Delhi, Pune, Bangalore and Chandigarh. The concept of this competition is different in the sense that tennis legends play alongside international ATP and WTA players and a selection of Indian tennis players. There is also special provision to include a top-ranked junior Indian boy or girl, with the idea being to spread the gospel of tennis across the country with the aim of finding new talent.

There have been some great names in Indian tennis: Anand and Vijay Amritraj, Mahesh Bhupathi and Leander Paes, and flying the flag now are Rohan Bopanna and Sania Mirza. Watching the best tennis players in the world on television is one way of appealing to a wider audience. I hope that tennis in India manages to fight its corner against the raft of other sports in the crowded market-place or we'll be in danger of saying prematurely 'Game, Set & Match' to a wonderful sport.

In recent years, we have seen the longevity of tennis players extend far beyond players of past eras. The thirty-somethings are playing as well as they did when they were twenty-somethings. The Williams sisters are simply phenomenal in all that they have achieved, and who knows when Serena will call it a day ? No-one could have seen the 2017 Australian Open finalists being four of the oldest competitors in the sport – the Williamses, Federer and Nadal.

Who is the greatest male tennis player of all time? How does one decide between the likes of Roger Federer, Rod Laver, Pete Sampras, Bjorn Borg, Jimmy Connors, Novak Djokovic, Rafael Nadal, Boris Becker, Roy Emerson: it's the kind of debate that makes for compelling television programmes. From a personal point of view, to have watched Roger Federer win his 20 Grand Slam singles titles is an experience difficult to express adequately in words. Is Roger Federer the greatest of all time? Will Rafael Nadal – now with 16 Grand Slam singles titles – catch him? The Spaniard is six years younger and has time on his side. Let's serve that one up for a tennis debate for the future. For heaven's sake, RF is still playing at an age when former champions had all retired! He is defying the aging process. Clearly he knows something the rest of the sporting world doesn't. Let's not change a thing. A sporting world without Roger Federer wouldn't quite be the same. Not in my book.

# 19

# Never a Good Walk Spoiled

*'Alan has an amazing command of the English language, with a passionate ability to tell the story of the moment and, when we work together, his professionalism helps to improve my broadcasting skills.'*

**Ian Baker-Finch**

He was just 19 years of age, thin as a pencil and, in the wet and windy conditions of an autumnal day in Wales, he was blown off his game to the extent that he didn't win a single point for the United States team in their 1995 Walker Cup match against the Great Britain & Ireland team. This was the 35th edition of the biennial transatlantic contest for leading amateurs, played on the superb Royal Porthcawl Golf Course in south Wales, but only the fourth time that the American team had failed to win. I was commentating for BBC Wales television and it was the first time we had seen Tiger Woods although, naturally, we had heard about his incredible amateur record.

Part of golf's appeal is the spectacular landscape of many courses. For a broadcaster, golf often provides working environments where you don't mind spending long hours on the job because the 'office' for four days can be a beautiful location. Top of the list in that respect is The Hills Golf Club in Queenstown, or Millbrook, on the South Island, which play host to the New Zealand Open golf tournament. Set over 500 acres of land across a glacial valley, the golf course highlights the dramatic elevation changes and rocky schist outcrops that are a feature of the area, and is surely one of the world's most spectacular settings for a golf course. It might take an entire day to get to New Zealand, but once you get to Queenstown, there are no complaints. If God has a garden, this is it. For four days of the year, I am one of the lucky people to work there for Sky NZ Television.

Back to Wales, and I had the honour of being invited by the Matthews family to be the inaugural captain for two years at the Celtic Manor Golf Resort in Wales. A local man and a highly successful entrepreneur, Sir Terry Matthews, had bought the old Lydia Beynon Nursing Home – where he himself had been born – on the outskirts of Newport and set about creating a landmark sports facility with golf taking centre stage.

Welsh golfer Ian Woosnam, the 1991 Masters Champion, was consulted over the design and he, with Sir Terry – and the American golf course designer, Robert Trent Jones Snr. – were the architects of the complex which boasts three of the finest golf courses in Wales. The international seal of approval for the Celtic Manor was its selection to host the 2010 Ryder Cup on the purpose-built '2010' course designed by Ross McMurray which produced one of the most dramatic Ryder Cup matches in history when the European team won by a point.

Having enjoyed the experience of broadcasting the South African Sunshine Tour when I lived in Johannesburg, I was naturally keen to get going with golf again when I moved to Singapore. Thankfully – since most golf tournaments were broadcast live on the ESPN Star Sports networks – the opportunity of working on Asian Tour golf quickly came along and for the best part of 12 years I worked across south-east Asia: Singapore, Malaysia, Indonesia, Philippines, Vietnam, Thailand and Brunei on the Asian pro-golf tour including frequent visits to the People's Republic of China, Hong Kong, India and South Korea: my passport was always on the move.

In the early years, most of this work was carried out with former tour professional, Dom Boulet, a Hong Kong-born golfer who found out that talking about golf was perhaps easier than playing it for a living. He picked up the profession of broadcasting with ease, and his knowledge of the game is excellent. I find that professional golfers and tennis players are scholars of their sport, and possibly know more of its history than professional cricketers do of theirs.

Unfortunately, my golf broadcasting took a hit when the Asian Tour decided not to renew its contract with ESS for the 2010 season. Since I was contracted to ESS, it was difficult to work for rival channels and although I believe an arrangement could have been reached, there was too much emotion involved and it was energy-sapping. So, in my later years in Singapore, I worked on tournaments for the newly-formed OneAsia tour, a rival to the Asian Tour.

The two camps couldn't have been more polarised, and golf in Asia suffered because of the intense rivalry between the two golf tours. I felt like a ball on the bagatelle board, so heaven knows how the professional golfers felt. The Asian Tour declared that no member of its tour could play on the OneAsia Tour. That's when the lawyers got involved, and it became unpleasant. For the OneAsia events I worked with Grant Dodd, an Australian ex-pro – a former winner on the European Tour – who again showed great aptitude for the job of commentary and hosting and, knows the history of the sport as well as anyone. He is a great guy with a different commentary approach to Dom Boulet, but each had their own style. Being the amateur golfer, it was my job to elicit as much from the professionals as I could. That is the job of the so-called 'lead' commentator, with the former professional adding their expertise on the technical aspects of golf and adding colour to embellish the story unfolding out on the course.

Ask any golfer where they would most like to watch, broadcast or even play and you'll get one answer – The Masters on the Augusta National golf course, host to the first of each year's four major tournaments. I don't think I have ever been more excited about a sporting event as I was for my first ever visit to Augusta for the 2007 Masters Tournament and, after 31 hours' flying time from Singapore, I don't think I have ever been colder at a sporting event, one of the coldest in the tournament's history.

The first time you see the course is an almost surreal moment, because all the years of watching The Masters on television do not prepare you for the sheer size of the real estate and the steepness of the elevations. It is a vast course, the pine trees are the tallest I have ever seen, the sand in the bunkers is whiter than any I have seen, and the colour of the flowers around the golf course is a spectacularly vivid Technicolor. The entire vista is strikingly breathtaking, so beautifully manicured and so aesthetic in every aspect, and here I was, working there. It wasn't just the once either, I was fortunate to visit Augusta for seven consecutive years from 2007 to 2013.

I am not sure of the price tag on a round there, because you play by invitation only, but the club does have a media day for selected individuals the day after the final round of The Masters. I was fortunate to have my name drawn following Bubba Watson's win in 2012. It was truly a lifetime experience.

I have often been asked which sport I prefer to work on, and it is always a difficult question to answer because, quite simply, I have derived so much pleasure from working on many sports across the board. I have enjoyed the variety of working on golf, cricket, tennis and rugby as, for one thing, it has helped me keep fresh, and the more I work on one sport, the more I want to know more about it, its history, the participants and how the sport has developed. I read more golf biographies than most sports, because I think it is only through a book that a great star of the game is able to divulge his secrets, if he has any.

I once had the real privilege of walking an entire golf course as an on-field reporter in 2010 at an event in Thailand to celebrate the King of Thailand's 60th year on the throne. The huge draw was Tiger Woods, returning to his mother's country of birth. Tiger was in good fettle, very relaxed and most forthcoming with his time and his words during the entire day. He might well have been less talkative at a major championship, but he realised that he was playing in Thailand in front of huge galleries and a big television audience. In this respect, Tiger was smart, and he was an absolute joy to talk to.

In more recent years, I count myself fortunate to have worked on events such as the 2013 World Cup of Golf at Royal Melbourne, having been invited to be part of the US PGA's world feed commentary team alongside Ian Baker-Finch, the 1991 Open Champion, and the 2015 Presidents Cup at the Jack Nicklaus Golf Club Korea, in Incheon, South Korea. Working with different commentators and with different production people is a real bonus, because the profession of broadcasting is an ongoing learning process. I have always felt that with each day at work on whatever sport, it is a learning process.

That was certainly the case at the 2016 Olympic Games in Rio de Janeiro, when golf returned to the Olympics after an absence of 108 years. Men's and women's individual strokeplay tournaments were played on the course at Barra da Tijuca, just outside Rio de Janeiro. Working 'on site' for the first time – I had hosted and commentated on the 2012 London Olympics and the 2015 Vancouver Winter Olympics from the ESS studios in Singapore – for the Olympic Broadcasting Services, the world feed commentary that went all over the world was a wonderful experience. There were three commentators, but what we lacked was a former golf professional, preferably a well-known golfing celebrity, who would have given the technical information that only a professional can provide. It is a highly technical sport with hundreds of nuances and component parts of the golf swing, and needs the expertise of the former professional. All you can do is to try your best on each given day, on whichever sport it is, and give the commentary, or the hosting, your best shot. You will not please everyone watching or listening. That we know only too well. Feedback, which used to come mainly from your executive producer or from a head of sport, now comes more immediately from modern social media platforms such as Twitter or Facebook.

Twitter can be an unpleasant place, full of vitriol, but I prefer to see the positive side of it. In golfing parlance, we would all love to hit the ball long and straight, chip to two feet and sink the putt, but it doesn't happen like that. Golf gets in your head probably more than most sports because that little white ball is not moving the way you want it to, and that's when a myriad of thoughts come into play. It's when it's easy to be negative about yourself, and your golf swing. It's when your confidence dips, and that's when your game can fall apart. Reading the trolls on Twitter is not an exercise I would recommend, and the more sensitive you are, the more the trolls can hurt. My advice to anyone starting off in this business is to listen to experienced people in the profession, but do not take heed of the vile comments that can come your way on public platforms. Give them a wide berth. There's enough to think about in the job itself.

Getting away from the sport is something I would also recommend. A long walk maybe.

When the sun is shining there's no better place than a golf course. It's you and nature and a little white ball. There's no point in worrying about which direction that ball is going to go once you've hit it, so the best way of coping with disappointment is to adopt an attitude of *Que Sera, Sera*, 'what-will-be-will-be'. Sure, we can practise our golf swing, we can go into the gym and build up our strength and endurance, we can work on our mobility, and we can think positive thoughts. A hundred components come together in the execution of a decent golf swing , which is why I love the game and its affinity with the natural landscape. For me, it's never a good walk spoiled.

# 20

# Stumps

'As a cricketer and then a broadcaster Alan has brought joy to millions of sports fans around the world. His is the modern voice of cricket and his passion for all things sport is inspiring and uplifting. It has been my privilege and great honour to call him friend.'

**Kumar Sangakkara**

Everything in life needs perspective, no matter what each of us has achieved, what career path we have chosen or what direction we've decided to travel. I have often heard the adage that 'life is not a rehearsal' and while I have not always adhered to that maxim, I certainly believe that life is short and that we should make the most of it every day the sun comes up in the morning because, for some, the sun does not come up the next morning.

I want to reflect on a journey that has taken me from a junior school in south Wales to parts of the globe that, early in life, I only experienced by collecting their nation's stamps. They were distant places 'on the other side of the world', but because I played cricket from an early age I managed to get a ride on the vehicle that eventually took me to places I'd always dreamt about. That vehicle was sport and although the ride hasn't always been the smoothest, I count myself fortunate that I was a passenger for long stretches along the way.

In my wildest dreams, I could never have envisaged a broadcasting career that would have coincided with the careers of three of the most iconic athletes of all time – Sachin Tendulkar, Tiger Woods and

Roger Federer – and that during my journey our paths would cross numerous times. Who said dreams didn't come true?

I owe so much to my parents, Anne and Haydn, for ensuring that if I didn't always take wickets or score runs, at least I looked like a cricketer and I was lucky enough to be given a perfect start to my sporting life. My mother ensured that my cricket kit was pristine for every match I played for my school. My father ensured that if I couldn't get to a cricket ground by bus or by train, he would take time off work to get me there. They both gave me unconditional love and support for me to play my sport – cricket and rugby in my early days – and they both shared my triumphs and my disappointments. Words can never express how much I owe my parents for my journey.

Pursuing a course of excellence, whether that be academic or sporting, lends itself to acts of selfishness along the journey. The very nature of striving to be better than the next person, as inculcated by my years at Loughborough, meant that personal sacrifices were made in the pursuit of goals and ambitions. There have been many personal disappointments and, if I had my time again, I would love to do things differently on many personal fronts. But everything is easier in hindsight. Each of us knows how much better we might have done on a personal or a working front.

What would I have changed? Well, I might have worked harder to bowl a bit quicker, to swing the ball a bit more, to bat with a bit more responsibility, to train harder than I did, but the fact is that I didn't. At the start of this book I said that I considered myself fortunate to have played cricket with and against the game's greatest players in the halcyon years of the sport, when seismic changes were taking place. In the years that I was lucky enough to be playing professional cricket in England, the Australian business tycoon, Kerry Packer, was changing the game at its very foundations. Menial cricketers like myself were all involved in the professional ranks whilst the likes of Tony Greig, Ian Chappell and Richie Benaud were in collaboration with Kerry Packer in a movement that transformed the game beyond recognition.

The razzmatazz of the modern game of Twenty20 cricket, which has spawned a new generation of cricketer and follower of the sport, was borne from the Packer revolution and his vision that cricket had to entertain both the television viewer and the paying spectator. Modern crickcters who are earning millions of dollars in the IPL and in other T20 leagues around the world owe their biggest debt of gratitude to Packer, Greig, Benaud and Chappell.

Television commentators like myself also owe the biggest debt of gratitude to those four innovators. We wouldn't be doing our job now had the game not undergone its tectonic transformation in the 1970s. I never met Kerry Packer, but I played against Tony Greig and had the pleasure of working alongside him and, the peerless Richie Benaud, and still have the pleasure of working with the imperturbable Ian Chappell: knowing him as a true friend. All four were visionaries of a sport whose popularity would not be what it is today had it not been for their actions.

As we head towards the end of 2017, the game of cricket is witnessing exponential growth and momentous changes. As Twenty20 cricket spreads its tentacles across the globe, there are calls for Test cricket to reduce its format to four days instead of five. The Caribbean Premier League (CPL) is seeking to expand its reach from the islands of the Caribbean towards the mainland of North America with a new T20 franchise based in Toronto or New York, whilst the latest member of the global T20 family is the South Africa Global T20, designed to occupy the last two months of the calendar year. Pakistan has just welcomed a World XI to Lahore in a bid to bring back international cricket to the country and in 2020 the UK will launch its new T20 franchise-based tournament that will change the way that cricket has existed for over 100 years amongst the traditional counties. Change is taking place at an astonishing pace and the ride – exciting as it looks – could prove to be a bumpy one.

My sporting journey was interrupted by a shoulder injury when I felt I was at my peak as a bowler. Some would argue that I never reached a peak, but I did have my moments in the sun and I can proudly say that I was given the opportunity to grace some of the most beautiful cricket grounds in the world as a player. Whilst, at the time of my injury despondency filled my world, looking back I have to say that it was the shoulder injury that turned my life in another direction, and gave me a start in a new career. Although I didn't know it at the time, 'no shoulder, no cry' became my mantra in life.

Some may surmise that over my time as a sportsman and as a broadcaster I have been a cantankerous so-and-so, baulking at authority along the way, but I have always been one to stand my ground when I believed in my actions, and I would rather have an animated discussion with a colleague or an adversary than keep feelings of resentment bottled up for a rainy day.

The South Africa issue was a vexing one for me. I wanted to go and see the country for myself and form my own opinions, rather than accept the views of others who had clearly had the opportunity to form theirs. For a few years in my life, the South Africa issue was a tortuous affair, but I have no regrets about having made the journey to visit and live in one of the most beautiful countries on the planet. I was fortunate to have been given that opportunity.

The journey is far from over. Having lived in Asia for the best part of 16 years, spending countless hours at 38,000 feet traversing the sporting globe, and having spent so much time in India, I still feel the urge to see parts of the world I have not been able to visit.

It's more than wishing to have more stamps in my passport, it is about meeting people in all walks of life and helping them along their journey. Life works in circles, and the journey we chose to take will one day bring us back to a place close to where it started, not so much physically, but more on a psychological footing when we know we have achieved certain goals and aspirations. It is a journey that never ends. We never stop learning. Our journey simply overlaps with those of others. We see signposts along the way and sometimes we go blindly past them, but eventually we reach destinations we strive to attain. Thank you for allowing me to share my journey with you. Good luck with yours.

# Selected Career Statistics

For the record, here's my cricket career 'at a glance' – it won't take long.

## First-Class Matches

| Team | Overs | Mdns | Runs | Wkts | BB | Ave | 5wi | From | To |
|------|-------|------|------|------|-----|-------|-----|------|-----|
| Glamorgan | 1252 | 234 | 4202 | 135 | 6-79 | 31.14 | 6 | 1976 | 1983 |
| Gloucestershire | 1024 | 232 | 3137 | 104 | 8-57 | 30.16 | 3 | 1980 | 1981 |
| Nrthn Transvaal | 28 | 9 | 73 | 1 | 1-27 | 73.00 | 0 | 1981 | 1982 |
| Eng XI Bengal | 46 | 14 | 97 | 3 | 2-60 | 32.33 | 0 | 1980 | 1981 |
| Total | 2350 | 489 | 7511 | 243 | 8-57 | 30.90 | 9 | 1976 | 1983 |

| | | |
|---|---|---|
| Best Bowling for Gloucestershire: | 8-57 v Lancashire at Old Trafford | 9.9.81 |
| Best Bowling for Glamorgan: | 6-79 v Hampshire at Southampton | 2.5.79 |
| Highest FC score: | 70 Notts v Glamorgan Worksop | 19.6.78 |

## Notable First-Class Dismissals (twice each)

| | | |
|---|---|---|
| Viv Richards | Ian Botham | Roger Knight |
| Sunil Gavaskar | Mike Brearley | Frank Hayes |
| Zaheer Abbas | Mike Denness | Mark Nicholas |
| Alvin Kallicharran | Graeme Fowler | John Parker |
| Bob Woolmer | David Lloyd | David Turner |
| David Gower | Clive Radley | |

## List A Matches (For Glamorgan & Gloucestershire)

105 matches 130 wickets. Bowled 54. Caught 53. LBW 23. 5w x 3, 4w x 4.

Best Bowling:   5-17 Glamorgan v Worcestershire B & H Cup at New Road 29.4.78
5-23 Glamorgan v Warwickshire Sunday League at Edgbaston 30.7.78

**Who Got Me Out**? (Top of a long queue)

Wayne Daniel (Middlesex & WI) 5 times
Graham Johnson (Kent) 4 times
Joel Garner (Somerset & WI) 3 times
Malcolm Marshall (Hampshire) twice
Michael Holding (Lancashire & WI) twice
And many others in between.

**List of Combined Dismissals** (First-Class and List A)

6 Phil Neale (Worcestershire)

5 Younis Ahmed (Surrey)
5 Peter Denning (Somerset)
5 Mike Taylor (Hampshire)
5 John Rice (Hampshire

4 IVA Richards (Somerset)
4 Alvin Kallicharran (Warwickshire & WI)
4 David Lloyd (Lancashire)
4 Derek Randall (Nottinghamshire)
4 Graham Barlow (Middlesex)
4 Brian Hardie (Essex)
4 Trevor Jesty (Hampshire)
4 Geoff Humpage (Warwickshire)
4 Nick Pocock (Hampshire)
4 Nigel Cowley (Hampshire)
4 Mike Selvey (Middlesex)

3 Gordon Greenidge (Hampshire & WI)
3 Ian Botham (Somerset)
3 Basil D'Oliveira (Worcestershire)
3 Barry Dudleston (Leicestershire)
3 Brian Davison (Leicestershire)
3 Clive Radley (Middlesex)
3 Andy Kennedy (Lancashire)
3 Gehan Mendis (Sussex)
3 Mike Smedley (Nottinghamshire)
3 David Turner (Hampshire)
3 Ian Gould (Middlesex)
3 John Birch (Nottinghamshire)
3 Joel Garner (Somerset)

# Index

# INDEX

# ST DAVID'S PRESS

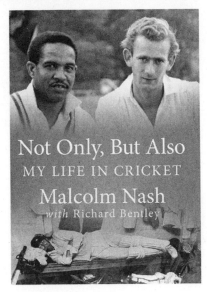

'Somehow one sensed that something extraordinary was going to happen when Sobers sauntered to the wicket.'
**Wisden**

'wherever I go, all I hear is: "Tell us about the six sixes".'
**Garry Sobers**

'People should remember that Malcolm was a wonderful opening bowler...in many of his peers' minds the best new ball bowler in county cricket'
**Peter Walker**

'A thoughtful and sensitive cricketer'
**John Arlott**

Malcolm Nash achieved sporting immortality as the bowler hit for a world-record six sixes by the legendary batsman Garry Sobers at Swansea in 1968 but, as Malcolm himself notes, although that single over made his name well-known, it should not define his long and distinguished cricketing career.

A highly regarded bowler, Malcolm played over 600 matches for Glamorgan between 1966 and 1983, taking over 1,300 wickets, had an England trial and was unlucky not to receive international recognition.

**pb - 978 1 902719 719 - £19.99 - 256pp - 207 illustrations/photographs**

# ST DAVID'S PRESS

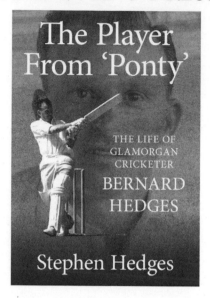

The Player From 'Ponty'

THE LIFE OF GLAMORGAN CRICKETER BERNARD HEDGES

Stephen Hedges

'Bernard was a true sportsman and played the game with an honesty and sense of fair play that stood out ... He was a good player but more than that, perhaps, he was a good bloke, easy company and willing to do anything for anyone.'
**Don 'Shep' Shepherd, from his Foreword**

'Bernard Hedges was an inspiration to a generation of cricket-mad Welsh kids. That was partly, of course, because he was such a steady batsman – who could weather any attack and punish every loose ball – and a marvellous fielder ... but our admiration was particularly strong because we knew that he was a 'valley boy' who'd had no special coaching or fancy equipment. That made Bernard really special. Truly, he was a hero who lived up to my expectations on and off the field. Every team in every sport needs a Bernard Hedges to make it whole.'
**Neil Kinnock**

The Player From 'Ponty' is the biography of Glamorgan cricketer Bernard Hedges, the talented sportsman from the valleys of south Wales who played rugby for Pontypridd and Swansea, represented a Great Britain side at football and became a widely respected cricketer for Glamorgan, who:

- Scored 17,773 first-class runs - Glamorgan's 7th all-time top run scorer.
- Hit Glamorgan's first one-day century, v Somerset in the Gillette Cup in 1963.
- Was one of only six Glamorgan players to score 2,000 runs in a season (2,026 in 1961).

Bernard's journey from his early days in Rhydyfelin – the eldest of eight children raised in a small council house – to the local grammar school, his National Service days, and to his professional career with Glamorgan is lovingly revealed by his son Stephen, who tells the story of the sporting life of a man who epitomised the 'unsung hero' by showing great grit and determination to make the most of the sporting talent he had.

pb - 978 1 902719 566 - £19.99 - 224pp - 100 illustrations/photographs

# St David's Press

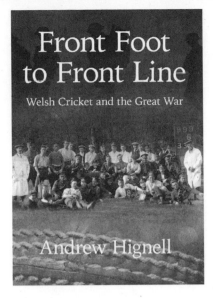

'We must never forget what these people did, either at the crease or in the trenches. As a tribute to their deeds either on the Front Foot or on the Front Line, this book is a most fitting one.'
**Hugh Morris, from his Foreword**

Front Foot to Front Line commemorates Welsh cricket's contribution to the Great War by chronicling the lives of 55 professional and amateur cricketers who left the friendly rivalry of the crease for the brutality and horror of the trenches, and lost their lives as servicemen on the bloody battlefields of Europe.

The distinguished author and the leading authority on Welsh cricket, Andrew Hignell, traces the major themes and battles of the First World War to provide a poignant snapshot of how Wales lost a generation of young men who were united by their love of cricket and their courage to serve their country.

**The cricket clubs featured in Front Foot to Front Line include:**
Blaina, Barry, Brecon, Bridgend Town, Briton Ferry, Cardiff, Cowbridge, Crickhowell, Denbighshire, Ferndale, Garth, Glamorgan, Llancarfan, Llandovery College, Llandudno, Llanelli, Monmouthshire, Neath, Newport, Pontypridd, Radyr, Swansea, Usk Valley, and Ystrad Mynach.

**pb - 978 1 902719 429 - £16.99 - 209pp - 85 illustrations/photographs**

# St David's Press

CRICKET IN WALES

**'LUCKY' JIM PLEASS**
The Memoirs of Glamorgan's 1948
County Championship Winner

**ANDREW HIGNELL**
Foreword by Robert Croft

'Reading this fascinating book, I can but only admire Jim's contributions during Glamorgan's Championship-winning summer of 1948 or his efforts with the bat against the 1951 South Africans at Swansea…[without him] I can only wonder at how different the course of Glamorgan's cricketing history might have been…But Jim was not only an unsung hero on the cricketing fields of Wales and England, he was also one of many thousands of people who heroically took part in the Normandy Landings of June 1944.'
**Robert Croft, from his Foreword**

This is the story of Jim Pleass, the last surviving member of Glamorgan's County Championship winning team of 1948, the first time the Welsh team won the highest honour in county cricket.

The Cardiff-born multi-talented sportsman, who was also an exceptional footballer and offered trial games for Cardiff City as a schoolboy, built a reputation as a solid and reliable team player at a time when Glamorgan was establishing itself on the first class cricket scene after the Second World War

In stark contrast to contemporary sport which is too often dominated by money and celebrity, Jim was a hard-working professional sportsman typical of his era, who simply enjoyed the camaraderie and of the game he loved.

**pb - 978 1 902719 368 - £14.99 - 128pp - 76 illustrations/photographs**

# St David's Press

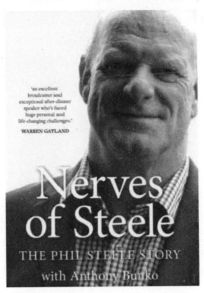

'I've been lucky enough to get to know Phil during my time as Wales coach. He is an excellent broadcaster who genuinely wants Wales and Welsh players to excel and I respect his friendly and personal approach. I also admire the fact that he has been able to do this while facing personal and life changing challenges.'
**Warren Gatland**

'Phil Steele embodies all that is great about the culture of Welsh rugby. His strength of character and sense of fun are all the more impressive given some of the dark and devastating times he has endured.'
**Caroline Hitt**

'In the early 1980s when Welsh rugby was not exactly overflowing with gifted players, I went to cover a match at Rodney Parade where one player that caught my eye was an unknown young full back named Phil Steele, he was a breath of fresh air.'
**Barry John**

Known to thousands of rugby fans as a knowledgeable, passionate and witty broadcaster, and as an entertaining and popular after-dinner speaker, Phil Steele's confident demeanour and humorous disposition mask a life-long battle against depression and anxiety heightened by heartbreak and tragedy in his personal life. Nerves of Steele is a remarkable story and reveals the real Phil Steele, a man known only by his very closest friends and family.

**pb - 978 1 902719 504 - £13.99 - 208pp - 32 pps of colour photos**
**eBook - 978-1-902719-53-5 - £9.99**

# St David's Press

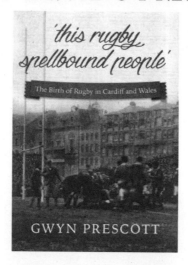

'...scrupulously researched [and] well written...Gwyn Prescott has given [rugby in Wales] a history to be proud of.'
**Huw Richards, scrum.com**

'Prescott paints a meticulous picture of Welsh rugby's growth in Victorian Britain'
**Rugby World**

'...a fascinating piece of research and a major contribution to the history of rugby.'
**Tony Collins**

'In December 1905, The Irish Times dispatched a reporter to cover the All Blacks game in Cardiff. Only a little over thirty years earlier, apart from a few young middle-class blades who took exercise by occasionally playing with an oval ball, the game of rugby was barely known in the town. Yet following the historic Welsh victory over New Zealand, that Irish journalist memorably described the excited, good humoured and wildly enthusiastic crowds he witnessed that day in and around the Arms Park as "this rugby spellbound people." He went on to declare that the Welsh were "undoubtedly the best exponents of the game".'
**from the Introduction**

Wales fell in love with rugby over 100 years ago, and this national affair with the game remains as intense and intoxicating today as it was in the late 1800s, when tens of thousands of passionate and expectant supporters would make their way to the Arms Park to see Wales play the best teams in the world and to enjoy the famous match-day atmosphere in Cardiff's bustling town centre. Rugby was undoubtedly the sporting heartbeat of Cardiff with over 230 clubs in 1895; but how did this obsession with rugby grip Cardiff and the industrial towns of south Wales, and why did the Welsh quickly become 'this rugby spellbound people'?

The Birth of Rugby in Cardiff and Wales is the essential guide to the importance of rugby in Cardiff and to the significance of Cardiff to the development of Welsh rugby in the nineteenth century.

**pb - 978 1 902719 436 - £16.99 - 304pp - 142 illustrations/photographs**

# St David's Press

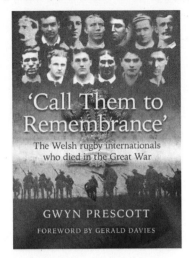

'These pages contain an unexplored and untold tale which, from the deepest anguish of the suffering born of their unquestioning bravery, pierces the heart...This book is [an] acknowledgment of the sacrifice made by 13 Welshmen....Theirs was a sacrifice which needs to be told....Gwyn Prescott, with meticulous and sympathetic attention to detail, tells the story. This narrative is an essential record'.
**Gerald Davies, from the Foreword**

'From the boisterous singing and exhilarating cheers of Cardiff Arms Park to the deafening roar of artillery shells and gunfire, these humbling stories describe thirteen individual journeys which began on muddy yet familiar Welsh playing fields but ended in the unimaginable brutality of the battles of the First World War.'
**Dan Allsobrook, www.gwladrugby.com**

'This is a book which moves as well as informs.'
**Huw Richards, Associate Lecturer in Sports History,**
**London College of Communication**

It is estimated that the First World War claimed the lives of 40,000 Welshmen, all of them heroes whose sacrifice is honoured by a grateful nation. 'Call them to remembrance', which includes 120 illustrations and maps, tells the stories of thirteen Welsh heroes who shared the common bond of having worn the famous red jersey of the Welsh international rugby team.

Gwyn Prescott's sensitive and fascinating book, the product of over ten year's research, recovers the memory of these thirteen multi-talented and courageous Welshmen who gave their lives in the Great War of 1914-18, detailing their playing and military careers.

**978 1 902719 375 - £14.99 - 175pp - 120 illustrations/photographs**

# St David's Press

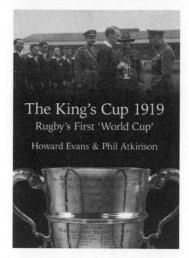

The King's Cup 1919
Rugby's First 'World Cup'

Howard Evans & Phil Atkinson

*'An intriguing retelling of a significant but largely forgotten chapter of rugby union history, superbly illustrated.'*
**Huw Richards, author of 'A Game for Hooligans: The History of Rugby Union'**

*'Howard is an authority on rugby's history and meticulous in his research'*
**Andy Howell, Rugby Correspondent, Western Mail**

At the outbreak of World War I in 1914, all rugby was suspended by decree of the individual rugby unions, with only inter-military encounters and fundraising games permitted. After the Armistice in November 1918, with the forces of the world's rugby-playing nations and many of their stars still stationed in Britain, and with the public desperate to see competitive rugby played again, an inter-military tournament was organised. King George V was so enthused by the proposed competition that he agreed to have the tournament named after him, and so The King's Cup was born.

Meticulously compiled by Howard Evans and Phil Atkinson, The King's Cup 1919 is the first book to tell the full story of rugby's first 'World Cup' which saw:

- the British military's decision to create a 'Mother Country' team rather than separate teams for England, Wales, Scotland & Ireland
- the confirmation of New Zealand's status as the dominant rugby-playing nation
- the first competitive game between teams representing New Zealand and South Africa
- the origins of pre-apartheid South Africa's refusal to accept black players in opposing teams

**pb - 978 1 902719 443 - £14.99 - 192pp - 140 illustrations/photographs**